Gender Fraud: a fiction

" … a gripping read … " Katya, Goodread

Impact

"Edgy, insightful, terrific writing, propelled by rage against rape. Tittle writes in a fast-paced, dialogue-driven style that hurtles the reader from one confrontation to the next. Chock full of painful social observations …." Hank Pellissier, Director of Humanist Global Charity

" … The idea of pinning down the inflictors of this terror is quite appealing …." Alison Lashinsky

"A deftly scripted novella by an author with a genuine flair for a riveting narrative style of storytelling that will engage the dedicated attention for women and men from first page to last … " Micah Andrew, *Midwest Book Review*

It Wasn't Enough

"Unlike far too many novels, this one will make you think, make you uncomfortable, and then make you reread it …." C. Osborne, moonspeaker.ca

"… a powerful and introspective dystopia …. It is a book I truly recommend for a book club as the discussions could be endless …." Mesca Elin, Psychochromatic Redemption

"Tittle's book hits you hard …." D. Sohi, Goodreads

Exile

"Thought-provoking stuff, as usual from Peg Tittle." James M. Fisher, Goodreads

What Happened to Tom

"This powerful book plays with the gender gap to throw into high relief the infuriating havoc unwanted pregnancy can wreak on a woman's life. Once you've read *What Happened to Tom*, you'll never forget it." Elizabeth Greene, *Understories* and *Moving*

"I read this in one sitting, less than two hours, couldn't put it down. Fantastic allegorical examination of the gendered aspects of unwanted pregnancy. A must-read for everyone, IMO." Jessica, Goodreads

"Peg Tittle's *What Happened to Tom* takes a four-decades-old thought experiment and develops it into a philosophical novella of extraordinary depth and imagination .... Part allegory, part suspense (perhaps horror) novel, part defense of bodily autonomy rights (especially women's), Tittle's book will give philosophers and the philosophically minded much to discuss." Ron Cooper, *Hume's Fork*

Sexist Shit that Pisses Me Off

"Woh. This book is freaking awesome and I demand a sequel." Anonymous, barnesandnoble.com

"I recommend this book to both women and men. It will open your eyes to a lot of sexist—and archaic—behaviors." Seregon, Goodreads

"Honestly, selling this in today's climate is a daunting challenge—older women have grown weary, younger women don't seem to care, or at least don't really identify as feminists, men—forget that. All in all a sad state of affairs—sorry." rejection letter from agent

Shit that Pisses Me Off

"I find Peg Tittle to be a passionate, stylistically-engaging writer with a sharp eye for the hypocritical aspects of our society." George, Amazon

"Peg raises provocative questions: should people need some kind of license to have children? Should the court system use professional jurors? Many of her essays address the imbalance of power between men and women; some tackle business, sports, war, and the weather. She even explains why you're not likely to see Peg Tittle at Canada's version of an Occupy Wall Street demonstration. It's all thought-provoking, and whether or not you'll end up agreeing with her conclusions, her essays make for fascinating reading." Erin O'Riordan

"This was funny and almost painfully accurate, pointing out so many things that most of us try NOT to notice, or wish we didn't. Well written and amusing, I enjoyed this book immensely." Melody Hewson

" ... a pissed off kindred spirit who writes radioactive prose with a hint of sardonic wit .... Peg sets her sights on a subject with laser sharp accuracy then hurls words like missiles in her collection of 25 cogent essays on the foibles and hypocrisies of life .... Whether you agree or disagree with Peg's position on the issues, *Shit that Pisses Me Off* will stick to your brain long after you've ingested every word—no thought evacuations here. Her writing is adept and titillating ... her razor sharp words will slice and dice the cerebral jugular. If you enjoy reading smart, witty essays that challenge the intellect, download a copy ...." Laura Salkin, thinkspin.com

"Not very long, but a really good read. The author is intelligent, and points out some great inconsistencies in common thinking and action .... may have been channeling some George Carlin in a few areas." Briana Blair, Goodreads

" ... thought-provoking, and at times, hilarious. I particularly loved 'Bambi's cousin is going to tear you apart.' Definitely worth a read!" Nichole, Goodreads

"What she said!!! Pisses me off also! Funny, enjoyable and so right on!!!! Highly recommended." Vic, indigo.ca

Critical Thinking: An Appeal to Reason

"This book is worth its weight in gold." Daniel Millsap

"One of the books everyone should read. A lot of practical examples, clear and detailed sections, and tons of all kinds of logical fallacies analyzed under microscope that will give you a completely different way of looking to the everyday manipulations and will help you to avoid falling into the common traps. Highly recommended!" Alexander Antukh

"One of the best CT books I've read." G. Baruch, Goodreads

"This is an excellent critical thinking text written by a clever and creative critical thinker. Her anthology *What If* is excellent too: the short readings are perfect for engaging philosophical issues in and out of the classroom." Ernst Borgnorg

"Peg Tittle's *Critical Thinking* is a welcome addition to a crowded field. Her presentations of the material are engaging, often presented in a conversational discussion with the reader or student. The text's coverage of the material is wide-ranging. Newspaper items, snippets from *The Far Side*, personal anecdotes, emerging social and political debates, as well as LSAT sample questions are among the many tools Tittle employs to educate students on the elemental aspects of logic and critical thinking." Alexander E. Hooke, Professor of Philosophy, Stevenson University

What If?...
Collected Thought Experiments in Philosophy

"Of all the collections of philosophical thought experiments I've read, this is by far the best. It is accessible, uses text from primary sources, and is very well edited. The final entry in the book— which I won't spoil for you—was an instant favorite of mine." Dominick Cancilla

"This is a really neat little book. It would be great to use in discussion-based philosophy courses, since the readings would be nice and short and to the point. This would probably work much better than the standard anthology of readings that are, for most students, incomprehensible." Nathan Nobis, Morehouse College

Should Parents be Licensed?
Debating the Issues

"This book has some provocative articles and asks some very uncomfortable questions ...." Jasmine Guha, Amazon

"This book was a great collection of essays from several viewpoints on the topic and gave me a lot of profound over-the-(TV-)dinner-(tray-)table conversations with my husband." Lauren Cocilova, Goodreads

"You need a licence to drive a car, own a gun, or fish for trout. You don't need a licence to raise a child. But maybe you should ... [This book] contains about two dozen essays by various experts, including psychologists, lawyers and sociologists ...." Ian Gillespie, *London Free Press*

"... But the reformers are right. Completely. Ethically. I agree with Joseph Fletcher, who notes, "It is depressing ... to realize that most people are accidents," and with George Schedler, who states, "Society has a duty to ensure that infants are born free of avoidable defects. ... Traditionalists regard pregnancy and parenting as a natural right that should never be curtailed. But what's the result of this laissez-faire attitude? Catastrophic suffering. Millions of children born disadvantaged, crippled in childhood, destroyed in adolescence. Procreation cannot be classified as a self-indulgent privilege—it needs to be viewed as a life-and-death responsibility ...." Abhimanyu Singh Rajput, Social Tikka

Ethical Issues in Business: Inquiries, Cases, and Readings

"*Ethical Issues in Business* is clear and user-friendly yet still rigorous throughout. It offers excellent coverage of basic ethical theory, critical thinking, and many contemporary issues such as whistleblowing, corporate social responsibility, and climate change. Tittle's approach is not to tell students what to think but rather to get them to think— and to give them the tools to do so. This is the text I would pick for a business ethics course." Kent Peacock, University of Lethbridge

"This text breathes fresh air into the study of business ethics; Tittle's breezy, use-friendly style puts the lie to the impression that a business ethics text has to be boring." Paul Viminitz, University of Lethbridge

"A superb introduction to ethics in business." Steve Deery, *The Philosophers' Magazine*

"Peg Tittle wants to make business students think about ethics. So she has published an extraordinarily useful book that teaches people to question and analyze key concepts .... Take profit, for example .... She also analyzes whistleblowing, advertising, product safety, employee rights, discrimination, management and union matters, business and the environment, the medical business, and ethical investing ...." Ellen Roseman, *The Toronto Star*

more at pegtittle.com

by Peg Tittle

fiction

Fighting Words (forthcoming)
Gender Fraud: a fiction
Impact
It Wasn't Enough
Exile
What Happened to Tom

screenplays

Exile
What Happened to Tom
Foreseeable
Aiding the Enemy
Bang Bang

stageplays

Impact
What Happened to Tom
Foreseeable
Aiding the Enemy
Bang Bang

audioplays

Impact

nonfiction

Just Think About It
Sexist Shit that Pisses Me Off
No End to the Shit that Pisses Me Off
Still More Shit that Pisses Me Off
More Shit that Pisses Me Off
Shit that Pisses Me Off
Critical Thinking: An Appeal to Reason
What If? Collected Thought Experiments in Philosophy
Should Parents be Licensed? (editor)
Ethical Issues in Business: Inquiries, Cases, and Readings
Philosophy: Questions and Theories (contributing author)

SEXIST SHIT THAT PISSES ME OFF

^

2nd edn

PEG TITTLE

Magenta

Sexist Shit that Pisses Me Off
2nd Edition
© 2014, 2021 by Peg Tittle

pegtittle.com
hellyeahimafeminist.com

ISBN 978-1-926891-83-5 (paperback)
ISBN 978-1-926891-84-2 (epub)
ISBN 978-1-926891-85-9 (pdf)

Published by Magenta

Magenta

Cover design by Donna Casey based on a concept by Peg Tittle
Formatting by Elizabeth Beeton

Library and Archives Canada Cataloguing in Publication

Title: Sexist shit that pisses me off / Peg Tittle.
Names: Tittle, Peg, 1957- author.
Description: 2nd edition. | Previously published in electronic format:
Sundridge, Ontario: Magenta, 2014.
Identifiers: Canadiana (print) 20210109556 | Canadiana (ebook) 20210109696 |
    ISBN 9781926891835 (softcover) | ISBN 9781926891842 (EPUB) |
    ISBN 9781926891859 (PDF)
Subjects: LCSH: Feminist criticism. | LCSH: Feminist theory.
Classification: LCC HQ1190 .T57 2021 | DDC 305.4201—dc23

Contents

Introduction

I came of age in the 70s when second-wave feminism was strong. By the early 80s, people were endorsing non-sexist language, revamping the white, male canon, and identifying, and cracking, the glass ceiling. Atwood's *The Handmaid's Tale* became a bestseller. Abortion became an issue. Women's shelters came into existence.

I happened to move to a backwoods area in the late 80s, and through the 90s, I attributed the sexism that I saw to regionalism — where I was, I thought, was just a bit behind the times (colleagues actually denied that the Montreal Massacre was misogynistic femicide). Also, because I was poor, and this was pre-internet, I lost touch with the rest of the world (I'd cancelled my subscriptions to feminist magazines, I'd stopped watching the news because it was so genuinely uninformative, partly because I could get only two local stations, etc.).

So I was surprised — bewildered and appalled, actually — when I saw in the 00s that all the ground we had gained, and then some, had been lost. 2014 feels very much like what I imagine 1950 to have felt like. (Worse, actually. I don't think crayons came in gendered boxes in the 1950s — though colours were gendered, of course, so maybe this latest development should be praised for 'outing' that sad state of affairs. Even so, 'tomboys' in the 1950s weren't pressured to think of themselves as transsexuals and undergo surgical 'transition'.)

What the hell happened? I'm still trying to understand it: is it just the cyclical generational phenomenon (each generation reacting against the former one), or is it that the easy access to pornography, courtesy of the internet, has conditioned men to be even more misogynistic (apparently they're watching it as early as eleven years of age, and contemporary pornography humiliates and degrades women *far* more than the centrefolds of *Playboy* ever did in its heyday), or is it that the 70s was just a fad and the boomers now in power never really were feminist, never really were against sexism ...

I think a lot of people believe we're now in a post-feminist (non-sexist) world, perhaps because of all the public changes (International Women's Day, Title IX, sexual harassment programs in the workplace, and so on), but we are so not there yet. Sexism has just gone underground, and because it's not as overt, it's harder to see. But sexist shit happens every day.

Sexist Shit that Pisses Me Off is an idiosyncratic collection: it includes only the stuff I've happened to think about, and what I happen to think about is typically dependent on what I happen to do or what happens to have been done to me. And I lead a rather ordinary, uneventful life. And yet — there are over a hundred angry pieces here.

If the collection were comprehensive, thoroughly representative of the most damaging and most prevalent and most important instances of sexism, there would be more in it about pornography (what is implied by the fact that so many men *enjoy* watching women being humiliated and degraded?) (for that matter, what is implied by the fact that so many of them enjoy watching other men get hurt and killed?), the sex 'trade' (what is implied by the fact that men buy and sell girls for their sexual use?), sexism in the workplace (I hate that men, on average, work less hard in school and obtain lower grades, and yet receive better job offers and higher pay), sexism in the schools (I hate the way men, on average, take up more conversational space, speaking slowly, repeating themselves, and making irrelevant comments that derail the discussion; I hate the way they automatically assume they know more than me — even when they're students in a class I'm teaching), sexism in the home, sexism in the rest of the world, the damage of sexism to men, and so on.

Fortunately, others are writing about all of that stuff, and finding it is just an internet search away. There are many excellent feminist, anti-sexism, anti-gender bloggers out there with reading lists. Find them. Read the recommended books. Then maybe you'll start seeing all the sexist shit in *your* life — prerequisite to doing something about it.

+ + +

I considered calling this book *Every Man Should Read This*. A presumptuous title to be sure, but I didn't think men would pick up, or click on, a book titled simply *Everyday Sexism*. (And at that point, I was hoping to interest one of the bigger publishers and thought they'd shy away from the title *Sexist Shit that Pisses Me Off*.)

But men should know that sexist shit happens. Every day. Every day women are 'put in their place' by it. Men are put in their place by it as well, but that place is almost always 'over' women.

And why do you, men, need to know? Because, assuming you agree that women should *not* be subordinated, that women *are* as intelligent, as capable, as worthy as men, it's almost impossible to get rid of sexism without you.

Partly, because a lot of the time you're the ones doing the sexist shit. And only you can change your own behaviour. And to those of you who are saying "Yeah, but not *all* men, not *me*" — okay, maybe (but I doubt it) (*I* still do sexist shit, and I've spent much of my life consciously thinking about this stuff — we're brainwashed from birth to pink and blue, so it's extremely difficult *not* to do it), but odds are you know someone who *is* sexist, who *does* consider and treat women *not* as peers: call him on it.

And partly, because you're the ones in power. *You're* filling parliaments, *you're* sitting in boardrooms, *you're* occupying management positions.

That said, every woman should read this too. We need to stop enabling. We need to understand what we're doing (for example, dressing to be sexually attractive as *a matter of routine*, rather than just when we really want to be), and what we're saying (for example, "Oh well, boys will be boys"), and what we're expecting (for example, that men know everything) — and we need to stop it. Perhaps most importantly, we need to reject the 'boys will be boys' mentality; boys, as well as girls, should grow up. We need to stop raising our sons to be sexist. And if their sexist behaviour is due to nature and not nurture, then we should raise them to *compensate* for their nature; consider it affirmative action.

So although it may seem like I'm criticizing men, I'm really criticizing what our social conditioning has turned them into. So yes, actually, I *am* criticizing *men*; I wish male human beings would just be *people*. I'm criticizing *women* too. I'm criticizing *anyone* who accepts the gender conditioning, who accepts the sexism, who agrees to become men and women (that is, human beings *identified primarily by their sex*) instead of people (human beings identified by their genuine interests, desires, values …).

Why? What's wrong with gender? It's a social construct that emphasizes and exaggerates, often to the point of grotesque distortion, differences between the sexes. *For no good reason.* Real or imagined differences, minor differences, differences that may or may not be innate (in many cases we have no way of knowing, no way of separating natural tendencies from socially imposed tendencies, *because* the conditioning begins at birth and continues, relentlessly, throughout our lives; only a few manage to resist, partly because to do so comes at a high cost, from 'mere' ostracization to physical assault resulting in death) — in a gendered society, males must be masculine and females must be feminine. Gender

4

thus limits our choices, our way of being, our way of living.

It also, by making sex so very prominent, enables a hierarchy based on sex; it enables the patriarchy we live in.

And, of course, again, by making sex so very prominent, it enables, it almost encourages, sexism.

If we get rid of gender — the rigidly oppositional bundles of attributes, behaviours, mannerisms, preferences, interests, desires, and values that we've labelled 'masculine' and 'feminine' — we'll go a long way toward getting rid of sexism, which is, essentially, unjustified differentiation on the basis of sex.

Unjustified because, simply put, one's sex is almost always irrelevant.

Mr. and Ms.

I'm in this world, okay, and the people identify each other by sex. All the time. It's like 'Female Person Smith' and 'Male Person Brown' or 'Person-with-Uterus Smith' and 'Person-with-Penis Brown' — I don't know the exact translation. But sex-identity is a mandatory prefix. They distinguish males from females. Before they do everything else. Before they do anything else.

It bothers me. It irritates me. It pisses me off. What's so damned special about my sex that it has to be part of my name? Surely my values, my interests, my abilities, my character — these aspects define my self more than my sex does.

And anyway, shouldn't *I* be the one to decide what parts of my self are important enough to be part of my name? Maybe I want to be identified by my ovaries, but maybe I want to be identified by my occupation. Hell, maybe I want to identified by my blood type.

The thing is, they consider it polite. Polite! To draw such relentless attention to details of my anatomy! In fact, they think that to call someone by just their name, without the penis/uterus prefix, is rude. So it's really hard to say anything. And it's even harder to *do* anything. I tried just saying "Dave" one time and everybody turned and stared at me. No kidding. I tried to hold my ground, but I heard myself say "Sorry, I mean, 'Mr. Brown'." And everybody smiled with relief.

I even tried variations once. I thought if I loosened up the custom a bit, it'd be easier to get rid of it altogether. Sort of like food that's dried onto dishes you haven't washed in a week.

So next time, I put on my best smile and said "Dickhead Brown". Everybody turned and stared. Worse than last time. Again, I found myself saying "Sorry, I meant 'Penis Person,

Male Person, Mr. Brown'."

Surely this can't be good, this obsessive marking of sex, this insistent separating of human beings into male and female. Talk about paving the superhighway to sex discrimination. I wanted to shout "Look, it's not like it has to be this way!" Why *not* just call people by their names, 'Dave' or 'Mary'? Too familiar for the formality-prone. Then how about using their surname, 'Brown' or 'Smith'? Too rude for the etiquette-addicted. How about an all-purpose sex-neutral prefix like 'Doctor' but without the professional implications; how about just 'Person' — 'Person Brown' and 'Person Smith'? As for the pronoun problem, they already have a sex-neutral pronoun: 'it'. But, stupidly, it's reserved for animals. Go figure. In this world, *animals* are accorded the respect of a sex-free identity, but *people* aren't.

Dolly

When Ian Wilmut's team was the first to successfully clone a mammal from a single adult cell back in 1996, they named the cloned sheep "Dolly" — because the cell had come from a mammary gland (and Dolly Parton is a famous woman who has relatively large breasts/mammary glands). I'm tempted, *on that basis alone*, to cast my vote against human cloning. Seriously, if that kind of short-sightedness or immaturity is going to be running things, they're bound to go horribly wrong.

Did they really not foresee that "Dolly" would become headline news? Or did they not even recognize how juvenile they were being? Mammaries = women = mammaries. We are not seen as people, let alone colleagues, certainly not ever bosses; we are nothing more than, we are only, our sexual parts. Really, need I explain the problem with that? It's all so old. And yet, grown men, brilliant men, on the cutting edge of science, who become headline news, are apparently still forcing farts at the dinner table and snickering about it.

So, cloning? I don't think so. Not until the other half of the species grows up.

(Then again, since cloning means we finally don't need them at all, not even to maintain the species, let's go for it.) (Could it be they never thought of that either — that cloning makes males totally redundant?)

Women's Fiction

I finished a novel by J. D. Robb the other day and also happened to read the back inside cover blurb: "Nora Roberts is the #1 *New York Times* bestselling author of more than one hundred novels. She is also the author of the bestselling futuristic suspense series written under the pen name J. D. Robb. With more than 145 million copies of her books in print and more than sixty-nine *New York Times* bestsellers to date, Nora Roberts is indisputably the most celebrated and beloved women's fiction writer today." Why the qualification — *women's* fiction? My guess is that with those numbers, she's a well celebrated and beloved fiction writer, period.

Besides which, what exactly *is* 'women's fiction'? Fiction *by* women? Unlikely. Harper Lee's *To Kill a Mockingbird* would be women's fiction then. As would be Ayn Rand's *Atlas Shrugged*.

Fiction *for* women? And what's that, fiction that women are interested in? As if all, or even most, women are interested in the same things. We are as different from each other as we are from each man. It's painfully clear to me that not all women are interested even in feminism/sexism. Just as not all blacks are interested in racism. (Is *Mockingbird* ever called black fiction?) And J. D. Robb's "Death" series, of which the book I read is part, is about a cop, murder, good and evil, justice — men aren't interested in these things? Since when? And her "Key" series, written under her romance genre pen name, Nora Roberts, is described thus: "Three women. Three keys. Each has 28 days to find her way through a dangerous quest. If one fails, they all lose. If they all succeed, money, power, and a new destiny await each of them. It will take more than intellect, more than determination. They will have to open their hearts, their minds, and believe that everything and anything is possible." Success, money, power, destiny — of interest only to women? Hardly.

Even if Roberts *does* write about romance and love — well, I can see that men aren't interested in romance, because it's a fantasy that features more benefits for women than men; men prefer the other fantasy, porn, which features more benefits for men than women. But we're in big trouble if men aren't interested in love. (Women, take note.)

Or is 'women's fiction' fiction *about* women? Well, yes, Robb's and Roberts' fiction typically, if not always, features a female main character. So, what, when the main player is female, men aren't interested? Wow. Let me say that again: *when the main player is female, men aren't interested.* That explains a lot. It also predicts a lot.

So fiction about men is men's fiction? I've never even heard the phrase 'men's fiction' — let alone heard it applied to fiction with male main characters. That would make *To Kill a Mockingbird* and *Atlas Shrugged* men's fiction. I've certainly read a lot of men's fiction, then.

And why is it that women are interested in both women's fiction and men's fiction, but men are interested only in men's fiction? That is, why is it that men are interested only in reading about members of their own sex? I suspect it's because it's not really, or not just, the case that they aren't interested in reading about women — it's that they don't consider women important/valuable. (Recall the Jane and John study done, what, thirty years ago? Two essays were presented to the participants, one written by 'Jane Smith' and one written by 'John Smith'; the one by John Smith was given higher grades by both male and female readers, despite being identical to the one by Jane Smith. Such studies have been replicated, with similar results, many times since — see Cordelia Fine's *Delusions of*

Gender.)

According to an article by Katha Pollitt ("Invisible Women"), op-ed editors wonder where the women are. ("In nine weeks, only 20 percent of pieces [in *The Los Angeles Times* op-ed pages] were written by women"; all five of *USA Today's* political columnists are male, all *Time's* eleven columnists are male, one of six in print and two of thirteen online for *Newsweek* ... .) Pollitt lists fourteen women op-ed writers 'off the top of her head'; I've heard of most of them — why haven't the mentioned op-ed editors? It seems to support what I'm saying: when a woman is the main player, men just aren't interested — it doesn't even register on their radar.

And consider *Washington Monthly* blogger Kevin Drum who apparently mused upon the absence of women bloggers and, says Pollitt, got a major earful from women bloggers, "who are understandably sick of hearing that they don't exist. 'I'm staring you right in the face, Kevin,' wrote Avedon Carol (sideshow.me.uk), 'and even though you've said you read me every day, you don't have me on your blogroll.'" Why are women so underrepresented? Because male gatekeepers don't see them, aren't interested in them, don't consider them important or valuable. Because they're writing women's stuff? Like women's fiction? About cops and murder — and good and evil and justice?

"Daddy, daddy, the house is on fire!" "Not now, sweetie, the game's on."

So about that guy in Taiwan who dropped his child in order to catch a foul ball at a baseball game ... I don't know whether to be more appalled at the man's action or at the media's framing of it.

Am I appalled that we condition our males to value sports over parenting? That they'd rather catch a ball than take care of a child? No. I myself would rather catch a ball than take care of a child. *Which is why I didn't make or adopt any.* The *appalling* thing is that a *father* would rather catch a ball than take care of his child.

(Yes, of course, it would be as appalling if it were a mother. But I can't resist suggesting that if it had been a woman who had dropped her child in order to catch a ball, they'd be hauling her ass into court, taking her kid away, and sterilizing her.) (Not — well, read on.)

Why do sports have such a hold over men? Is it the competition and the possibility of winning? And is that so bloody attractive because that's the way we raise our boys? Or is it simply because they're hardwired to compete? Either way, if their upbringing or their testosterone (or whatever) makes them choose catching a ball over holding on to a child, something's seriously wrong.

Or is our obsession with sports an indication that we are so very desperate to be heroic? Have our daily lives become so bereft of significance? (And why is that?) And has the mere catching of a ball become a heroic act? (What does that say about us?)

Or is it just that men will reach out to catch a ball, even if it means putting a child at risk, because like many animals, their attention is captured by anything that moves. Which is a good thing if you're a Neanderthal hunting for your next meal, but — we're not. Neanderthals hunting for our next meal. So does this mean that contemporary men are unable to suppress their primitive brain? If so, we shouldn't let them — run the world, for starters.

Men, if this (dropping a child in order to catch a ball) isn't a wake up call to question and reject your conditioning and/or to recognize and resist your biochemistry, what is??

And then there is the commentators' response. Laughter, first of all. A child is dropped — and they laugh.

And they laugh in a 'boys will be boys' way. Men, don't you find it insulting? To have your irresponsible, immature behavior accepted as inevitable?

Or they laugh because, hey, it just goes to show that men aren't cut out to look after kids, best leave it to the women. Oh please. (Like they can never do a good job of cleaning the toilet either. And yet the car gleams.)

Then there are the giggling comments about his wife's 'death stare' and how he's gonna get it now. What is he, twelve? Apparently. And what's his wife, his mom? Apparently he needs one. Still. (If I were a man, I'd be pretty pissed at the implication that I am to be *scolded*.)

And then, there are the endless snickers about how 'he's going to be in the dog house' or 'sleeping on the couch'. A child is dropped, and the big concern is that he won't have sex for a while. *What is wrong with you people??* (And that whole marital dynamic — if he's good, he gets sex; if he's bad, he doesn't — that's okay with all of you?) Where are the men who are wincing at all of this? Where are the men who would confront this guy and tell him to grow the fuck up??

Truthfully, and unflatteringly, I'm not surprised. (Men, are you not ashamed that we're not surprised? Not surprised

14

you would put a child at risk in order to catch a ball, not surprised at the depth of your irresponsibility, at your 'me-first' behaviour, at your priorities ...) I expect shit like this in the States and Canada. But it happened in Taiwan. And the Taiwanese commentators giggled and snickered just like the American commentators. (In fact, the similarity was chilling.) Could it be that the gender role conditioning that is so prevalent here is damn near universal? A scary thought. Or is that universality evidence that it's not a matter of nurture, but of nature (testosterone, the Y chromosome, the primitive brain, whatever).

Either way, the conclusion has to be that men are, universally, children. Or idiots. (Or both.)

War Rape

It's not just an enthusiastic spillover of violence and aggression. The act of sexual intercourse is too specific, too far removed from the other acts of wartime violence and aggression. Shooting a person twenty-five times instead of once or twice would be such a spillover; forcing your penis or something else into a woman's vagina is not. Furthermore, war rape is often not a spontaneous, occasional occurrence; apparently it's quite premeditated and systematic.

And it's not, or not *just*, a matter of ethnic cleansing. If men truly wanted to eradicate the other culture, (and if they believed ethnicity was genetic), they'd just kill the women along with the men. (Women *are* killed, but as I understand it, they're usually raped first.) (Or, sometimes, after.) (And men are castrated, but not nearly as often as women are raped.)

And if they truly wanted to increase their own numbers, they'd hang around and see that the kid reached maturity. (Raped women *are* sometimes kept prisoner until the child is born — but unless the kid is subjected to specific and exclusive cultural conditioning, how is their purpose achieved? They'd have to look after the kids themselves for ten years.) (Which is unlikely.)

And it's not, or not *just*, a property crime against the enemy. If men sought merely to destroy their enemy's property, they'd, again, simply kill their women and children, along with their livestock. Before or after they burned their houses. (Unless, of course, they wanted to confiscate their property — in which case, they'd enslave the women rather than rape them.)

So what is it? What can explain this peculiar practice of male soldiers forcing sexual intercourse with enemy civilian women? Some insight can be gained if we consider that for men, sexual intercourse is an act of conquest. But then we must ask, since one army of (mostly) men conquers another, why don't the soldiers rape each other as an act of conquest?

Perhaps men are so afraid of being considered homosexual, they rape the enemy women instead of the enemy men. (So only homophobia prevents men from raping enemy men? Note the vested interest women have, then, in discouraging homophobia: maybe then men *would* rape each other instead of us.)

Or perhaps the conquest involved is not that of one person over another, but that of one person over another's property — and women are men's property. And as long as conquest, rather than destruction, is the point, the property will be occupied, not destroyed. And in sexual intercourse, men *literally* occupy women's bodies — they thus occupy the enemy's property.

But all of this is nothing new. One might persist, however, and ask how men can continue to regard women as property when legal and economic conditions no longer support that interpretation. The answer lies in attending not to the ownership part of property, but to the inanimate part of property: to be property is to be a thing.

Clearly, men do not consider us as equals — otherwise, we would be the enemy, not the enemy's property. And they'd kill us as they do the men (or they'd rape the men as they do us) (well, except for the homophobia bit).

They don't even consider us as inferior human beings, say, as children. Children are either spared or ignored. (Or, increasingly, drafted.)

We aren't even considered (non-human) animals. They too are either spared or ignored. (Or just killed.)

We belong to a special category — that of cunt: we are a vagina, and sometimes a uterus; we are a sexual body part, a sort of subhuman thing. Rape is not so much *im*personal as *a*personal. It's

17

no coincidence that one protests, or tries to escape, rape by claiming the characteristics of personhood: you're hurting me! (sentience); I have a name! (identity); I have a life! (interests). (One might wonder how the husbands and fathers can renounce their raped wives and daughters — don't they recognize it was against their will? Of course not: subhumans don't have will, don't have volition.)

Greer once said something like women have no idea how much men hate them. To be hated would be a step up. I say women have no idea how much men fail to see them as anything but their sex. On the basketball court, playing with a bunch of high school boys, a pick by me is not just a pick: it's a pick *by a girl*, and so it elicits extra humiliation and anger, it elicits shame and rage. And the next time I set a pick, the boy aggressively plows me out of the play. In the university classroom, teaching to male students, a critique of an argument is not just a critique: it's a critique *by a woman*, a challenge to one's masculinity, and so it elicits strong defensive action. Complaints are made to the Dean. And a suggestion to a colleague, a male colleague, is not just a suggestion: it's a woman telling you what to do, and so at best, it's not taken seriously. (At worst, it too is taken as a challenge.) It's certainly not accepted. Thus our agency in, our interaction with, half the world is denied. Men's insistent perception of us as *female* limits us, because to be female precludes being a person.

Such a perception may indeed be irrational — and the consequent behaviour, such as rape, may indeed be primitive and/or pathological. But it *is* their perception, and women would be wise to understand that. (Even more wise would be the men who understand it: for enlightenment and/or imprisonment is surely not going to be brought about by anything we subhumans do.)

Casual Day at the Office

Every second Friday is 'Casual Day' at the office — the principal lets us wear jeans to school. I need two degrees to do my job, but apparently I just can't seem to dress myself.

In addition to infantilizing the subordinates, Causal Day underscores the tradition of hypocrisy, the tradition of pretending: financial advisors who work on your portfolio at home probably do most of their work in jeans and a sweatshirt; they just change, they just put on the façade, the uniform of authority and competence, when they're in their office. Do they think we're idiots? Do they think we judge a book by its cover, do they think we're fooled that easily?

Well, yes, they do. And they're right. Behold the power of a suit coat and tie: it says 'I'm to be respected'. Anyone up on charges who borrows a suit for his day in court knows that. Oh, but the judge would be a fool to be suckered in by that. Yes — and so are we.

We also fall for the laser-printed resume over the merely photocopied one, the custom-made business card over a name and number written on a piece of paper, the bass voice speaking with grave pauses over the soprano who inflects upward at the end of each sentence. We even have a word for prioritizing pretence over substance: professionalism.

Another disturbing thing exposed by Casual Day is that the more formal the attire, the more gendered it is. Formal dress is rigidly male or female: a three-piece suit and tie or a dress and high heels. Less formal attire is less gendered: slacks and a blouse or jeans and a shirt. The most casual is completely ungendered: the old 'sweats'. The thing is this: a suit coat and tie outranks a dress and high heels. (Women wear pseudo-suits; men never wear pseudo-dresses.) So as long as formal attire is required, men will outrank women. (In perception.) (Which apparently is all that matters.) A male teacher once said he was so very grateful for his suit coat and tie during his first year of teaching because it gave him the authority he needed to control his class. It didn't occur to him that female teachers can't depend on attire for the authority they need; nor did it occur to him that perhaps he thereby contributes to their 'inability' to control their classes.

As one who has often been reprimanded, and even suspended, for 'inappropriate attire', let me just say that I think the whole thing is rather pathetic: what does it mean when the word 'subversive' can actually apply to fabric choices?

Bang Bang

Ya gotta love Christmas. Peace on earth, goodwill toward men, and record sales of toy guns.

But, my friend says, her son, and all of his friends, will make a gun out of any old thing. The problem isn't the toys.

Okay, so it's the boys. Seems they're hardwired with a propensity toward killing. Why is this not a problem? A stand-up-and-scream problem. Not a sweep-it-under-the-carpet boys-will-be-boys problem.

Why does it not bother parents that their son considers pretending to kill to be *fun* (that is, that he derives psychological *pleasure* from *pretending to kill*)?

Why does it not bother them that their son considers killing a *game* (that is, an appropriate activity for make-believe)?

'No, it's just the noise and the chasing that's fun, he doesn't associate the action with killing' — is that supposed to make it *better*? That he pulls a trigger on a gun and *doesn't associate the action with killing*? Maybe you should take him to an ER and let him see what a bullet does to a body. He might think twi — he might *think* then before so casually making that pulling-a-trigger motion.

I wonder whether parents would be as blasé if their son as repeatedly put his arm around someone's throat and swiped a piece of stiff cardboard across it? Is it just that people have become desensitized to the shooting-a-gun action?

Further, I am puzzled by the 'doesn't bother me' response not only because of the psychological and philosophical implications, but also because of the practical ones: first, once he's fourteen or sixteen, the action (the mere action) becomes illegal. (Then again, it might be illegal at all ages and maybe it's just that when a *kid* points a fake gun, no one presses charges.) (Because boys will be boys?) (So the men who do so are also boys?)

And, second, such an action may well get him killed. 'Cuz I have to tell ya, since real kids have access to real guns these days, if I were walking down a city street and a kid jumped out at me pointing a gun, I'd shoot first and ask questions later. If I had a gun.

Which I don't. So instead I'd just break out in a cold sweat and frantically try to figure out what to do. In order to end up alive. And then when the kid laughed and lowered his arm, telling me it's just a toy, I'd haul him off to his parents and give all three of you a huge piece of mind. What right do you have to let your kid terrorize me like that? What the hell is wrong with you??

Surrogacy — Why Not?

Sure, women should be allowed to be surrogates. We all do work with our bodies, some of us also include our minds in the deal (some of us are *allowed* to include our minds in the deal), so why not? As long as they get paid for service rendered.

Being a surrogate is sort of like being an athlete. You have to be and stay physically healthy, for the duration: you have to eat and drink the right stuff, and not eat or drink the wrong stuff; you have to get the right amount of physical activity. And so on. It's important. Use during pregnancy of illegal drugs (such as crack cocaine and heroin) as well as legal drugs (such as alcohol and nicotine) can cause, in the newborn, excruciating pain, vomiting, inability to sleep, reluctance to feed, diarrhoea leading to shock and death, severe anaemia, growth retardation, mental retardation, central nervous system abnormalities, and malformations of the kidneys, intestines, head and spinal cord (Madam Justice Proudfoot, "Judgement Respecting Female Infant 'D.J.'"; Michelle Oberman, "Sex, Drugs, Pregnancy, and the Law: Rethinking the Problems of Pregnant Women who Use Drugs"). Refusal of fetal therapy techniques (such as surgery, blood infusions, and vitamin regimens) can result in respiratory distress, and various genetic disorders and defects such as spina bifida and hydrocephalus (Deborah Mathieu, *Preventing Prenatal Harm: Should the State Intervene?*) To be an elite surrogate, you have to have a good genotype — no genetic diseases, etc. And elite athletes — professional football, hockey, basketball, and baseball players — are paid around $3 million dollars per season.

I think many people justify that level of income because of the risk of physical injury that such athletes incur. Okay, fair enough (let's say) (because coal-miners don't get paid $3 million). Being pregnant incurs the risk of nausea, heartburn and indigestion, constipation, incontinence, backaches, headaches, skin rashes, changes in sense of smell and taste, chemical imbalances, weight gain, dizziness and light-headedness, diabetes, anemia, embolism, stroke, circulatory collapse, and cardiopulmonary arrest.

Athletes are, further, paid what they're paid because their career is over by around thirty or thirty-five. (I don't agree with that reasoning, but it's the same reasoning used by construction workers and other seasonal workers who charge higher-than-average hourly rates. I used to teach piano, a September to June thing; in the off-season, I just had to find other work.) Similarly, women are pretty much toast as surrogates by thirty-five, forty tops.

In addition, *unlike* being a professional athlete, being a surrogate involves, typically, some sort of emotional expense. (The extremes and the attachment are typically 'artificially' triggered by estrogen, progesterone, oxytocin and other drugs produced by the body — so there's that to deal with as well; by 'that', I mean the uncontrollability during and the 'withdrawal' after ...)

And, then there's the labour. Perhaps if professional athletes had to undergo knee surgery without anaesthesia at the end of the season —

Lastly, there's the value of the service provided. Football, hockey, basketball, and baseball players play a game whose outcome is of no consequence whatsoever. Surrogates create a human being. I'm going to make a modest proposal here and suggest that, given this difference alone, surrogates should be paid ten times what professional athletes are paid. $30 million.

And *that's* the problem with women being surrogates: we wouldn't be paid what our work is worth.

School Crossing Signs

You've seen the signs I mean: silhouette figures of two children about to cross the road — one boy, one girl. How do we tell? One's wearing a skirt. (That'd be the girl.) (Really, do most girls still wear skirts to school?)

So, yes, let's emphasize *sex*. Boy and Girl. Ms. and Mr. *Nothing else matters.*

And nothing else is possible.

Note that the boy is taller. 'Oh, but they are.' Not at that age! Taller suggests older which suggests more mature, wiser. And just in case you miss this not-so-subtle suggestion of male authority, look, he has his hand on the little girl's shoulder — guiding, protecting, patronizing. It will be there for the rest of her life.

Just to make sure of that, we have this social understanding that in a couple, the man should be two or three years older than the woman. Such an arrangement gives the illusion, and the excuse, of the man being in a position of authority over the woman — after all, he's older. (But since, as they say, women mature two years ahead of men, such an arrangement merely ensures the two are 'equal'. If they were the same chronological age, they'd see in a minute that the woman should take the lead, being more mature intellectually, emotionally, and socially.)

And to really *really* make sure the message of male authority gets through, mothers encourage their boys to be the man of the house. So a fourteen-year-old boy comes to consider himself more knowing, more capable, than a woman twice his age (his mother). Is it any wonder that at eighteen, he assumes he's more knowing, more capable, than *all* women?

Now I confess that if the crossing sign had things the other way around, a taller, older girl guiding a younger boy, I'd protest the nurturant mommy-in-training role model. Which just goes to show we can't win. As long as we insist on pointing at everything and saying 'male!' or 'female!' As long as we live in an apartheid of sex.

The ironic thing is that the signs point the way to (or from) *school*, the institution at which we supposedly become educated, enlightened. Looks like we just learn how to colour — in pink and blue. (In black and white.)

Grey's Anatomy, Flashpoint, and Who knows how many others (I don't — and this is why)

Why didn't Bailey get the Chief of Surgery position? For the same reason Ed jokingly says to Greg, when he questions his rank, "Should I get you a dress?" — and they both laugh.

Because in the 21st century, being a woman (still) (STILL!) (STILL!) (*STILL!*) means being subordinate.

I love that on *Grey's Anatomy*, so many main characters, surgeons every one of them, are women. Actually they outnumber the men. 8:6. And yet Owen gets the Chief position. Richard, then Derek, then Owen. 3 of the 6 men get to be Chief. 0 of the 8 women. Bailey's been there longer than Owen. And longer than Sloan, the other contender. And yeah, okay, Kepner got the Chief Resident position even though she was there longer than Karev, but he didn't want it. (And we see it primarily as a position of responsibility, not power.) At one point, Chief Webber said he was grooming Bailey for Chief of Surgery — what happened?

And on *Flashpoint*, Sam gets to be team leader in Ed's absence. Not Jules. Again, she has more seniority. And she's just as competent (if not more so — she can shoot *and* she can negotiate a crisis).

This is why I stick to *Murphy Brown* and *Commander-in-Chief* reruns.

(We're going in the wrong direction, people.)

(And just when, and why, did we turn around?)

Short Men

I recently watched, with horrified amusement, a tv program about short men who choose to undergo excruciatingly painful surgical procedures (which basically involve breaking their legs and then keeping the bones slightly apart while they mend) in order to become a few inches taller.

Asked why they would choose to undergo such a drastic, and excruciatingly painful, procedure, they said things like 'Do you have any idea what it's like to go through life as a short person? To sit in a chair and only your toes reach the floor, you can't put your feet flat on the floor? To not be able to reach stuff on the upper shelves in grocery stores? To be unable to drive trucks because you can't reach the pedals properly? To have people always looking down at you? Do you know what that's like?'

Well, yes, actually I do. I'm a woman.

Oh, but that's different, I suppose. Why? Because we're *supposed to* go through life inconvenienced? Feeling subordinate?

Ah. That's the real problem. These poor guys can't take their rightful place *over women*. (As one man, 5'6" before the surgery, explained, "I'll be a better father and husband and son." Yup. Sure you will.)

Sex and Salespeople

Given that the people who use washers, dryers, ovens, dishwashers, and the like are usually female, I find it puzzling that the people who sell these items are usually male. Especially because it's inconsistent with the rest of the sales world, in which men tend to sell things men use, such as hardware and men's clothing, and women tend to sell things women use, such as cosmetics and women's clothing.

Hypothesis #1 — The current sexist state of affairs is just a carry-over from the days when all salespeople were male. Gee, I don't think men *ever* sold cosmetics or women's clothing. (And even if this were so, why is the field of kitchen appliances the last to evolve?)

Hypothesis #2 — These are big heavy items and so the superior strength of men is needed. Well, the salespeople don't have to *move* 'em, they just have to *sell* 'em. (And even if they did have to move them, your average appliance salesman isn't exactly Arnold Schwarzenegger.) (And anyway, ever hear of a lever? A cart? And, hang onto your hats, a forklift?)

Hypothesis #3 — Men sell the more expensive things — because they want the higher commission, or because they need the higher commission, or because only they are responsible enough to handle such large sums of money. Wedding gowns often cost more than a washer and dryer put together, but women sell these.

Hypothesis #4 — These are machines — and men know more about machines. Despite its lack of truth (at best, this is *generally*

29

true), this is, so far, the hypothesis most consistent with the rest of reality. But what about sewing machines? Who sells sewing machines? And coffee-makers? (Men don't seem to know that these machines even exist.)

So where are we — what, to judge by sex in the sales field, is still considered the man's domain?

1. Big things. Well, that's no surprise. The size thing is really *really* hard to get over. (Get over it, already!) Most people still think men are generally bigger than women. Yes, generally they weigh more. And yes, generally they're taller. But inch for inch, I'm not sure they take up more space than women (*real* women): our chest measurement is often larger, our hips are broader, we've got bigger thighs, and we've got bigger asses.

2. Expensive things. Also no surprise, this is a relic of the breadwinner days despite its obvious non-applicability today. My guess is that there are as many self-supporting women as men and that in most mixed sex families, both the man and the woman provide financial support.

3. Machine things. What is it about things that plug in or make a lot of noise that women do not or can not or will not get comfortable with — or men do not or can not or will not think women can get comfortable with? Socialization? Dick used the lawnmower, Jane used a dustcloth. Education? Dick took shop and got to see what a gear and a circuit board look like and how they work; Jane never got to do that — they remain a mystery. Is it that machines evolved along with outdoor stuff? (When women were inside with the babies — washing diapers by hand.) (Tell me again why washers and dryers took so long to invent.)

Put it all together and you get the ultimate male domain: cars. They're big, expensive machines. Which is why, perhaps, a woman on the showroom floor is so very *very* radical. (Wait a minute. Women drive cars, don't they?)

All in all, the division of sales by sex is illogical. (And they say logic a male thing.) My guess is if you put a few women on the showroom floor, be it with cars, computers, or stereos (or washers, dryers, ovens, and dishwashers), your customer base would double — so the division of sales by sex is also bad for business. (And isn't taking care of business a male thing?)

Games for Girls (Seriously? In 2012?)

Okay, so I went to bored.com, clicked on Games, then clicked on Girls. Mostly because I was irritated that there even *was* a separate section for Girls (and surprised there wasn't a separate section for Blacks) — alongside Popular, Animations, Stickman, Shooting, Escape, Puzzle, Action, Skill, Walkthru's, Mobile, and More. (How many category mistakes can *be* at one website?)

Why do girls need a separate section? Are they not interested in any of the other sections? Are none of the other sections 'for' them?

Anyway, so what do I find when I click on the Girls tab? This:

> *Sugar and Spice and everything Girl! Play celebrity, dress-up, cooking, sports, and puzzle games designed just for little ladies young and old alike! Like to run restaurants? Become a princess? Go on a hot date with the boy of your dreams? It's all here!*

Seriously? In 2012?

I'm a girl, or at least female-bodied, and I have to say I'm very interested in Action. Specifically, Shooting. Failing that, Escape.

Marriage: A Sexist Affair

Marriage, by its very (traditional) definition, is a sexist affair: it involves one of each sex — one male and one female. And I suppose this is because, traditionally, the purpose of marriage was to create a family— to have and raise children.

This view is fraught with questionable assumptions, glaring inconsistencies, and blatant errors. I'll give one of each: the connection between having and raising children is not at all necessary, hence the 'one male and one female' is not at all necessary; if the purpose of marriage is to create a family, why do couples who do not intend to have children nevertheless marry; the marriage contract goes well beyond family concerns — indeed, it barely approaches family concerns — one pledges to love and honour one's spouse, not one's children.

Notwithstanding the very mistaken connection between marriage and family, I'd like to suggest another reason for the sexism in marriage. Assuming that marriage entails love, and love entails 'looking after', sexism makes things 'easier'.

Consider this: needing to be looked after suggests one is a child or perhaps an invalid; if both people are looking after each other, well, how can a child look after — another child? (It makes marriages rather like the blind leading the blind.) (Not an entirely unapt analogy.) There has to be a difference, some sort of distinction. The distinction is, surprise, sex: the husband is the father, he looks after his wife with respect to the male domain — he fixes things for her, he tells her stuff, he makes the money; the wife is the mother, she looks after her husband with respect to the female domain — she feeds him, clothes him, reminds him.

This sexist division also avoids a second problem: without it, they'd each feel, as indeed they are, treated like a child. How does a wife feel when her husband lets her know what colours go together? How does a husband feel when his wife changes the spark plugs? Inadequate, insulted, put down. No doubt responding with an eight-year-old's 'I know that!' or 'I can do it!' The sexist division of labour justifies ignorance and incompetence within a certain domain; it therefore allows people to remain children, without embarrassment, within a certain domain. And this enables the other to take care of them, in that domain, without offense. (I suspect, therefore, the more whole a person is, the less feminine or masculine, the worse they fare in a marriage. And if women tend to be more whole than men, well, that would explain why men need marriage more than women do — I'm thinking of happiness/suicide studies — aren't unmarried men the worst off?)

Now of course I wonder how same sex couples look after each other. Do they all negotiate some sort of butch/femme split? Or — and wouldn't this be simpler, wouldn't it be healthier — does their concept of love between adults not entail, not require, such nurture?

Kids Behind the Wheel

The other day, I was walking on the gravel/dirt road I live on. It's a back road that might see a dozen cars in a day. As one such car passed me, I noticed that a kid was at the wheel in dad's lap. Proud dad, happy kid.

What is it with that? Why, of all the adult things, do parents push their kids into that one? Mis-asked the question. It's not the *parents*, it's the *dads*. And usually, it's their sons, not their daughters.

Given that men are worse drivers than women (ask the insurance companies — why do you think young males pay such a high premium?), perhaps it makes sense: boys need all the practice they can get. But surely it would be better to take them to a go-cart track.

'Proud dad, happy kid.' I get the impression it's not practice. Is it a rite of passage to manhood? But women can, do, and should drive as well. There's nothing gender-specific about driving a car. So why would it be a rite of passage to *man*hood?

Maybe it's the vroom vroom that confuses men. It's a surrogate roar. They think they're intimidating when they make a lot of noise. (Actually, they're just annoying. As hell.) And they want to be intimidating because ... ?

Or, also, attendant with a roar, maybe their primitive brain triggers the production of adrenaline, and the adrenaline makes them feel good. Perhaps that explains the appeal of the Indy. And the adolescent males who take the mufflers off their trail bikes.

Or maybe it's the speed that confuses them, makes them feel like they're chasing prey (or fleeing predators) and again, their primitive brain produces feel-good adrenaline.

35

So why doesn't their modern brain recognize this and veto the primitive response? Noise and speed matter little to *homo sapiens* living in the 21st century.

'Proud dad. Happy kid.' Oh aren't you the grown-up. No, you're not. You shouldn't be behind the wheel until you're sixteen and then you should approach the task with fear and trembling. *Driving is not fun. A car is not a toy. One wrong move and you could kill someone.*

I'm not a feminist.
Feminism is so over.
We live in a post-feminist world.

It used to be that men pressured women to have sexual intercourse with them. And despite the fact that it meant risking years of unhappiness for us (unwanted pregnancy, unwanted children), for ten seconds of happiness (or relief) for them, we'd do it. How stupid was that?

Of course, without the weight of our conditioning under the patriarchy, fewer of us would've done it, but still. (And I am including in that conditioning the social bit of being raised to yield to men and the economic bit of having to marry one in order to have children. Oh, and the bit about intercourse resulting in ecstatic orgasms. For women. Right.)

But now? Nothing's changed. Damn right you're not feminists, as all you young things proclaim with revulsion. Because you're still servicing men. Only now it's with blow jobs. You're still trading your pleasure for theirs. (Your clitoris isn't in your throat.)

When a boy makes a girl come and keeps his own pants on, when a boy becomes popular (or a professional) because he knows what to do with his hands and his tongue, *then* you can say it's so over.

On the Radfem Doctrine
of Separatism

Here's the thing. Men are already separatists. (So really we have no choice.)

Men already exclude women from anything, everything, important. (Any inclusion is tokenism: a false symbol, a PR move.)

Men already refuse to get involved with 'women's issues', whether personal or political. That feminism itself is considered a special interest indicates that. (It shouldn't be. And it wouldn't be if 'women's issues' were typically *included* in 'issues'. That we have to establish them as 'add-ons' proves that 'issues' are really 'men's issues'. See? Separatism.)

Canterbury's Law

When the pilot episode of *Canterbury's Law* aired, I was really annoyed. The main character was an intelligent, powerful woman (a lawyer). Good. Who is shown obsessing over her appearance, albeit grudgingly, wondering whether the color of her suit brings out her eyes. Within the first hour, we also see her going to her husband for comfort and mourning a lost child.

The main character, a man, in *Law and Order?* I didn't see the pilot episode, but I'll bet it didn't open with him fretting over his tie, I'll bet he's never shown seeking, let alone getting, comfort from his wife, and I'll bet being a father is probably not a defining aspect of his character. He's just a damned good lawyer.

Why can't women just be damned good lawyers?

(Because the men who write the scripts and/or the directors who direct them and/or the producers who fund them are insecure — they can't be *men* unless women are *women*. And being a woman means being a(n aspiring) beauty queen, a wife, and/or a mother.)

A Man Shaken by a Bomb

I picked up a sci-fi novel the other day at a used bookstore (*Alas, Babylon* by Pat Frank). The jacket said it was set after a nuclear war and written by someone who'd rubbed shoulders with a lot of military people. Well, I figured it'd be interesting to see what *they* imagined life'd be like after a nuclear war. (The pages weren't blank.)

What can I say, it was slow reading. For example, the author said, "A man who's been shaken by a bomb knows what it feels like." So I had to stop and wonder why a woman wouldn't know. Is he saying women never get shaken by bombs because they're never in bombed areas? Or they are, but for some reason, they don't get shaken by them? Or they do, but they nevertheless don't know what it feels like?

And that was just the preface. Chapter one introduced Florence. Who gossiped. She didn't design state of the art mp3 players. And she certainly wasn't looking for the cure to cancer. She gossiped. However, "If your sister was in trouble and wired for money, the secret was safe with Florence. But if your sister bore a legitimate baby, its sex and weight would be known all over town."

Only if *my sister* was in trouble? What about me? I realized then that this guy hadn't even *imagined* the *possibility* that *women* might read his book. And, well, we might. After all, we *can* read.

And apparently it didn't occur to him that someone's sister, a *woman*, might have money of her own. Or that she might ask another *woman* — not a man, not her brother — for a loan.

Then of course we have the phrase "in trouble". Being pregnant, having a life begin to grow inside your body — that's not being "in trouble". It's either amazingly wonderful or incredibly devastating. But it's not being "in trouble".

Then there's that word "legitimate". First I had to back up and figure out that being in trouble meant, to him, not only being pregnant, but also being unmarried. Which would make the baby 'illegitimate'. Right. As if men alone confer legitimacy on life. My, my, aren't we a little full of ourselves. ('Course that might explain why they feel they have the right to take it so often, so capriciously. Coupled with the gross underestimation of its value indicated by the phrase "in trouble" to describe its creation...)

And what precious information would Florence, otherwise, spread far and wide? Whether his sister survived the birth? No, apparently that's not important. What's important is the sex and weight of the baby. And presumably it's important that it be *male* and that it be *big*. And why is *that* important? Well, the best I could come up with was that the guy has in mind a world in which food and shelter is gained by one-on-one physical combat (not our world), and the combat is such that brute force is an advantage (what, no weapons? no martial arts skill?), and he's assumed positive correlations between maleness and size and capacity for said brute force (not a valid assumption).

Okay, onto the next couple sentences...

Christmas Elves

Generally speaking, I don't do Christmas. At all. But when I see an ad in the classifieds for "Three female elves to work in a mall during the Christmas season", well, I have to say something.

And the first thing I have to say is, I don't think they're going to find any — male *or* female. They may find three women to play the part, but I doubt they'll find three elves.

Which brings me to the second thing I have to say: why do they have to be female? What must a Santa's elf do that a man can't do?

One, Santa's elves are industrious; they're notorious for being hard workers. Well, men are hard workers. (No, seriously, some are.)

Two, elves are pretty handy in the workshop, making all those toys. Again, I think men can meet this requirement. (Some are even quite good with their tools, given a little instruction.)

But in the mall, Santa's elves will probably have to stand on their feet all day long. I must admit that I think women have an edge here. At least they do if I'm to judge by all the checkout cashiers and bank tellers I see, *all* of whom are women, and apparently subject to some insane rule that prohibits them from sitting down on the job. (I've never understood that one: surely their work wouldn't worsen if they were able to sit down; in fact, it would probably improve — freedom from chronic back pain would have that effect, I should think.)

And, well, Santa's elves have to smile a lot. All the time, actually. And I'm afraid women again have the advantage. Unfortunately, smiling has become second nature for women; those caught *not* grinning like the idiots men like to believe them to be are often reprimanded. Now I'm willing to grant that men, because of their much-publicized superior strength, would be able to handle the standing. *And* the smiling (I suspect that it takes fewer muscles to smile than to maintain that tough and serious look so many men seem to favour).

But can they handle the subservience? Santa's elves get paid minimum wage, which is less than what Santa gets paid, and they pretty much play the part of Santa's subordinates.

Despite that, Santa's elves are really quite important. Ask any Santa who's had to work with an elf with an attitude. (I can give you some names.) A good elf intercepts the sucker that will get stuck in the beard; a good elf tells Santa the difficult names so the kid won't start bawling because Santa doesn't even know his name; a good elf has 'pee-my-pants radar' and uses it at all times. And a good elf does all that while *appearing* to be merely ornamental. I'm not sure men would be very good at that. Most men I've known who are important act like it. ('Course, so do the ones who aren't important.)

Lastly, let's not forget that Santa's elves must be good with kids. And this one really makes me hesitate. Men can *make* kids, with hardly a second thought. But can they *interact* with them? *Can they pay attention to kids — for eight hours at a time?*

I'm going to go out on a limb here and say yes. Yes they can. Oh I know they don't, most of them. I've read the stats on dead-beat dads who keep up their car payments while ignoring their child support payments. And I've read the stats showing that fathers spend, what is it, less than an hour a day with their kids (their *own* kids — it hasn't escaped me that Santa's elves have to pay attention to *other* people's kids — to phrase it in a way apparently significant to men, other *men's* kids). But well, just because they don't doesn't mean they can't. After all, if women can be lawyers and mechanics, why can't men be Santa's elves?

43

The Condom Recall

Back in the '80s when condom recalls first made headlines, which was when AIDS also first made headlines, the reason given for the recalls was that the old condoms didn't meet the new standards. Companies felt a certain social responsibility, they said. Ah. How nice. How very good of you.

Before, when a defective condom could fuck up a woman's life (either way, her life would've changed forever — to abort and suffer the anguish before and how long after, or to give it up and know forever she or he was out there somewhere, or to keep it and give up her own life for a good fifteen years) — well, that was okay. That was an acceptable risk, apparently.

But *now*, now that a *man's* quality of life is at stake, now the condoms have to be better. (Better than what exactly, I'm wondering …) In fact, now they can even be advertised, now they're even in the school washrooms. (Hey wait a minute, wouldn't she or he have been *your* kid too?) (Which reminds me of that judge who ordered that prostitutes be tested for AIDS, but not their customers.)

New standards, you say? They sound just like the old ones to me — double.

Whose Violence?

I read the other day that "Violence in our society continues to be a problem." One, duh. Two, no wonder. I mean, we haven't even got it *named* right yet.

"Violence in our society." It sounds so — inclusive. So *gender*-inclusive. But about 85% of all the violent crime is committed *by men*. The gangs are made up of men, the bar brawls are fought by men, the corner stores are held up by men, the rapists are men, the muggers are men, the drive-by shooters are men. This is sex-specific. The problem is *male* violence.

So it does no good to look at 'society', to look at our schools, our workplaces, our televisions. We need to look at our *boys*. We need to look at how we raise them — *to become men*. Because our *girls* don't grow up to commit assault and homicide on a regular basis.

For starters, let's admit that we stunt their emotional growth. From day one, we encourage outright denial: big boys don't cry. They don't cuddle and hug either. So hurt, pain, love, and affection are — not cards in the deck they're playing with.

And then there's the development of empathy. A grade eleven male student once told me that I'd wrecked hunting for him, because I'd described in some detail the awful last few hours of a wolf that'd been shot. The boy said he'd never thought about it before. Seventeen years old, carrying a loaded gun, and he's never thought about it. (Then again, it's no wonder — you can't imagine in another what you can't even see in yourself.)

Now as any reflective human being will know, hurt and anger reside pretty close to each other. So if you're blind to the hurt, all you'll recognize is the anger. And anger seems to need

45

explosive expression — if not verbal, then physical. Which brings us to communication skills. As any teacher will tell you, boys lag behind girls in language skills. Why is this? Even if it *is* innate (a boys-are-better-at-spatial-tasks-girls-are-better-at-verbal-tasks thing), well, that's just a reason for doing *more*, not *less*, with boys and communication skills. Because if they *can't* talk about, they *will* fight about it.

And let's look at nature. What if male violence *isn't* the result of a double standard in nurture? What if it's the testosterone? Or the Y chromosome itself? Maybe it's the *men* we should be over-tranquillizing. If we can manipulate estrogen levels, surely we can control testosterone levels.

Of course, you're horrified at the thought of such chemical castration. Well, hell, *I'm* horrified! We have an epidemic of violence that's clearly sex-linked and everyone seems to be busy oohing and aahing at the emperor's new clothes. The truth is *masculinity kills*.

Arrogance, I think

Fresh from the office of my supervisor who persists in gently giving me unsolicited advice, despite being neither older nor wiser, I'm struck by Rousseau's tone (in his "Marriage"): "Extreme in all things, they [women] devote themselves to their play with greater zeal than boys. This is the second defect. This zeal must be kept within bounds. It is the cause of several vices peculiar to women, among others the capricious changing of their tastes from day to day. Do not deprive them of mirth, laughter, noise and romping games, but prevent them tiring of one game and turning to another. They must get used to being stopped in the middle of their play and put to other tasks without protest on their part." I have as much trouble imagining the absolute certainty, *the arrogance*, required to initiate, let alone sustain, such pontification as I do imagining myself putting an arm around the shoulder of the guy who works in Accounting, and telling him what he should be doing with his life. Even if I were his supervisor. I simply could not go on and on like that, not even to students, nor even to children. Not even at forty.

At least not without the qualifier 'I think ...', that recognition of subjectivity — the absence of which is the presumption of objectivity, of omniscience. Can you spell 'ego'? I recall one of my philosophy professors stroking out every single 'I think' in my paper, calling it wordy, but no doubt judging me to be lacking in confidence or certainty to 'hedge' so much. But his corrections left me with lies — with presentations of opinion as presentations of fact.

And I now recognize that omission as the quintessential male lie; it's how we come to consider them as authorities, on

47

everything. Refusing to accept one's ideas as opinions means refusing to accept the possibility that they're incorrect or insignificant. (Particular shame on epistemologists for this. I now understand that, compared to my philosophy professor, I was subscribing to the more mature epistemology — *not* arrogantly equating or ignorantly assuming that my (subjective) thoughts and perceptions were *the* (objective) thoughts and perceptions.)

Or maybe the absence of the 'I' is simply the denial of, the failure to take, responsibility. Compare "Your postal code is indecipherable" to "I can't read your postal code": the first, without the 'I', doesn't even *consider* the possibility that the fault may rest with the reader.

Perhaps there's yet another explanation. Owen Flanagan notes that "Insofar as reflection requires that we be thinking about thought, then an 'I think that' thought accompanies all experience" — but he goes on to qualify that, saying, "There is no warrant for the claim that we are thinking about our complex narrative self. We are not *that* self-conscious" (*Consciousness Reconsidered*). Well. He may not be. But I am. And I dare say men in general may not be that reflective, but a great many women are.

Smile!

If I had a dollar for every time someone (i.e., a man) told me to smile, I'd be rich. (And if I had *five* dollars for every time that same someone did *not* tell a *man* to smile, I'd be *really* rich.)

Why is it that women are told, are expected, to smile a lot? (Or at least a lot more than men?)

Could it be that there are (still) some men who believe women are their responsibility, theirs to look after, care for, and protect (these are the men who call us 'dear') — and so for them, an unsmiling woman is a reproach, an indication of the man's failure? 'Smile!' means 'Tell me I'm a success!'

Could it be that women are (still) perceived to be the species' emotional barometers? Men are not allowed to be emotionally expressive (forget for a moment every hockey game and every soccer game you've ever seen men watch — I never said our society was logically consistent); a *smiling* man, especially, is effeminate. So when men feel happy, the women have to smile.

Could it be that women are (still) perceived as having the responsibility for the emotional health of the relationship, the family, and well, the world. And men want to think (not necessarily to know — different things) that all is well. They want us to smile.

Well, for someone to smile that much, they'd have to be in denial about cancer rates, ethnic cleansing, teenage violence, political corruption, big business subsidies, population growth rates, the nuclear industry, and, well, the world. They'd have to be pretty sick, psychologically, to be able to smile with all that.

Or they'd have to be hypocrites.

Or they'd have to just not know about all that — they'd have to be pretty ignorant. Or children.

Ah, maybe that's it. Men, when they tell us, expect us, to smile all the time, are telling us, expecting us, to be childish.

Next time a man tells me to smile, I'm going to tell him to fuck off.

To the Morons who Wear Make-up

First, there's the ageism you're perpetuating: make-up is intended, to a large degree, to make one look younger. In many respects, younger *is* better, but in many respects, it isn't (and anyway, make-up merely gives one *the appearance* of being younger). True, at some point in time, being old is completely the pits, but hey, that's life, deal with it — *without* delusion or deception (or implied insult).

Second, if make-up were merely intended to (attempt to) make one beautiful, I suppose there's no harm in that — the world can always use a little more beauty. But I despair at the pathetically low aesthetic standards in use if a blue eyelid is considered beautiful — let's at least see a glittering rainbow under that eyebrow arch! Further, I despair at the attention to beauty of skin if at the expense of beauty of character.

However, make-up is intended as much, if not more, to (attempt to) make one sexually attractive. I'm thinking, for example, of reddened (and puckered) lips — what is that but an advertisement for fellatio? And the rouged cheeks, suggestive of the flush of arousal. Consider too the perfume (especially if it's musk rather than floral), and the earrings (earlobes as erogenous zones), and the bras that push up and pad — all are part of the woman's morning grooming routine, her 'getting ready'. The phrase itself begs the question 'Ready for what?' 'Sex!'

There's nothing wrong per se with being sexually attractive. But there is something wrong — something sick — about wanting to be bait (sexually *attract*-ive) *all day long*. *Especially* when those same women complain about the attention they receive for their sexual attractiveness — the looks, the comments, the invitations. Not only is there a serious self-esteem problem here, there's a serious consistency-of-thought problem here.

Third, combine the first point with the first part of the second point and we see another problem: make-up endorses the '(only) young is beautiful' attitude.

Combine the first point with the second part of the second point: make-up endorses the '(only) young is sexually attractive' attitude.

Add the shaved legs and armpits (and eyeliner, for that baby doe-eyed look), and we see we're not just talking 'young' as in twenty, but 'young' as in *pre-pubescent*: only prepubescents are hairless, only prepubescents have such smooth skin. And that's *really* disturbing — endorsing the idea that prepubescents are sexually attractive.

Why is it that men find young women, girls, sexually attractive? I doubt it's just the 'they're healthier for childbearing' thing. Because actually, it's *not* healthy for girls to bear children, and it's not even *possible* for prepubescents to do so. (And it's not like the men follow up in nine months to claim their progeny.) (But then I'm assuming rational behaviour here.)

I suspect it's the power thing. Men can have power over, feel superior to, children more easily than adults. So in addition to encouraging sexual abuse of children, women who shave their legs and otherwise appear/act prepubescent are reinforcing the 'sex as power' instead of 'sex as pleasure' attitude (though of course I guess for many men power *is* pleasure).

Last, compounding all of this is the custom that only women wear make-up. Which reinforces the whole patriarchy thing: women are sexual *objects* while men are sexual *subjects*. (Of course, without make-up, and the loss of about 30 pounds, and, well, major surgery, most men couldn't cut it as sexual objects anyway.)

Let's Talk about Sex

I used to deejay for parties and other events, and on any given night, one or two of several things might happen. For a long time, I never gave them much thought. But when all of these things happened during a single night, it suddenly seemed clear to me that all those hitherto separate things were, in fact, related. They were all related to my sex.

On the night in question, I had agreed to fill in for a friend, to do his regular gig at a basement bar. When I arrived early for a show-and-tell with his system, I was immediately struck by — size. Mike and I had started out as deejays at the same time: we went through the training together, we apprenticed with the same outfit, and then we each bought out our identical systems and started our own businesses. I had pretty much kept the same system — a couple cassette players, a search deck, a mixer, an amp, and a pair of 12" x 16" speakers on tripods, with a microprocessor. Mike, I saw, had added. And he'd added big: he now had *two* pairs of speakers, each 3' by 2', a second amp of course, and a couple CD players.

What is it with men? They get suckered in to the 'bigger is better' mentality every time. (And it's not just immature, it's dangerous: look around — continual growth is *not* good, we *can't* keep expanding, getting bigger and bigger, using more and more.) I asked him if the smaller set-up wasn't loud enough, if he'd gotten too many complaints. Of course he had to say no. But this looks better, he says. And that *really* pissed me off. Most people — most men — are stupid that way: they see Mike's huge array of equipment, compare it to my little set-up, and figure he's a better deejay. There's no logic to it. And either Mike knows it and he's taking advantage of it (and making it that much harder for the rest of us who refuse to be taken in by size) or he doesn't know it and he's just as big a fool as the rest of them (unknowingly at my expense).

Whatever, he walked me through and in a few minutes I was fine — unless I got a lot of requests. And this is another problem with more, more, more: there were at least four different places in which to look up a title — there was one directory for the old cassettes, a separate directory for the new cassettes, a third directory for the CDs (except for the ones which weren't listed anywhere), and a fourth 'hits' directory. This is crazy, I thought as he left. I took some time to familiarize myself with what was where, and saw a ridiculous amount of duplication — there had to be at least a hundred songs I could find in at least two places. And altogether he had ten times more music than he could ever hope to play in a night.

Well, the requests started coming in at 10:00. The bartender told me to play Seger's "Rock and Roll", "Dance Mix 95", and the "Macarena". Gee, none of those would've occurred to me, thanks. Then the other bartender came up and asked for something. A little later I got a note with seven or eight titles on it. It occurred to me at that point that I was getting a lot more requests than Mike usually got. (He'd said this gig would be a piece of cake, no one ever bothered to make a request.) And I wondered, is it because I'm a woman, so people think I'm more approachable? Or is it because I'm a woman, so probably I have to be told what to play, because I probably don't know. (And half the time it is just that: I'm *told*, not asked, to play such-and-such.)

At around 10:30, this guy came up to chat. He opened with 'So are you Mike's helper?' Excuse me? Mike's *helper*? I told him no, I have my own business (I gave him my card), I'm just doing this gig for him tonight as a favour. The guy continued the small talk. I was trying to be polite, but I was also

54

listening for the end of the current song, and trying to find at least *one* of the requested songs in at least one of the directories or boxes of music — and then it dawned on me that this guy was really trying to stretch out the conversation, he was, in fact, 'hitting on me'. And I was, in fact, trying to work.

The same thing happened again later on. Only with the second guy, we got into this ridiculous competition of 'I know more about deejaying than you.' I'm sure you know the type, there's one in every crowd who comes up to tell you 'Yeah, I used to do this, how many watts do you have?' But this guy *really* wanted to win — and it occurred to me that the male-female thing was getting in the way again, it was complicating simple shop talk, he refused to lose to a woman. Listen, I'm trying to *work* here —

And then a *third* guy came up and said, 'Play some rock, this stuff is shit.' I smiled and said, 'This shit was requested, but I'll certainly put on some rock for you.' I did so within two songs. He came up again, and this time sat himself down in my chair, behind my table (I've never seen *anyone* do that to a *male* deejay). He told me he had been drinking since 2:00. He thought he was bragging rather than proclaiming how pathetic he was, and I realized, geez, he's hitting on me too. 'Play some rock,' he said again. I said, 'I've *been* playing rock, what specifically do you want to hear, what do you mean when you say 'rock'?' '*Any* rock,' he exploded, then insulted, 'Anyone knows what rock is!' He came up a third time, and said he'd taken a survey and no one wanted to hear this shit ("Dance Mix," requested three times), play some rock and roll! By now, I was just trying to ignore him. I'd already played Seger, Springsteen, the Stones, Cochrane, and Adams; I'd played Tragically Hip and Pearl Jam; I'd played Hootie and I'd played the Smashing Pumpkins. This was one drunken asshole I would not be able to please. He persisted from the end of the bar, yelling 'Rock and Roll!' every time I put on some dance or country (also requested several times).

I almost lost it when at around midnight the bartender came up and asked me to play some rock and roll — 'He keeps asking us to come up and tell the girl to play a little rock!' Any man pushing forty would be, I think, insulted to be called a boy. Wake up call, guys: most adult women are (or should be) just as insulted to be called a girl.

Shortly after, the first guy came back up to tell me he thought I was doing a fine job, he saw the shit I was getting from the other guy. Part of me wanted to take that at face value; that was a really nice thing to do. But another part of me was thinking 'Yeah but he's only nice like that because you're a woman': there's a subtext of either making the moves on me or patronizing me. (Did he think I was about to burst into tears? Actually I was thinking about just hauling back and decking the drunk — but I didn't want to have to pay Mike for damage to his equipment.)

The night finally ended; I packed up and left.

The next night, I had a wedding to do. And it was just like any other wedding I'd done, but after the previous night, well, it was just like that night…

'I don't think this is gonna go, you should play something faster,' I heard someone say to me. I looked at him and wondered if he thought his being male and my being female gave him the right to criticize, to give advice to someone old enough to be his parent. Thirty seconds into the (slow) piece I'd chosen, the dance floor was full. Have I proved myself? Of course not — I just 'lucked out'. 'Again', I mused sarcastically.

Another guy came up, walked around my table, and stood beside me. No, he didn't have a request, he just wanted to introduce himself, say hi, how's it going. He stayed, there, in my way, for three whole songs, oblivious to my suggestions that he join the party, it looks good.

A little later, an older guy, fifty-something, gave me a gentle warning, 'You can't please everyone, but just try a bit of 50s and 60s.' 'I know,' I told him, not pointing out that I'd already done a 50s-60s set, 'I've been doing this for over five years now.' 'Oh you *have?*' He was so surprised. What, do I have 'novice' written on my forehead? Did the way I set up my equipment suggest that I didn't know what I was doing? (Single-handedly and in fifteen minutes flat.) No — I'm female — so it just goes without saying that I probably don't know what I'm doing.

I just wanted to be a deejay. But people, especially men, kept insisting by their behaviour, that I was a *female* deejay. Sex shouldn't make a difference. But they make it make a difference. Are male deejays expected to chat pleasantly while they're working, not just once or twice but through the whole night? Do they have to deal with a constant stream of guidance, a constant stream of unwelcome and unnecessary advice?

Frankly, it's irritating, it's insulting, and it's exhausting.

King of the Castle

Octavia Butler got it right in *Xenogenesis* when the aliens identified one of our fatal flaws as that of being hierarchy-driven (they fixed us with a bit of genetic engineering) — but she failed to associate the flaw predominantly with males.

And Steven Goldberg got it right in *Why Men Rule* when he explained that men are genetically predisposed to hierarchy (fetal masculinization of the central nervous system renders males more sensitive to the dominance-related properties of testosterone) — but he presented that as an explanation for why men rule and not also for why men kill.

And Arthur Koestler got it right in *The Call Girls* when, recognizing that the survival of the human species is unlikely, a select group of geniuses meet at a special 'Approaches to Survival' symposium (and fail to agree on a survival plan) — but I'm not sure he realized (oh of course he did) that one of his character's early reference to a previous symposium on 'Hierarchic Order in Primate Societies' was foreshadowing.

The reason the human species will not survive is simple: the males can't help playing King of the Castle — all the time, everywhere, with everyone. Discussion about aggression and violence, or greed, is all very good, but these things are secondary: aggression and violence are means to the end of becoming King of the Castle; and it's not really that men are greedy, they just want more than the next guy, they want to be better, higher than the next guy, then the next, and the next, until they get to the top.

And once they *become* King of the Castle, they see, from up there, that there's another castle to become King of. Once they've got the one-bedroom apartment, they go for the two-bedroom. Then the duplex, then the single-family dwelling.

Once they get a house, they need a cottage too. And once they get the cottage, then they need a summer home. Then a yacht. They can't stop adding and upgrading. Whether it's homes or cars, stereo systems or computers — nothing is ever (good) enough. Nothing satisfies. Sold one million? Let's aim for two million. This year's profit is X? Let's set a target of double X for next year. Consider the business graph of success — more, more, more... They cannot 'say when'. Contentment forever eludes them. The only joy in their lives is that which is associated with achievement, with getting a toehold a little higher on the hill, winning an extra inch. They can't play without keeping score. They can't go canoeing without a destination *and* an arrival time. They cannot concede, surrender, or lose without shame.

It's not about the pursuit of excellence, don't let them kid you: there's no standard of intrinsic quality involved; comparison is all. And it's not about self-improvement: being King of the Castle seldom improves the self.

The end result to this deadly game they play will be the same, whether it's achieved by genocidal war, environmental destruction, or the global marketplace: loss of diversity. It's the kiss of death for any, for every, species. (Unless, of course, some Nero goes nuclear first.)

Playing Basketball

I play basketball Monday nights. It's an all-comers thing, but mostly it's students who show up — team members of the high school in whose gyms we play. The boys' team. And there's a handful of older guys, some ex-students, and some acquaintances of the coach/teacher who 'runs' the night. And there's me — and two other women.

When I first showed up and saw that I'd be playing with/against predominantly sixteen to eighteen-year-old males, I prepared myself for a good cardio challenge. I wasn't prepared for everything else.

First of all, the coach/teacher's division into teams. He'd carefully put one tall person on each team; he'd also split up the senior hotshots, the new and clued-out grade nines and tens, and the over-twenty men. And then he'd put one woman on each team. I wondered why our gender disqualified us from the height/skill/age categories. Certainly the attributes were not exclusive: one could be female and also be over or under 5'8", one could be female and also be skilled or unskilled, one could be female and also be over or under twenty. But our height/skill/age was irrelevant — our gender was all that mattered.

This view was also held by most, if not all, of the players there. Once in teams, two teams per gym, we'd face our opponent team and sort of pick who our 'man' would be (we always played a one-on-one game). The tall guys picked each other, the hotshots paired off, the nine/tens stood together, and it was always assumed that the two women would guard each other.

When I objected one night, I was told no, no, it's not because you're both women, we decide on the basis of height. Bullshit. One of the hotshots is the kind of player I used to be:

a speedy little guard that lasts forever, with great reflexes and superb co-ordination — the terrier of the team. He's about 5'6". Audrey's 5'1". I'm 5'4". Did you guys fail arithmetic?

Furthermore, when there wasn't a woman on the other team, they'd match me up with the youngest newest littlest grade niner. So I knew the matching was on the basis of perceived ability; and not only were the women perceived to be of equal ability because we were women, we were perceived to be of lower ability than the men. Any of the men. All of the men. How humiliating. I set six track records at my university, I used to lift weights and coach gymnastics, and I'm still a dancer (so among other things I can run backwards, quickly). Even without all of that, a thirty-five-year-old body has a cardio-vascular and muscular system much more developed than a thirteen-year-old body. They'd never think of matching Jack with a kid (Jack's about my age, probably five years older in fact, and an ex-basketball ref.)

Not only is their perception/practice humiliating and unfair, it leads to a real stupid situation. What happens is this. When two perceived-to-be-poor players are matched up to each other, they have nothing to do but play a great defensive game — because their team-mates never pass them the ball. So, not having to worry about anything else, such as getting the ball and scoring, Audrey (or Billy) guards me so closely I can never get clear; so my team-mates never pass me the ball; so I never get to shoot; so I'm perceived to be a poor player; so I get matched with Audrey (or Billy) ...

A couple times I managed to match with one of the hotshots. Was he ever pissed. Usually another hotshot is guarding him, and that other hotshot is so busy trying to get the ball that his man is often in the clear. So of course he gets the passes, and the shots. I, however, stuck to him like glue (having nothing else to do) — so no one passed to him. And if they did, he was too far away to make a good shot. Goodbye hotshot status. I have also frustrated a tall player, with my superior speed and/or co-ordination and/or endurance — and intelligence (anticipation). And that's what should be happening: the best defensive players should be put on the best offensive players. But of course it would be humiliating for any male player, most especially the good ones, to be paired with me.

I must say though, that at least at the beginning, it might've been wise to match the women with each other because our playing style is so different from that of the men. In fact, for a few months, I was a poor player because the way I played, the way I was taught to play, just didn't work when playing with men.

For instance, when I went through school, girls weren't taught how to do a jump shot: our feet either stayed on the ground or we jumped *as* we shot — we never practiced, let alone mastered, the 'jump, then while elevated above your opponent, shoot' kind of shot. Consequently, all of my shots were blocked merely by someone's raised hand. (Remember that most, not just some, of the other players were taller than me.)

Furthermore, I was taught to shoot from the chest, not from over my head (probably because it was believed then that girls didn't have, couldn't develop, the necessary arm strength). Again, my (female) way destined me for failure (in a world dominated by men).

However, I adapted. I figured that since it was hopeless to try to shoot from within the key (it was even hazardous to play in there because of the elbow-in-face possibilities), I decided I'd learn to shoot from outside the key. So I quickly developed a pretty accurate three-point shot. (My hand-eye co-ordination has always been pretty good and with a few weeks of weights and push-ups I regained enough shoulder power to support that co-ordination for the two hours of play.)

62

It worked. I was finally accepted as an okay player. Not good, mind you — just okay. Note that I had had to develop above-average ability (most of the guys can't shoot as consistently as me from the three-point line) just to be considered okay.

Then again no, actually, it didn't work at all. You need the ball before you can shoot. And my team-mates just wouldn't pass it to me. No matter how much or how often I was in the clear. They'd rather make a risky pass to someone else than a safe pass to me. Like guys, am I invisible? Yes. We're not the second sex, or even just the silent sex. We're the invisible sex.

And this led to another stupid situation. Eventually, when I realized I was only going to get the ball a few times, I'd make a shot every time I could, even if it was a bad shot. After all, it might be the only shot I'd get all night. And so of course making poor shots, that missed, made me seem even more of a poor player. And so they passed the ball to me even less. I hardly even got the chance to dribble. Without in-game practice, I couldn't improve; without improvement, I wouldn't get the ball for in-game practice. Eventually I reamed out a few guys for not passing to me. And, eventually, a few changed and began to include me in the game. (It's too bad it had to take a display of anger, but 'When you understand another language, you just let me know!')

Another difference between the female and male playing styles is strategy. The guys seem a lot more devious. The feint I learned, way back when, was a very obvious pretend chest pass in one direction followed by a real pass in the other. I see guys feinting with their shoulder, their eyes — it's second nature to them to pretend to go up, wait till their guard is in the air to block the shot, then as he's coming down, go up for real. And shoot. And score. I was never taught to do that. Then again, were they taught or does such 'deeking out', such deceit, just 'come naturally'? Do boys' games involve more deceit than girls' games? Good question. Playing house requires imagination. Skipping, hopscotch — these are games of pure skill. But cowboys and Indians? Cunning is needed to catch someone. And hockey and soccer involve strategies of deceit similar to basketball. Hell, poker, the consummate man's game, positively *depends* on bluffing.

There were other differences, between male and female, that worked to my disadvantage. For instance, their ball is bigger. I didn't even know that until just last year, when I saw one guy discard, with some disgust, a ball he had chosen from the cart. It had GIRLS written on it. I couldn't believe what I'd seen, and I said 'What's the big deal, for god's sake, if a ball has the word GIRLS written on it? Afraid you're going to get pregnant or something?' He said 'It's smaller.' I picked it up. It *was* smaller. (Though of course that doesn't explain the disgust accompanying his discard.) I used it for shooting practice that night. My accuracy jumped from 50% to almost 80%. So, apart from the disadvantage of playing with a ball differently-sized from what you've learned with and used for ten years, given my hand size, a larger ball is simply a bit harder to dribble, pass, and catch with any speed. (I've often thought NBA games have become so boring because the court size, net height, and ball size haven't changed in proportion to player size and height. If I could play on a court I could cover in what, ten strides, with a ball I could grip with one hand, shooting at a net I could reach just by standing under it, my stats might be a little more impressive too.)

And then there's the bit about shirts and skins. Always the figuring out that the team with the woman on it had to be shirts. That really bothered me. I started playing in September after spending several months shirtless (it's legal now). And then suddenly it's a big deal — I have to keep my shirt on. So I spoke up. I said 'I resent the fact that your upper body is considered acceptable for public display, and mine is considered obscene.' One guy chided me with a smile that said I was being a naughty child, 'Ah let's not hear any of that!' 'Any of what?' I asked. He didn't reply, as if my question was rhetorical. I was about to ask then if they'd object to my being shirtless if I'd had a bilateral mastectomy — but they had started the game, dismissing my objection, dismissing me.

And legs. I wore long pants the first year, mostly because my short track shorts simply didn't fit like they used to. Then I bought another pair of shorts, longer and looser, and wore them — in spite of my increasing dismay with my legs: as long as I felt they had a half-decent cut, I had the guts to go unshaved; but now, for the first time in my life, I felt a little self-conscious of their increasing, and I imagined, comparative shapelessness. (Of course they still had shape — just a different shape than they used to!) Part of it is simply the female layer of fat, I told myself, and part of it is age; and part of it is you simply don't run forty miles a week or lift weights anymore. But — and here's the thing — my legs look exactly like a lot of other legs out there on the court, hair and all. Seventeen-year-old legs and thirty-seven-year-old legs. Male legs. And it occurred to me, of course! Why should we expect a female leg and a male leg to be shaped differently, why should we even expect a big difference in hair? And I'll bet *they're* not self-conscious about the shape of their legs. Hell, they're probably not even *conscious* about the shape of their legs. Learning that, knowing that, took away my self-consciousness.

I learned a lot of other things, things about myself, playing basketball Monday nights. I thought I had overcome most of the negative aspects of my feminine conditioning, and I realized I hadn't.

I was still waiting to be noticed, not making myself noticeable. It's not enough to be in the right place at the right time, you have to yell about it and wave your arms.

I was still waiting for someone to pass the ball, to give the ball to me. Instead of just taking it.

And I was still being nice, still being polite. I'd let a player go by rather than interrupt, rather than block his path. When both of us were running down the court I didn't cut in front to block potential passes, I almost said 'After you!' Even for rebounds, it's still hard to butt in, to step *in front of* someone; I had to be there first in order to be in front. And I didn't reach out for the ball, grab it, and hold onto it; if it didn't come right into my hands, it didn't come into my hands at all. And certainly, I didn't grab the ball if it was intended for someone else — I went after it only if it was a 'free' ball.

I learned it was my habit to share, to co-operate. I recall a rule, hopefully from gym class and not from team play: 'When dribbling, you can't bounce the ball more than three times without passing it to someone else.' And so I'd pass the ball to another player more often than try to move in and take the shot myself.

And I learned I'm still ... tentative. The guys pass the ball harder, they grab it more aggressively — they play with more conviction. And I see a guy who last year was a grade nine and worse than me, this year trying moves I still don't dare. Where did he get the confidence? From being male? From being encouraged? (Are the two related — still?)

Lastly, I learned I was still deferring to men. Men half my age for god's sake. When a ball went out of bounds and I retrieved it to pass it back into play, or when I had it to bring up the court, often one of my team-mates would say, in a helpful tone, 'Here, I'll take it'. And for a long time I automatically handed it over. I mean, someone asked me for something (no, they didn't *ask*), something I could give to them, so I gave it to them. But why should he take it? Can't I throw the ball to someone and get it remotely close to target? Can't I bounce a ball and run at the same time?

Every Man, Woman, and Child

There's an interesting phrase. Man, woman, and child: those are my options, are they? Identifying oneself by one's sex is a prerequisite for adulthood: if I don't want to identify myself by my sex, as either a man or a woman, I'm left with identifying myself as a child. How interesting.

Actually, it explains a lot. I have neither of the traditional signifiers of fulfilled womanhood — a husband or children. Nor do I have the traditional signifiers of manhood — a breadwinning income or a family (the wife and kids). And, it seems to me, I have often been treated like a child, like an insignificant, like someone to be seen and not heard, to be dismissed at will.

Once, when I called a garage with questions about rustproofing my car, I got superficial and incomplete answers that were of no help at all in deciding whether and where to have the work done; a male friend of mine called the same place, spoke to the same guy, and was treated to the adult version, a clear and substantial explanation of the advantages and disadvantages of wax-based and oil-based undercoating.

A female friend of mine once explained that introducing herself as *Mrs.* So-and-So made a big difference with stuff like that. And I recalled then the following incident. After recently moving to a semi-rural area, as I walked to the mailbox cluster for my mail, a neighbour stopped to walk with me and chat. Her first question was 'Is So-and-So your husband?' No. 'Are So-and-So your kids, then?' No. 'Oh, you're So-and-So's girlfriend, aren't you?' No. End of conversation. I couldn't be connected to husband or kids (even husband-potential would've sufficed), so I didn't exist. I became invisible.

I am a bit of an androgyne. For whatever reason, having followed my inclinations, my preferences, I have about as many masculine traits as feminine ones. And while most people recognize me as female, I have been taken for a man on several occasions. This doesn't bother me, because if I were to describe who or what I am, my sex would be rather low on the list: I am a lot of other things before I am a woman/man. And — this is important — *all of these other things are very adult.*

The Pill for Men

'Outrageous!' That was the word used way back in '85 in response to the expectation that men take a contraceptive that had a side-effect of reduced sex drive. Hello. Let me tell you about the contraceptive pill for women. Side-effects include headaches, nausea, weight gain, mood changes, yeast infections, loss of vision, high blood pressure, gall bladder disease, liver tumours, skin cancer, strokes, heart attacks, and death. Oh, and reduced sex drive. (Thing is, and get this — do not pass go until you do — taking the pill is, for many of us, preferable to getting pregnant.)

But, you know, that's okay, that men refuse to be responsible for their reproductive capability. They wouldn't remember to take the pill every day anyway. What with their busy life of going to work and coming home again. So we'd end up being responsible for reminding them — perhaps after we pick up the kids on our way home from work, and make dinner, and do the dishes, but before we start the laundry and see that the homework comes before the tv. Which sort of defeats the purpose.

'Course if it were meat-flavoured and chewable, like, say the beef jerky treats my dog scarfs down...

And it would have to come in regular and extra-strength so men could boast about their virility ('I need the extra-strength to subdue my guys!').

And it would have to be available without a prescription of course ('Don't need to see no doctor to tell me what I can and can't take!'). At all hardware stores. And beer st— hey, wait a minute! Why not put it *in* the beer!

69

I can't possibly be strong

The other day, I stopped to help a neighbour whose car was stuck in his driveway. (It was winter. Snow.)

"Want me to push while you give it some gas?" I offered.

"Do you think you can?" he replied.

Well, if I didn't think I could, I wouldn't've offered. Numbnuts.

On another day, I heard another neighbour say that he'd seen the small tree across the path alongside my cabin (dragged there in an attempt to discourage ATVers), but he didn't think I'd put it there. He apparently thought to himself it was "too heavy for Peggy".

(And yes, note the 'Peggy' — I've never introduced myself to *anyone* as 'Peggy', but he is not the only one to have gone for the diminutive version — do I call him Bobby instead of Bob?).

Here's the thing. Both neighbours see me kayak every spring/summer/fall afternoon — *all* afternoon. They both see me hiking through the bush every winter afternoon — *all* afternoon. They both know I used to be a marathon runner, they've seen me go running. They both know (or would if they'd actually thought about it) that I shovel my own driveway and split my own wood.

And yet pushing a car and moving a small fallen tree is apparently beyond my capabilities.

But not, apparently, beyond *their* capabilities. Because they're male. Even though one is in his 70s and the other is in his 60s. Which means I'm several decades younger. Still, they *must* be stronger than me. Their worldview depends on it.

The Gender of Business

Business is male. Make no mistake. Everything about it smacks of the male mentality.

First, the obsession with competition. You have to be #1, you have to outcompete your competition. So hierarchy, rank, is everything. As is an adversarial attitude. It doesn't have to be that way. Business could be a huge network of co-operative ventures, each seeking to better the whole. But no, we have to be better than, stronger than, faster than —

Bigger than. Business is obsessed with size. Mergers, acquisitions, expansion. Bigger is better. Bigger wins. The business suit has padded shoulders to make its wearer look bigger. They're always talking about new opportunities for growth. Unlimited growth. They never talk about cancer.

Closely related to size is number. Business measures success in numbers, in quantifiable units. (And the numbers must be big.) Units manufactured, units sold, profits, paycheques. (Not customer service reps though.) It also measures value in numbers. It puts a price on beautiful views. And lives. Again, it doesn't have to be that way. When some people say something is priceless, they mean it.

Another characteristic, derivative of the obsession with competition, is the obsession with power. Power over others. Responsibility is the flip side of power, but the only responsibility business talks about is the responsibility to shareholders — to be competitive, to be big, to produce high returns. All other responsibilities are swept under the carpet and called externalities.

And of course if you're going to compete, you have to take risks. Business is all about taking risks. Yet again, it doesn't

71

have to be that way. Safe is good. The system could be set up so risk isn't required. (Actually, as it is, it isn't — if you're big enough. Bail-out.)

And it almost goes without saying that, given competition, the emphasis is on the self. Business is egotistic. One collaborates only in order to compete, to win. Communalism and socialism are dirty words. Altruism is simply denied.

And perhaps the most dangerous: women are devalued. Half the species just doesn't count, as far as business is concerned. 80% of male city finance workers visit strip clubs for 'corporate entertainment' ("On Bankers and Lap Dancers" M. Lynn, *International Herald Tribune* Jan 12/06).

This is why men go into business. It has what they are. It's also why business is male. They are it. It's a vicious circle.

That's why we're never going to change business, we're never going to stop its crippling effect on the quality of our lives. We'd have to stop making men first. (We could, you know. We could make just people instead.)

The Sexism Compensation Index

I suspect that even with today's rigorous interview and job performance appraisal techniques, which require that all applicants be asked and scored on the same questions, multiple standards still interfere with merit as the sole criterion for hiring and promotion.

How? Suppose the interviewers are asked to rate the candidates on 'friendliness'. On an absolute scale of ten, the averagely friendly woman is, or is thought to need to be, at, let's say, 6. So for a female candidate to be rated 'very friendly' as opposed to just 'friendly enough', she must score 7 or better. The averagely friendly man, on the other hand, men tending of course to smile less, chat less, be more product-oriented than process-oriented, etc., is at, say, 4. So for a male candidate to be rated 'very friendly', he must score only 5 or better. There you have it: suppose both a male and female applicant score 5 on the friendliness score — the man will be perceived as '*more* friendly than' and the woman as '*less* friendly than'.

The same might go for appearance: the man who spends ten minutes to get ready for work, to shower and put on clean clothes, is deemed presentable; the woman who does the same is told she should've dressed up a bit (what, no make up? no styled hair? no jewellery?).

The assertiveness scale probably works the other way: say both candidates are at 5 — the man may be deemed 'not a go-getter' or 'lacking in confidence', the woman, 'pushy' or 'arrogant'.

And on and on.

How do we correct this? Many interviewers take great pains to be fair, to be consistent, to stick to the list of questions — so what, exactly, is the problem? Well, it's usually not the questions, but the answers — it's how the answers are heard. Most of the interviewers were raised in sexist times and so differentiating on the basis of sex is second nature to them; and it's hard to shed one's formative years overnight. Or even over a decade, apparently.

Gender blind interviewing might help, but without expensive voice scramblers and screens, this is impossible. And I suppose, to some extent, these measures would defeat the purpose of the interview.

However, if all items but those which couldn't possibly be measured except in a face-to-face encounter were measured prior to the interview, that would go a long way. Cover letters and resumes could be identified by number only (as is the case with anonymous review for publication). Calling people listed as references would, unfortunately, reveal gender (damn our language and names), so perhaps the conversation or at least the comments could be translated to gender-free language by someone not doing the actual scoring. This wouldn't eliminate the gender bias of the person called, but it would minimize what gets passed on.

Another solution might be to adjust the scores, after the interviews, to compensate for the sexism: one could apply an SCI, a Sexism Compensation Index, whereby all of the scores would be adjusted up or down a few points depending on the sex of the applicant, the item scored, and perhaps the sex of the interviewer. So, for example, the woman's friendliness score of 5 will get boosted to 6 or 7 to reflect the higher standard that is sexistly expected of women; 7 compared to 5 makes it clear that the woman is actually the friendlier of the two.

Am I serious? Not really. But sort of — knowing this, considering this, during the interview and at any other gender-known stage, might alone effect the necessary adjustment.

In Praise of AIDS

AIDS can be a good thing.

First, if we need a 'die off', if we need a major decrease in the human population, in order for the planet (the human species included) to survive, then AIDS gets my vote.

War would do it. But, whether biochemical or nuclear, it would also destroy a lot of the environment. Which kind of defeats the purpose. Furthermore, a lot of innocent people tend to die in wars.

And that's the problem with major environmental catastrophe, another contender. Sure, a lot more earthquakes or droughts would do it — droughts are especially effective because they can cause mega-famines — but again, a lot of innocent people would die.

There are other diseases which, in epidemic proportions, would do the trick. Tuberculosis and the Bubonic Plague, for instance. But here's where the beauty of AIDS comes in: those other diseases can be caught quite accidentally, because they're airborne or spread by very casual contact; to get AIDS, you have to do something pretty definite, pretty intentional. Except for in utero transmission, blood transfusion, and rape, getting AIDS can never be called an accident; getting AIDS is always voluntary.

And, that makes for a pretty neat self-selection thing: if you're the kind of person who's stupid enough not to know that HIV is transmitted by having sex (or even stupider, to think that having sex is worth dying for), or if you're the kind of person who shoots up with any old needle, then frankly, you're the kind of person the human species can do without.

Second, AIDS is the best thing that's happened to women in a long time: it can make rape the equivalent of murder. And the significance of this lies in the law regarding self-defence: typically, killing in self-defence is justified as long as you think your life might be at stake and you believe, on reasonable grounds, that you have no other way of protecting yourself.

How do I know my rapist-wannabe isn't HIV-positive? It's reasonable to assume he has a sexual history of multiple partners and a history of rough sex. And it's reasonable to assume he's not going to put on a condom. Or if he does, that it'll break. So it's reasonable to assume that any rape could turn out to be murder — he might be killing me while he's raping me. Consider it death by lethal injection. So, thanks to AIDS, I now have legal licence to kill the sonuvabitch.

The Soaps vs. The Game

While both 'the soaps' and 'the game' have been criticized as poor viewing choices, only the soaps have been dismissed as fluff. However, a close examination reveals that, in fact, the soaps have more heft than the game.

In both cases, the central theme, and that which drives the action, is winning. In the soaps, what the players are trying to win is money, power, love, and/or happiness. These are pretty substantial goals. In the game, however, the players are trying to win — the game. Frankly, it verges on circularity (you play the game in order to win the game), which comes close to utter triviality.

And while both sets of players use strategy, often involving manipulation, the strategy of the soaps is considerably more complicated than 'Fake left, then go right.' In fact, I would venture to say that the soaps is to the game what chess is to checkers.

With regard to setting, the soaps have a bit of an edge: while a well-furnished room is the norm, at least the set does change. (One has the well-furnished office, the well-furnished den, the well-furnished living room...)

With respect to dialogue, again the soaps have the edge: there *is* some. (Actually, I expect the game players speak to each other too, but for some reason we never get to hear their dialogue; instead, we are privy only to a voice-over commentary, explaining the action, rather like a Greek chorus — as patronizing now as it no doubt was then.)

While the characters of the soaps are more gender-inclusive, the characters of the game are more race-inclusive. (And in both cases, they're rich.) I'd call it a tie here.

77

As for plot, again I'd call it a tie: in both cases, the events are terribly predictable. I'd venture to say one is hard put to distinguish one game from another or one soap from another — only the characters give it away.

In the cinematography category, the game is superior for its long shots, but the soaps are superior for their close-ups. Again, a tie. However, in the soundtrack category, the soaps walk away with the prize.

As for sex and violence, I think the soaps lead the game on both counts. There is simply no sex in the game — unless you count the occasional ass-pat (but that is so very elementary, it hardly even counts as foreplay). And while there is a lot more physical contact in the game, of a violent-seeming nature, and while injury must therefore be frequent, it is seldom permanent; in the soaps, however, people get hurt all the time, in rather long-lasting ways. Death is even rarer in the game; not so in the soaps.

One might point out that the game is real, whereas the soaps are not, and on that basis alone claim victory for the game. Unfortunately this very 'advantage' backfires: given the level of injury and death in the soaps, it's to its credit that it's *not* for real; in the game, however, real people get hurt.

Tally up the points and I rest my case: the soaps are pretty substantial stuff compared to the schoolyard play of the game.

Almost Psychopathic

I realize, spurred to reflection by an incident at Monday night basketball when, after I set a very successful pick, the young man involved fussed and fumed and threatened to 'plow me over next time!' — I realize that yes, I fear men. But it's not their superior strength or physical abilities I fear. We are *homo sapiens*: we have gone beyond brute force with our use of tools, as weapons if need be.

Rather it's their anger, their lack of control, their tendency to tantrums that I fear. Combined with their relative self-centredness, a focus on rights over responsibilities, and a certain lack of ability to empathize, that tendency makes them capable, more capable than women, of causing great pain.

The man who may some day get back at me by kicking or shooting Chessie causes pain not as much because of his malicious intent as because of his ignorance: his ignorance of Chessie's value to me, of my love for her, of our incredible, amazing bond. Malicious intent is there, certainly, but it is intent to cause just X amount of pain — it's just a dog. His action will, however, cause tenfold X pain — it's *Chessie*.

I'm reminded of the man in *The Piano* who, in a fit of rage, a tantrum, cuts off the mute pianist's finger: he has *no idea* of the damage he's done, absolutely no understanding of the irrevocable loss he has caused — it *wasn't* just a finger. Not by a long shot. A very long shot.

There's something very frightening about this kind of capacity to injure: to hurt with intent is at least to act with responsibility, and it shows a sort of respect for the other, an appreciation of the harm caused; but to hurt spontaneously, recklessly, casually, without bothering to even be aware of it, aware of the magnitude of the injury, adds a sort of insult to the injury (I think this is why victim impact statements are so important: we want the other person to *know* just what he's done, to take on that burden of responsibility). Indeed, to hurt in that off-hand cool sort of way — it's almost psychopathic

What's so funny about a man getting pregnant?

I recently read *The Fourth Procedure* by Stanley Pottinger, in which, during a surgical procedure, a man is given a uterus containing a fertilized egg. He is enraged when he finds out, afraid that if it becomes public knowledge he'll be a laughing-stock. Turns out he's right. But I don't get it. What's so funny about a man getting pregnant?

Is it like laughing at the guy who slips on a banana peel — laughing at another's adversities? For when pregnancy is unwanted and occurs in a world without abortion, it is certainly an adversity. Forget going to college, forget that career. You're screwed. (The double meaning of that phrase is no coincidence.) Even if you give the child to someone else, a good year of your life has been derailed.

It takes — I was going to say immaturity, but that's an insult to the many children who do *not* laugh when another kid falls down and hurts him/herself. And then I was going to say it takes a lack of empathy — but those who laugh at others' adversities seem fully aware that they *are* adversities. So what is it then? Well it's sick. (There's a philosophically precise term.)

But perhaps it's not the adversity that's funny; maybe it's the unexpectedness. But there are many unexpected things we don't laugh at, so that can't be right.

Then I read that one of the characters who laughed at the situation called the guy a 'wuss' — which, of course, means the man is effeminate, feminine, womanly, womanish, whatever. So how does that fit in? To be pregnant is to be female, and to be female is — laughable?

And why is that exactly?

Freakonomics Indeed

In *Freakonomics*, Levitt and Dubner present an astounding connection between access to abortion and crime: twenty years after Roe v. Wade, the U.S. crime rate dropped.

Astounding indeed. That men are so surprised by that! Just how clueless *are* you guys? About the power, the influence, of parenting, about the effect of being forced to be pregnant, to be saddled with a squalling baby you do not want, on an income you do not have, because you've got a squalling baby you do not want ... What did you guys *think* would happen in situations like that? The women would get "Mother of the Year" awards for raising psychologically healthy adults?

What *I* find surprising is that lack of access to abortion (common, despite Roe v. Wade) isn't related to infanticide. Pity. Given the *Freakonomics* boys.

Bare Breasts: Objections and Replies

Thanks to Gwen Jacobs, since 1991 it has been legal in Ontario for women to go shirtless. Even so, the choice to do so is often met with one or more objections. To which I offer the following replies.

1. *It's immoral.*
   Why? What is it about a woman's breasts that makes it immoral for them to be uncovered?

   a. *They're sexual.*

      i. If this refers to their role as fast food outlets, not every woman's breasts *are* — and to legislate against *all* because of *some* (and actually a very small percentage at that, at any given time) is unreasonable.

         Further, a McDonalds in Ethiopia is surely more immoral than such a breast in the park.

      ii. If 'sexual' is intended to mean 'sexually attractive', no they're not. At least, not to me. Nor to any homosexual man I know. So it seems the original law prohibiting shirtless women was made by and for heterosexual men. (No surprise there, really.) (Except that you'd think the original law would *require*, rather than *prohibit*, baring breasts.)

         And actually, by and for *only some* heterosexual men — I understand that some are 'tits and ass men' while others are 'leg men'. And since it's not illegal for us to bare our legs — in fact, doing so, wearing dresses and skirts, is encouraged (were the 'leg men' in on that?) — the law is inconsistent, at the very least.

Doubly inconsistent, at the very least, because *I* find *men's chests* sexually attractive, and yet there is no law insisting they cover up. (Well, *some* men's chests. As is the case, I expect, even with those 'tits and ass men' — surely they don't find *all* women's breasts sexually attractive. And if not, then again, the law prohibits all because of a few.)

But let's back up a step. Who determines whether a body part is sexual at any given time or place — the owner of the body part or the other person? When I am shirtless on a hot day out on the lake, I'm not considering my breasts to be sexual. When I'm with someone in private, I may. It's *my* call.

And anyway, what if they *are* sexually attractive? Well, you may answer, men are sexually aggressive; it's for your own protection. Well, I say back, if a man has so little control that I must fear assault whenever shirtless, do something about the man, not my breasts. (Surely the provocation defence is pretty much dead and buried by now.)

b.   *The Bible says*

i.   *— that it's immoral for women to bare their breasts.* Okay, so Jewish and Christian women shouldn't go shirtless. They don't have to — I'm not arguing for a law that *insists* women go shirtless; I'm arguing to eliminate the law that *prohibits* it. So you'll still be able to follow your religious beliefs. I, however, don't share your religion. So why should I have to follow your religious beliefs?

ii. — *that it's immoral for men to see women's breasts.* This would make it more difficult for men to follow their religious beliefs — if women at large were to be shirtless. I guess you'd have to spend a lot of time indoors. But again, I don't share your religious beliefs. On what basis do you limit *my freedom* so you can follow *your religious beliefs?*

2. *It's disgusting.*

a. Not according to me. Why should your aesthetic rather than mine be legally supported? (And while we're invoking personal aesthetics, what I find disgusting — much to my shame, so I'm working on this — is men's guts that look nine months pregnant; so to be consistent, there ought to be a law insisting they cover *that* up.)

b. If women's breasts are disgusting, why is Playboy thriving? (The articles, oh right, I forgot.) Let's pursue this for a moment. I'll bet that the same man who ogles Candy Cane's breasts in the centrefold would get all upset if Candy Cane did a Gwen Jacobs. Do men have some psychological problem such that they can't handle the real thing? And is it as boring as the need to control, the need to be the centre of the universe? The real thing is okay in a strip bar, it's okay if a woman does it *for a man,* but if she does it merely *for herself,* well, we can't have that.

85

3. *It's just custom, that's all.*

   'That's all' is right — appeal to tradition is not sufficient for anything, let alone a law. (We've always bashed our babies' brains out, so let's have a law saying we must continue to do so. It's just our way.)

4. *It will lead to topless beaches, then nude beaches, then pretty soon everybody will be walking around buck naked.*

   I sincerely doubt it, but — your point? (See 1, 2, and 3 above, if all you're saying is that naked bodies are immoral, disgusting, or contrary to custom.) (Otherwise, check out the slippery slope fallacy: X *need not* lead to Y.)

Let's admit that men have breasts too: women's are more developed and have the potential to produce milk, but *both* sexes have two areas of tissue density on the chest, each centred by a nipple.

Given then that the distinction seems to be based on a difference in development, pre-pubescent girls should be shirtless, by custom, as freely as boys. The custom is, however, that girls as young as two years of age are dressed in two-piece bathing suits — what's the point of the top piece? Could it be the insane need to differentiate on the basis of sex? Pink and blue, girls and boys, Ms. and Mr. — secretaries and presidents.

Gay Bashing

Gay bashing. Now there's something (else) that doesn't make sense. 'Queers are disgusting, men touching other men, that's really sick.' So, yeah, go beat 'em up. Get real close and touch 'em all over. (And they say men are the logical ones.)

But of course it's not just the no-necks roaming the streets at night. It's also the ones in the offices during the day. Consider these words of a cable television program manager: " ... men French kissing and ... caressing ... thighs ... the scene [was] offensive ... [and in] bad taste." But men hitting each other, bruising and breaking bodies with fists, and men killing each other, spattering blood and guts with bullets and knives — that's, what, *good* taste? I'd rather see men kissing each other than killing each other any time. (But then I'd *really* rather see *Boston Legal* reruns.)

It's weird, the relationship between sex and violence. I don't understand it. Mitch, the bouncer, says "They're either gonna fuck or fight." *He* understands it. Okay, think like a man. (I can't, it hurts.) (Yes you can, try harder.)

Okay, they both involve physical contact. So do football and ballet; the former, laced with violence, is okay, but the latter is not.

They're both tension releasers. Isn't that flattering: she thinks they're making love; he's just releasing tension. (Men, where do you get all that tension from?)

They're both opportunities to display dominance — heterosex in a sexist society is an opportunity to display dominance. (I see, you're tense because you're *not* dominant.)

So what does all this have to do with gay bashing? I have no idea. Told you, I don't get it. I understand why (some) men beat up gays. Maybe their problem is they never learned "Rub a dub dub" when they were kids. Maybe the problem is they did. Maybe, they figure homosex means one of them has to be *not* dominant — is that why they fear it, why they must attack it? (Right. Get over yourself. He's so not into you.)

Wait a minute, gay bashers are often white supremacists, aren't they? Hm — and misogynists. Could it be as simple as 'If it's different, kill it'?

I hope the aliens get it.

Macho Music for the Mensa Crowd

Music and men has always been an iffy combination. If it involves banging on things and making a lot of noise, well, that's definitely male, on both counts, so being a drummer is okay. And if it involves plugging something in — that ultimate test which separates the men from, well, from the women — that's good, so playing the guitar, lead or bass, is okay. Especially since holding your hand at cock level is involved.

But what if your tastes are a little more classical? What if you're a little more intellectually-inclined? Fear no more! Electronic music is here!

To begin, like all good little boys, electronic composers are obsessed with *how*. Their program notes are paeans to process: "The harmonic matrix for this construction was established with a dominant to non-dominant ratio of 7:5 and intra-note relationships determined according to a chance-randomized method ... "

And yet, it sounds like shit. But then they probably just forgot to consider the end product. Kinda like Oppenheimer and the gang at Los Alamos, so absorbed by the sweet technicalities of the process, it wasn't until they exploded the thing that they thought 'Gee, this could hurt a lot of people!'

And what about the *why*? *Why* did you write such a piece of shit? (And why oh why are you playing it in public?) Despite their claim to superior logic and rationality, men, macho men, are notoriously inept when it comes to reflective reasoning. 'Why? Whaddya mean "why"?' It's not a question they're used to, apparently. Their professors (and make no mistake, classical music is music's ivory tower — you need a Ph.D. to get in — and electronic music is its engineering department) never asked them *why* they wrote a certain piece. And they never ask themselves. As in all locker rooms, concert hall dressing rooms are filled with competitive claims about equipment and technique, not rationale. Certainly, reasons are nowhere to be found in program notes.

The notes do reveal, however, a certain attention to complexity. Failing that, to *apparent* complexity. The composers make what they do sound as complicated as possible. "Intra-note relationships determined according to a chance-randomized method"? Heads it's major, tails it's minor. Why bother telling us at all, I wonder, since communication is so obviously not your purpose. Ah. Because you don't really want us to understand — you want us to applaud: 'Look at me, I'm so clever, I understand something too difficult to explain.' Actually, what you're saying is 'Look at me, I have *no* communication skills whatsoever.'

People who think 'complexity good, simplicity bad' have obviously never heard Bach's *Prelude I*. Or the wheel.

Maybe the idea is that if you make it complicated enough, no one will be able to replicate it. So you'll be the first and only to have composed such a piece. But what's the big deal about being first? I have never understood that. In *any* context. First to land on the moon, first to discover insulin, first to cross the finish line, first to get on the bus — first to discover where that land mine was.

Truth is, the first to do X is often merely the first to be *recognized* as doing X. Do you really think that Bannister was the *first* person ever to run a mile in under four minutes? Talk to the descendants of the guy who *wasn't* on the cheetah's lunch menu that day.

And what's the big deal about being the only? Why the desire to be unique, singular, with no company, no community. Ah. The myth of the unconnected male. Can you spell 'denial'?

Good thing the first guy to write a piece for the piano didn't worry about there being others who could do the same thing. (And good thing the second guy to write a piece for the piano didn't let not being first stop him.) Different isn't necessarily better. Ask any black living in Alabama.

It's a quantity thing, really. Do you guys see that? And the first (quantity) is seldom the best (quality). For example, the first time I walked — well, I can tell you I'm much better at it now. I almost have it mastered. What *is* it with you guys and this obsession with number, with quantity, with size.

Consider the speakers. Have you seen the size of the speakers at an electronic music concert? They're bigger than those commonly found in a single guy's apartment. They're even bigger than the deejay's. Why so big? (I've heard that there's a direct relationship between penis size and foot size. Or is it hand size. Whatever, I suggest that there's an *inverse* relationship between penis size and speaker size.) And why so many? I've seen eight at one concert, spread out around the room.

I recall someone asking an electronic composer once why all electronic music was so loud, and he said something like "Do you mean apart from the obvious answer that all electronic composers want badly to fill empty spaces with lots of sound?" *Obvious?* But okay, so it's not just an obsession with size: the obsession with size is connected with the obsession to fill a space, to occupy. Sex comes to mind. And what my dog would do to those eight speakers spread out around the room.

Then there are the machines. Have you ever looked at the liner notes of an electronic music recording? Fairlight CMI, Emulator, Moog 55, Arp 2600, DX7, Prophet V, OB-Xa, Simmons SDS V, SequencerMax, EMS Vocoder, Boss PRO SE 150, Korg DDM 110. And that's just for one piece. (Writers don't usually list the equipment they use.) (Microsoft

Word.) But this is *macho* music. Real men play with machines. They tinker and twiddle and tune — What *is* it with men and machines? I mean, just look at their behaviour with the remote control.

Ah — that's it. Remote *control*. Real men have control. And if they don't, they take it. I've always wondered why electronic composers mix their pieces in public. Why not get the perfect mix once and for all in the studio and then just press the 'Play' button in the concert hall? I understand that some adjustments need to be made to compensate for the unique acoustics of the hall, but these can be made during the sound check, can't they? Yes, but then they can't do the 'See me control this sound, this console, this computer' thing. Really, is anyone impressed anymore to see someone with their fingers all over a bunch of knobs, looking oh so serious?

Now of course all these huge speakers and fancy machines are expensive. The more expensive, the better. Another macho thing. Real men have money. Too bad they're really bad at managing it. Could be part of that unconnected thing. They incur huge car payments and then, poor boys, can't afford the child support payments. (See what happens when you turn your back on the *simple* things — like addition?)

And speaking about looking oh so serious, why is electronic music considered *serious* music? What's serious about it? SOCAN classifies music as Serious and Non-Serious (serious music gets higher royalties), but unless there are words, how do you decide? If it's played in concert halls, it's serious, but if it's played in sports arenas, it's not? If the performers are wearing tuxedos, it's serious, but if they're wearing spandex, it's not? If a piece lasts for a really long time, it's serious? (A hundred bottles of beer on the wall...) If it uses more than three chords (or, alternatively, if it uses no chords at all), it's serious? If it takes more than a day to write, it's serious? (There goes most of Mozart.) Electric violins are serious, but electric guitars are not? (Because guitars come in red?)

Even if there *are* words, it's hard to tell. Consider *Orpheus and Eurydice*, a piece of serious music. Basically the lyrics are 'She's gone, I miss her a lot, so I'm gonna get her back.' Sounds like your typical country and western ballad to me.

Electronic composers, discoursing at great length about how they created their very complicated pieces, fiddling with the faders on their expensive machines that feed into their huge and many speakers, and being oh so pretentiously serious about it all — it's macho music for the mensa crowd.

Impoverished Scientists

To read the science journals, one would think that animal life consists of nothing but predation and reproduction, both thoroughly competitive in nature. The absence of any capacity for pleasure, or at least for non-competitive pleasure, is frightening. Lining a nest with warm and soft material is not for comfort, but to "increase the survival rate of offspring" and arranging for others to watch the baby during long and deep dives is not from affection but to "maximize reproductive success".

This is of concern for two reasons. First, to judge by my own life and that of the dog with whom I live, that view is, to say the least, narrow and thus incomplete.

Second, what does it reveal of the scientists? Do they really see nothing but predation and reproduction — nothing but competition for food and sex? If it's true that we see what we want to see, why do these people want to see nothing but that? Is it a projection of their own view of life? How awful — how impoverished one must be — to see life — to live life — as nothing but a competition — and, worse, a competition for nothing but food and sex. If that's all we think there is, that's all we'll see, and if that's all we see, that's all we'll think there is. Socializing not as a reproductive strategy, but for companionship; playing not as practice for evading a predator or capturing prey, but for fun; lying in the sun not to regulate one's body temperature, but simply because it feels good — why are these things so unthinkable?

Or perhaps these things *are* thinkable, are visible, but are considered unimportant, trivial. What a value system that reveals! Not only that food and sex are more important than beauty and laughter, but that competition is more important than cooperation.

These are our scientists. These are the people who are collecting information, amassing knowledge, constructing our view — or rather, imposing their view — of the world. Surely a little more responsibility, a little more maturity, is called for.

Why isn't being a soldier
more like being a mother?

Motherhood is unfair to women in a way fatherhood most definitely is not. Not only are there the physical risks (pregnancy and childbirth puts a woman at risk for nausea, fatigue, backaches, headaches, skin rashes, changes in her sense of smell and taste, chemical imbalances, high blood pressure, diabetes, anemia, embolism, changes in vision, stroke, circulatory collapse, cardiopulmonary arrest, convulsions, and coma), there's the permanent damage to one's career: if she stays at home, she suffers the loss of at least six years' experience and/or seniority; if she doesn't, she suffers the loss of a significant portion of her income, that required to pay for full-time childcare. (And even if she can swing holding a full-time job and paying for full-time childcare, she probably won't get promoted because she typically uses all of her sick days, she's reluctant to stay past 5:00 or to come in before 9:00 or on weekends, and she occasionally has to leave in the middle of the day, perhaps even in the middle of an important meeting. In short, she can't be counted on. Such a lack of commitment.)

Either way, it's necessary, then, for all but a few mothers to be attached to another income (typically a man's) in order to even *be* a mother: very few women make enough money to support themselves and a child, let alone a full-time childcare provider. A mother must be a kept woman; she must become dependent, financially, on a man. (So *of course* after a divorce, the man's standard of living increases 42% and the woman's standard decreases 73% — he no longer has to support *two* people, and she is no longer supported, she has to pay her own way, and start from scratch to do so.)

96

Cut to the man who becomes a soldier. After all, notes Barrington Moore, Jr., "for a young man it's much more fun to prance around with a gun, or to kill several enemies with a bomb, than it is to sit at a desk day after day, bored by a dead-end job" ("How Ethnic Enmities End"). What if he weren't paid to do all that prancing around? Would he be so eager to do so then? Why should we pay men to *be* a soldier when we don't pay women to *make* a soldier? Why should we pay men to actualize *their* hormonal impulse when we don't pay women to actualize theirs? (I say hormonal because neither desire is very rational. Before she 'signed up', she really didn't like kids much — now she wants to be with one 24/7? Before *he* signed up, he probably didn't give other people the time of day — now he's willing to die for them?)

How many men would do it if they lost six years of seniority or work experience (let's say the experience they gain is considered as nontransferable to, as not useful in, the workplace as the experience gained by women as they raise a child)? How many would do it if they didn't get paid for the duration? How many would do it if they had to depend on their wife to buy them their food and accommodations, their guns and bullets?

97

Making Taxes Gender-Fair

Since men commit 90% of the crime, they should pay 90% of the tax that supports the judicial system. Prisons are expensive to build and maintain. As are prisoners — they don't work while they're in prison, so we have to support them. Then there's the expense of the police forces and courts that get them there. We already require that men pay the bulk of car insurance premiums because they're the worse drivers. So what's stopping us from going further, making the system even more fair?

And since a large percentage of their crime is violent, it follows that men are responsible for far more ER visits than women (assuming no gender differences with regard to illness and other injury) (actually, since men take more risks than women, there probably *is* a gender difference with regard to other injury) (don't forget the driving thing), so men should pay more of the tax that supports the healthcare system.

Oh, and the military. Men are the ones who thrive on aggression, they get off on the excitement of fighting. They *want* to join the military. They *want* to go to war. So let *them* pay for it. Let *them* pay the $530 billion required by the military budget.

Then there's all the environmental stuff. All those beer cans, empty cigarette packs, fast food cartons — most of the litter along the highways was put there by men. As they continue to drive their big gas-guzzlers with the high emissions. And the companies that dump toxic waste, and clear cut forests, and dam river systems? All run by men.

We could call it the Gender Responsibility Tax — a $5,000 surtax could be levied on each and every male. Payable annually, from birth to death. (By the parents, of course, until the boy reaches manhood.) (They chose to make the boy, after all.)

Suicide, Insurance, and Dead Sugar Daddies

I've been thinking that, with the exception of those who are paralyzed or severely physically debilitated, people who seek euthanasia are cowards. They are grossly inconsiderate and amazingly irresponsible. If you're ready to die, then die. Do it yourself. Don't ask someone else to kill you and then live with it. What an awful request to make, of anyone! It's *your* life — it's *your* death.

However, just recently the insurance connection clicked into place: if you suicide, the company won't pay — so it's for the sake of your loved ones that you endure or entreat ...

So all these intellectual and ethical gymnastics we're sweating over — passive/active, terminal sedation or physician-assisted suicide, the double effect — it's all because the insurance companies won't pay? Wouldn't it be so much easier, and, I suspect, cheaper, to simply legislate that they must? (Especially when the suicide simply hastens a looming death?) The financial desires of a certain private sector industry should not override our freedom to die!

Well, they don't really. We still have the legal and moral right to die. The insurance companies just override our desire to capitalize on it. Which makes me think instead that we should simply legislate against life insurance. Consider it: we're putting a monetary value on an individual life.

And just a little less questionable is the expectation that one's spouse — whether dead *or* alive — provide one with money. Sure, if there are children, they must be taken care of; in that case, I can understand the desire to have insurance against the potential loss of income that enables such care (but then let's call it income insurance — life is surely a little different, a little more, than income). But I'm beginning to think this whole privatized parenthood thing isn't such a good idea. Perhaps we as a society should take on the responsibility for their support — right from the beginning. (But then we'd have to have the right to provide some input into that beginning in the first place...) And if there's no children, well, GET A JOB like everyone else! (And let your husband — or wife — die when and how he — or she — wants to.)

Hockey Brawls
(and other cockfights)

Do you remember that all-out hockey brawl during which one guy beat another into unconsciousness? Shocking, everyone said, quite surprising. Indeed. Surprising it doesn't happen more often. Just like that Somalia kid incident.

Consider the similarities: both the military world and the sports world are nothing but teams of hyper-emotional men who are fixated on winning at any cost.

Men — hyper-emotional? Haven't I got that backwards? It's *women* who are the emotional ones. Right. Anyone who says men aren't emotional hasn't seen a game. Or a fight. What do you think motivates the players, the soldiers — the calm, cool voice of reason? Thinking for oneself, should this be possible, is openly discouraged on both the playing field and the killing field; success of the team depends on uncritical obedience.

The very structure of the league/legion is irrational: 'the enemy', the guys you are expected to beat, have never done anything to you and there's little proof they ever will. Hell, the enemy changes at the flick of a — a dollar: players are traded like the performing commodities they are, today's good buddy is tomorrow's target; and lest we forgot, the Gulf War reminded us that any nation's soldiers are really just mercenaries. (Hell no, we won't go, we won't fight for Texaco! Did you notice that the announcers are now saying *Molson* Leaf Hockey?) Given such a vacuum of rationality, no wonder the men are in emotional overdrive most of the time.

Oh but I can hear the coaches protesting: 'We *always* say winning isn't everything, it's how you play the game!' Well, coach, actions speak louder than words: who gets the applause, who gets the trophy, who gets the money — the loser?

And how *do* they play the game? Like the real men they're taunted to be — with all the aggression they've got. And if testosterone, and ten years of Ninja Turtles and big-boys-don't-cry, and another ten years of how-far-d'ya-get isn't enough, then put back a coupla six packs and pump some steroids to bring out the beast in you.

Oh sure, there are rules — don't forget fouls and the Geneva Convention. Again, right. The only rule is Don't-Get-Caught.

So why the surprise when the players do exactly what they've been trained to do: hate and hurt (and kill), for no real reason, and not care about it.

What do you expect at a cockfight?

Sex and
So You Think You Can Dance

When *So You Think You Can Dance* first started, they had one winner. In season 9, they decided to have two winners: one male and one female. I thought it was because they realized the odds were stacked in favour of male dancers since most of the viewers/voters were female (and, presumably, heterosexual) (and, presumably, not voting for dance ability as much as for sexual appeal). However, in the preceding eight seasons, there were four female winners and four male winners. The runner-ups were a bit more skewed, with two female and six male.

Then I read in an interview about the change, this comment: "Girls dance totally differently than guys." Yeah, if that's what their choreographers demand. (Who may, in turn, be providing, what Nigel Lythgoe and the other producers demand.) I have to say I am so very sick and tired of almost every dance being a presentation of the stereotyped (i.e., gender-role-rigid) heterosexual romance/love/sex scenario, right down to the music, the costumes, and, of course, the moves.

But now, they've reverted to one winner — suggesting that sex is irrelevant to dance. Does that mean they're going to make the dances — the music, the costumes, the moves — as sex-independent? Not likely.

Pity. Because I, for one, would love to see more like Mark Kanemura's "Bohemian Rhapsody" audition piece and Mandy Moore's "Boogie Shoes" (the latter was, like the former, pretty much just asexual fun with music and movement *despite* the gendered costumes — cutesy skirt/dress for one, long pants for the other, pink shoes for the one, blue shoes for the other —

yes, yes, we must *must* MUST separate, distinguish, the girls from the boys, the patriarchy depends on it, the subordination of women depends on it!). (And that's another thing: would they PLEASE stop calling 18- to 30-year-olds 'girls' and 'boys'?)

They (the *So You Think You Can Dance* people) really should make up their minds. If sex is important to what they want to be doing, then they should have best male and best female dancer awards, continue to pair in male/female, and continue to insist the males look and dance in a hypermasculinized way and the females look and dance in a hyperfeminized (which in our society means in a pornulated way).

If sex isn't important to what they want to be doing, then they should have best dancer award, and pair at random — actually, since the heterosexual mating concept would no longer be the central motif, they wouldn't have to be limited to pairs at all — and let the dancers dance with strength, balance, coordination, musicality, and skill, with beauty, drama, fun, and quirkiness, *regardless of their sex.*

So you want to be a nurselady ...

And even though you don't know any other guys who want to be nurseladies, you persist. Because quite simply, you think you'll like nursing, as a career, a job, an endeavour. So you take your high school maths and sciences, you do quite well, and you get accepted into nursing school.

Where almost all the students are women. You feel like you don't really belong, you feel odd, you stand out. There are a few other men in the class and at first you hang around with them, but you don't really like them. Part of you thinks you *should* like them, but, well, you just don't. You try hanging around with some of the women, and they're pleasant enough and they talk to you, but you never get included in their group things outside of class. So you become a loner, part of nothing, sort of invisible. But you persist, you keep coming to class.

All the profs are women and they keep saying things like "Well, ladies..." as if you weren't there. There's one who makes a point of adding, as a cute afterthought, "and gentlemen", but something in her tone bugs you and you'd rather she just stick to "Well, ladies". And there's another one who asked once why, with your build, you weren't playing football instead. You were speechless. But you persist, you don't drop out. (Even though you wonder sometimes at the average marks you get for work you think is above average.)

There's only one men's washroom in the whole building. On particularly bad days, it annoys you when you have to go to a different floor just to go to the washroom.

And it seems that some knowledge is assumed as background. Things like how to hold a baby. How are you supposed to know what they haven't taught you yet?

And there are no nursing uniforms for you in the campus shop. Something special has to be ordered. It's different, of course, and makes you stand out even more, as someone who doesn't really belong with the group. This is especially bad in the training hospital — people keep thinking you're security or something. Sometimes it seems you have to spend so much time and effort just getting accepted as a nurse, you don't have anything left to actually do any nursing.

But you persist. Even though you probably won't get a job when you graduate — men are thought to be not as emotionally sensitive, you've already been criticized for being gruff (you swear you were just speaking normally). And if you do get a job, it'll probably be in some no-name hospital god-knows-where with no chance for advancement. None of the head nurses in any of the hospitals you've been in were men. But you persist.

One day it occurs to you that it would help if they stopped calling it 'nurselady' and just called it 'nurse'. When you suggest that, you get weird looks as if you're obsessed with sex or over-reacting (or both). A few agree to use just 'nurse', but the way they say it defeats the purpose. The same sort of thing happened when you said something about the uniforms and the washrooms. You were criticized for making a fuss. But you persist. Because damn it you want to be a nurse!

Against the Rape Shield

Sexual assault, like many other crimes, often occurs when no one's watching. Given the absence of a third-party witness, how are we to decide guilt/innocence?

Circumstantial evidence is typically not helpful because consent, that which differentiates between legal and illegal sex among adults, is essentially a mental event, and of this there can be no evidence: a brain scan won't show us whether or not a person consented.

Considering consent as a behavioural event, a gesture or a word expressive of consent, is not much better: evidence is possible, but unlikely — even if an audio or video tape of the event exists, one must establish the absence of coercion for any apparently consensual gestures and words.

In a way, things were better when force and resistance differentiated between legal and illegal sex: evidence of this is easily available — torn clothing, bruised body parts, etc. However, we recognize that force and resistance, and perhaps more often torn clothing and bruised body parts, may be part of consensual sex; we also recognize that force may not be physical and resistance may not be wise.

Left without such circumstantial evidence, we must therefore base our decision of guilt/innocence on credibility — specifically (1) which person is more likely to be telling the truth, and (2) which story is more likely to be true. In both cases, the rape shield law hinders rather than helps our decision. Questioning the accuser about her/his sexual history, as well as about her/his character and motive, may indeed provide relevant information. Questioning the accused about his/her sexual history, character, and motive may *also* provide relevant information. *Both* lines of questioning should be common in cases that must be decided without circumstantial evidence.

Consider Woman A: she is sexually active and often goes to bars to pick up men; she cruises, chooses, and queries — if he consents, they drive to her place. Suppose she changes her mind on one occasion, and the man persists. She may, quite reasonably, decide not to lay charges of rape; she would not expect anyone to believe her. Given her past practice (her sexual history), it would, in fact, *not be reasonable* to believe her.

Consider Woman B: she is celibate and solitary. Suppose a man were to enter her residence and rape her. She, reasonably enough, *would* lay charges; she would expect to be believed. Given *her* past practice (her sexual history, or rather the lack thereof), it would be *very reasonable* to do so. It is crucial, therefore, for that past practice, the fact of her long-term celibacy and solitude, to be admissible.

Likewise, the past practice of the man should be admissible: a history of habitually raping women, for example, is relevant; a history completely devoid of aggression is also relevant.

Such information is relevant, however, only insofar as we are creatures of habit, people with tendencies. To say past practice is relevant is to assume that people by and large are consistent in their behaviour. This may not, in fact, be the case: people are inconsistent, people change, people do things for the first time, people do things out of character — all of this is true. Just because a woman consented to sex with twenty strangers before this one doesn't mean she consented to this one. And just because a man raped twenty women before her doesn't mean he raped her. Just because the sun has risen every day until now doesn't mean I can *know with certainty* that it will rise tomorrow; but *probably* it will. And probabilities are all we

108

have, especially when there are no witnesses. If a person typically gets drunk on Saturday night and becomes very generous, lending cash and car keys, then his/her charge of theft some Sunday morning is going to be a tough one to make stick; people will *reasonably* conclude that *probably* s/he consented to the transaction.

Yes, information about one's past may be misused; but this isn't a good reason to prohibit its use: baseball bats can be misused too, but we don't therefore make them illegal. Rather, it's up to the court officials to say 'Wait a minute, that's a *non sequitur*, that's irrelevant'. And if the case in question involves consent, sex, and a stranger, probability based on past practice with regard to consent, sex, and strangers is what's most relevant; information about such past practice should, therefore, be admissible. (Similarly, if the case in question involves consent, sex, and someone known to the woman ...)

It may, however, be the *only* information that's relevant: arguments to character are of questionable validity — 'She's sexually active, therefore she's a slut, and sluts lie'; 'She's a teacher, therefore she must be morally upright, therefore she would *not* lie'; etc. Arguments to motive are also questionable, if only because this takes us back to the unknowable mental event.

Most of the items mentioned in discussions about the rape shield would also be irrelevant — medical records, adoption files, child welfare records, and abortion files. A personal diary, however, *may* be relevant: if the woman had written in her diary the night before the alleged rape, "I intend to get laid tomorrow night and it doesn't matter by who — and the more it hurts and the more afraid I am, the better — and I'll lie about consenting just to make my life a little more interesting", then that entry should be admissible; likewise, if the man had written in his diary "Tomorrow is Victim Number Ten — I've got my knife

109

sharpened and ready to go — I get hard just thinking about raping whoever it'll happen to be", then that should be admissible.

If judges order irrelevant records to be turned over, then *that's* the problem — and the solution is not a restriction on the admissibility of all personal records/history but mandatory Logic 101 for court officials. To use one example, drug use does *not* show general disregard for the law.

To summarize, (1) we can't have certainty, we can have only probability; (2) past practice *can be* (not *is*) relevant to probability; therefore, (3) information about relevant past practice, of *both* the accuser and the accused, should be admissible in court.

Dangerous Sports

'Sports are too dangerous for women; they might get hurt.'

This from the sex that makes beating someone senseless *part of the game.*

And has its reproductive vitals hanging by a thread at bull's-eye of the body with nary a half-inch layer of fat for protection. (What's next in the evolution of the male, a brain growing outside the skull?) (Oops, been there —)

The sex that got the girls' and boys' bicycle designs backwards.

And competes on the pommel horse, voluntarily.

Do I need to point out that women's musculature is generally more elastic, rendering it less prone to injury?

And that women seem to have a better developed survival instinct? We duck. We run the fuck the other way. And we don't make insupportable claims about our opponent's sexual preferences or those of her parents.

Why are Women
More Religious than Men?

Why are women more religious, in belief and in practice, than men? I can think of a few reasons.

One, religious belief is more of an emotional thing than a cognitive thing. (Consider the fact that merely thinking about religious beliefs is usually sufficient to reveal they're unwarranted.) And women are raised to be more emotional than cognitive; men are raised to be more cognitive than emotional (in fact, they're encouraged, even taught, to deny their emotions).

Two, religious authority figures, mythological (God, Allah, Zeus, and so on) and real (priests, rabbi, ministers, and so on), are male. And since women are raised to be subservient to males, to regard males as authorities, it's easy for them to accept God, for example, as an authority and to subordinate themselves to him. Men, on the other hand, are encouraged to *be* the authority; they're also encouraged to compete with other men. So to accept God, for example, as an authority and to subordinate themselves to him would not be easy — in fact, it would be emasculating. (Which is why the macho Promise Keepers came to be.) (And why the movement's popularity didn't last very long.)

Three, except for the war element (note that men are okay with claiming religious belief when it's associated with war), religion is very much about morality. (Or so people think.) And it's *women* who are the designated moral guardians: young women are the 'gatekeepers' when it comes to pre-marital sex (often considered immoral), wives are referred to by their husbands as 'their better half' ('better' referring to some quality of moral goodness), and mothers are assumed to have the primary responsibility of teaching their children right from wrong.

When a man introduces the matter of morality, questioning, for example, whether it's right to do whatever it is that's about to be done, he is accused of 'going soft', or being weak, or being a 'boy scout', or being a 'bleeding heart', and so on. Note that the last accusation, with its reference to the heart, connects morals with the emotional realm, which neatly connects this point with the first one — as does this excerpt from a novel, whose author I unfortunately failed to note: "The boy's nothing more than a bleeding heart waiting to cry over this injustice or that!...you'd think we raised a bloody priest."

Making Kids with AIDS

What has been glaringly absent in news stories about children with AIDS in Africa is comment about *why* there are so many children with AIDS. "We are going down," a woman says, "Theft will go up, rape all over will be high. People — " Wait a minute. Back up. "Rape all over will be high"? And that's just one more unfortunate circumstance beyond their control, is it? What, as in 'boys will be boys'?

Excuse me, but when someone knowingly infects another person with a fatal disease, he's killing her. And if someone takes away someone else's right to life, I say he forfeits his own. And not only is the HIV-infected rapist guilty of murdering the woman he rapes, he's guilty of murdering in advance the child he creates (whether he himself is HIV-infected or whether he rapes an HIV-infected woman). There's something incredibly sick about knowingly creating a human being that will die, slowly and painfully.

So, the solution? Drugs, yes. But the kind vets use when they put an animal down. (Or, if mere prevention rather than justice is the goal, castration. At the very least, vasectomy.) Let's have some accountability here! Those 20,000 kids with AIDS didn't just appear in a pumpkin patch one morning. *Someone made them. With a conscious, chosen, deliberate act.*

First (and last) Contact

Women have a long tradition of being diplomats. "Historically ... marriage has been the major alliance mechanism of every society, and little girls are trained for roles as intervillage family diplomats ... the married woman straddles two kin networks, two villages, sometimes two cultures" (*The Underside of History*, Elise Boulding).

Many women have decades of experience, settling a dozen disputes a day. To whom do the kids go crying "It's not fair!"? Mom. She's the mediator, the negotiator extraordinaire.

Girls develop language skills before boys, and their level of proficiency continues throughout their lives to be superior. Women in languages and linguistics degree programs outnumber men. Translators? Women. Writers? Women. In short, women are better at communication.

(And) (So) We talk a lot. (Well, when we're not interrupted by men.) Although 'gossip' can be superficial and mean, much talk among women is unjustly dismissed with that term — when women talk, they're doing social cohesion work.

But of course communication doesn't involve just words. And women are also better than men at reading facial expression and body language. And they go deeper: men actually avoid any kind of psychological understanding (of themselves as well as others); women actively embrace such knowledge ("But *why* did you do that?").

Lastly, women, whether by nature or nurture, are more predisposed to cooperate, whereas men are more predisposed to compete. We prefer a win-win solution; men love a win-lose one.

So why is it that when presidents fill their ambassador and diplomat positions, they appoint men? Is it because their ambassadors and diplomats will be talking with men? And men are more comfortable talking to other men? That would mean ambassadors and diplomats are men because they're men.

Or is it (also) because the goal of a diplomatic exchange is not to cooperate, not to resolve conflict, but to conquer, to come away 'one up' on the other? Diplomats are really just smoke screens; mediation isn't the goal at all.

And why is that? It could be as simple, and as awful, as (1) Women are good at mediation; (2) Whatever women are good at is devalued; therefore, (3) Mediation is devalued.

But look at where that's gotten us. Planet-wide, we spend more on weapons than food, clothing, and entertainment put together. Unless of course you consider weapons to be entertainment. Which apparently men do. (Turn on any tv show during prime time, and nine times out of ten a gun will be fired in the first five minutes.)

But hey, when *the aliens* come, NASA's first contact team had better include a bunch of women. Because please, guys, all those weapons of yours? They will surely be but slingshots.

Paying Stay-at-Home Moms

Every now and then, we hear the proposal that women be paid to stay at home and be moms. The fact that women are paid to be surrogate mothers suggests that regular mothers also deserve payment. So. Should we pay regular mothers just as we pay surrogate mothers?

For starters, who is this 'we'? Surrogate mothers are paid by the people who want their labor. Who wants the labor, the service, the children, of non-surrogate mothers? The state? If so, for what? There is no shortage of civil servants. We aren't at war. And if we were, we would need more soldiers, not more children. So the job paid for should be not 'making a child' but 'making a soldier'.

Because if we're going to pay, it would be a job. You'd have to wait for an opening and then apply. So not only would the state, should it be the employer of mothers, have the right to be quite specific about the job description ("Women wanted to make soldiers ... "), it would have the right to be quite specific about the qualifications ("Genetic make-up must include average IQ or lower, above average physical health and fitness, pliant personality ... ."). And it would have the right to be quite specific about the performance standards — no drinking on the job, or substance abuse of any kind except that prescribed by the employer, etc.

You want to be paid for being a mother? Well, he who pays the piper picks the tune.

An End to War

At one time, bank tellers and secretaries had a certain prestige — the time when such positions were held by men. Schoolteachers used to be schoolmasters — before women entered the classroom. People who boast that many doctors in Russia are women fail to mention that doctoring in Russia, well, someone's gotta do it.

Whenever women enter an occupation, it becomes devalued. It loses glory. It loses funding. It loses media coverage. It becomes unpopular, even invisible. So if we were serious, really serious, about ending war, we'd fill the military ranks with women. When becoming a soldier has about as much appeal as becoming a waitress (another archetype of the service sector industry) —

An added bonus would be that if the enemy army were (still) male, they'd start killing themselves. Because better that than be killed *by a woman*. It would certainly save on ammunition.

On the other hand, if the enemy army were (also) female, more often than not, the wars would probably just sort of fizzle out into some sort of stalemate. We just don't have the equipment for pissing contests. But since no one would really care, or even know, because it would be a woman thing, that'd be okay.

We could live with that.

Men and Illegal Words

Lying is illegal when economic interests are at stake: libel, slander, fraud, misrepresentation, false advertising. For example, libel (written) and slander (oral) both refer to false statements that injure a person's reputation, and you can bet that the reputation being talked about is that which enables the person to make money, not one's reputation as a good person. (Women don't have reputations. Except sexual reputations. And they can't sue if some guy writes her name on the locker room wall. Wait a minute though. Traditionally, her sexuality was her ticket to income, either through prostitution or marriage, so why don't we find such cases in the history? Oh. Right. Forgot. Women weren't persons under the law until — when?)

Why isn't lying illegal otherwise? Why is loss of income more subject to compensation than, say, loss of self-esteem (which may, of course, result in loss of income)?

Words are illegal when physical violence is involved: uttering threats, 'fighting words', intimidation, criminal harassment. Why aren't they illegal when psychological violence is involved? "Acts which inflict severe mental pain or suffering" *are* illegal as part of torture (CCC 269.1(1)) — but that's only when such acts are committed in order to obtain information (the presumed purpose of torture).

Emotional pain and suffering are routinely included in civil suits. Why not in criminal matters? Why is economic and physical injury, but not psychological injury, a matter of public interest — a crime? Why, when it comes to illegal speech acts, is there an emphasis on economic and physical injury?

119

Is it just that the male mode has ruled? Males engage in business, income-generating activities — making money is traditionally their role, their legitimator. Men also engage in physical contests of all kinds.

Also, loss of income is more measurable than loss of self-esteem; physical injury is more measurable than psychological injury. And males are more engaged in, more comfortable with, quantitative activities than qualitative activities.

Furthermore, loss of income is less emotional than loss of self-esteem; psychological injury is often all about emotion. And males, of course, are uncomfortable with any emotion other than anger.

Some may scoff at criminalizing psychological injury. Surely physical injuries are more serious. But are they? I suggest not, especially if the verbal assaults are ongoing. Many of us spend our whole lives crippled by apparently permanent injuries to our self-esteem, our belief about what we can and cannot do. The consequences of psychological injury can be as severe as, if not more severe than, those of physical injury; they're just much harder to see and harder still to link to the cause. (And harder to recover from.)

Maybe the exclusion is justified on the basis that if you punch my body, no matter how strong I am, my body will bruise, but if you punch my psyche, if I am psychologically strong, if I am mature and have a firm sense of my self, that punch need not injure me. So it's our own fault if we're injured by insult. As for other kinds of psychological injury, we are responsible to a large extent for our thoughts, opinions, beliefs, values, and attitudes and, thus, our psychological response to injury. So again, it's our own fault if we're injured. But a punch will break, not bruise, a less strong body. Just how strong, psychologically speaking, are we expected to be?

And anyway, physical aggression is considered illegal even when it doesn't injure. It's the action, not the consequence, that determines its illegality. If you punch me, whether I bruise, or break, or neither, I can still charge you with assault. Why doesn't insult have the same legal weight? Because men aren't into words — unless there's money or a fight involved?

Take Her Seriously

I used to think that the problem with rape was that women weren't being explicit — they weren't actually saying no, partly because men weren't actually asking. Perhaps because there's (still?) something shameful about sex that makes people reluctant to come right out and talk about it. Or maybe that would destroy the romance. Whatever.

I still think that a pre-sex explicit question-and-answer might be a valuable social custom, but I'm now thinking that a much bigger part of the problem is that women *do* say no, implicitly *and* explicitly, and men *do* understand that 'no means no' (I suspect the prevalence of the 'no means yes' belief is grossly exaggerated, if not completely fabricated, by men for men), but men don't hear us: they continue to think that women, like children, should be seen (okay, looked at — all the time, everywhere) and not heard. And when they do hear us, they don't take us seriously. We've all read the studies about how a woman will say something in a meeting. Silence. Then a little later, a man will say the same thing. Excellent idea, Bob! You're promoted! Here's a raise!

Lucinda Vandervort ("Mistake of Law and Sexual Assault: Consent and *Mens Rea*" in *Canadian Journal of Women and the Law* 2) presents a hypothetical sexual assault trial in which the defendant maintains that all of the woman's neutral as well as non-cooperative behaviour really indicates consent. The hypothetical defendant may have been *honestly* mistaken in his belief that the woman consented (which is accepted as a defence in Vandervort's hypothetical). But given the woman's behaviour (she said no, she did not say yes, she did not co-operate), surely he was being *unreasonable*, not to mention arrogant, selfish, immature, or just incredibly stupid — to believe as he did.

And in fact, a standard of reasonable *is* used: "When an accused alleges that he believed that the complainant consented to the conduct that is the subject-matter of the charge, a judge, if satisfied that there is sufficient evidence and that, if believed by the jury, the evidence would constitute a defence, shall instruct the jury, when reviewing all the evidence relating to the determination of the honesty of the accused's belief, *to consider the presence or absence of reasonable grounds for that belief*" (Criminal Code s.244(4), my emphasis).

But Vandervort says that a case such as her hypothetical would probably be screened out as unfounded by the police or rejected for prosecution by the Crown on the grounds that the mistaken belief in consent was not "*sufficiently* unreasonable" — that is, the defendant's belief is deemed not only honest, it's considered reasonable enough. What? What planet do you guys live on? Oh. This one.

On a non-patriarchal planet, the man's belief in consent, despite what the woman says ("I have to leave", "Stop") and does (she struggled, she pushed him away), as well as what she doesn't say ("I want to" "Yes") and doesn't do (undress), would surely be considered unreasonable. And delusional. At the very least, 'wilfully blind' (and thus *un*acceptable as a defence).

Further, Vandervort states that in sexual assault cases "the reasonable person standard ... focuses on the type and degree of violence used by the assailant and compares it with that used in normal sexual encounters of a similar nature" and notes, somewhat dryly, that "normal sex appears to include some quite extraordinary forms of interaction, some of which are quite violent." Indeed, according to Lorenne Clark and Debra Lewis (*Rape: The Price of Coercive Sexuality*), most men (against whom rape complaints were laid with the Metropolitan Toronto Police

123

Department in 1970) consider violent behaviour to be normal for a sexual encounter. I wonder how many women would agree. (Though perhaps 'preferred' should be substituted for 'normal': it could be that a similar finding — that most women also consider violent behaviour to be normal for a sexual encounter — merely reflects the reality of sex because it usually involves a man.)

Even so, one has to wonder just who's being consulted about what's normal? Consider Robin Weiner's comments: "What is 'normal' according to male social norms and 'reasonable' according to male communication patterns and expectations does not accord with what women believe to be reasonable .... A woman may believe she has communicated her unwillingness to have sex — and other women would agree, thus making it a 'reasonable' female expression. Her male partner might still believe she is willing — and other men would agree with his interpretation, thus making it a 'reasonable' male interpretation .... The use of a reasonable person standard thus has a basic flaw. Courts do not clarify the perspective from which the 'reasonableness' standard should be applied" ("Shifting the Communication Burden: A Meaningful Consent Standard in Rape" in *Harvard Women's Law Journal* 6, 1983). And anyway why isn't what's *acceptable* used instead? Just because everyone does it that way (it's normal) doesn't mean it's right.

Look, guys, we take you seriously. We can't help but do so. Your repertoire of facial expressions and your body language are limited to 'serious' and 'more serious'. And when we don't take you seriously, when we laugh at you, for example, you get really pissed off.

So, please, show a little respect. Acknowledge that we too have brains. That we know what we want and what we don't want. That we can express ourselves accurately. Take us seriously. We get really pissed off when you don't. (We just don't come after you with a gun.)

124

Brunettes, Blondes, and Redheads

So the other day I started reading *Iron Shadows* by Steven Barnes. He's apparently a bestselling author. Which is really disturbing.

Because four sentences in, he describes a woman as "a small wiry brunette". Seriously? Does anyone actually identify women by their hair colour any more? That's so—1940s. Isn't it? I check. The book's copyright is 1998. Okay. Guess not. Guess the tradition of objectifying women lives on.

We don't do that with men. We don't objectify them by their hair colour (or anything else, for that matter). Their *hair colour* for godsake. She's *a* brunette. Or *a* blonde. Or *a* redhead. As if all women with brown hair are what, interchangeable? Because they're completely defined by—the colour of their hair?

Not only that, but he had to mention her size. *Small.* Of course. If she's going to be a heroine, she has to be small. I'm surprised he didn't tell us how large her breasts are.

And whereas she's small, he's "enormous". Of course he is.

Could we just reverse the description with nothing odd happening, that test for sexism? "The man, a small, wiry brunette with an ugly bruise on his left cheek, wore a yellow unisex utility uniform. The woman was enormous, but barely conscious." Not only do you find it odd to hear a man called "a small, wiry brunette", you no doubt found it a bit disgusting to hear the woman called "enormous".

I am, goddammit, still a little forgiving, so I read on.

But the very next woman—or maybe it's the same woman, since the next bit happens two months earlier—the very next woman "nibbles" on dry wheat toast. Because we can't have a woman actually eating with guilt-free enthusiasm.

And she has "an oval face framed by a cascade of small soft blonde ringlets". *Small* again. And *soft*. And *blonde*. And *ringlets*. Ringlets?!

In case we missed it, "Her habit of peering out from behind them sometimes *made her resemble a* mischievous *child* peeking through a fence."

In 1998. And published by Tor.

No wonder women can't get published. As long as this insulting crap is deemed worthy. Is bestselling.

When will men finally get it? When will they finally get it right?

Robert J. Sawyer. He's the only one. The only male sf writer who's smart enough to create a non-sexist world.

Kept Women (and Men)

There is something objectionable about a perfectly-capable-of-working adult being 'kept' by another adult. It seems to me the epitome of laziness and immaturity to be supported by someone else, to have someone else pay your way through life.

But, I suppose, if someone wants to pay someone else's way, if a man wants to 'keep' a woman (or vice versa), and that woman (or man) wants to be 'kept', I suppose that's no business of mine.

But then why should I subsidize their keep? What has your wife (or husband) ever done for me? And yet I must subsidize her discounted income tax. Her discounted car insurance. Her discounted health insurance. Her discounted life insurance. Her discounted university tuition. Her discounted club membership. Hell, even her discounted airline ticket.

If he wants to pay her way, fine, but her way should cost the same as mine. Why is her way discounted just because she's not paying it herself? Even if she *is* paying her own way, why should she have to pay less than me just because she's married? Why should spouses get a discounted rate on all those things? Why do we roll out the red carpet for kept women?

(In particular, access to company benefits irks me: you don't even work here, why should you be covered?)

Two married adults should pay the same as two single adults. End of story.

Porn's Harmless and Pigs Fly

The fact that 'you' claim porn doesn't harm women is proof that it does. Such a claim indicates that you're so accustomed to seeing women sexually subordinated you think there's nothing wrong with it. Such a claim proves that that porn has skewed your perceptions so much you actually *believe* the women are enjoying, asking for, whatever it is you see. (They're *pretending*, asshole. They're *acting*. According to some guy's fantasy script. And they're doing so because they're getting *paid*.)

Such a claim also proves you haven't read the research: for example, compared to those who do not watch porn, men who watch porn are more likely to have aggressive and hostile sexual fantasies, more likely to say that women enjoy forced sex, less likely to be bothered by rape and slashing, and more likely to consider women subordinate and submissive.

(And if that's not important, consider that the more you watch porn, the less able you will become to be aroused by real women. So, your choice: fake, vicarious sex or real, actual sex.)

Population Growth (i.e., rape)

I am amazed at the number of population growth analyses that don't mention rape. So far I've read — none. And if they don't even *mention* rape, they sure as hell can't consider it *a major causal factor*. Do you really believe that millions of women *want* to be pregnant for five to ten years? Do you really believe that most women would actually *consent* to child number four when the other three are still under six?

And look! The lower the status of women, the higher the birth rate. Compare Bangladesh's birth rate of 3.7 with Sweden's 1.9. Coincidence? "Women of low status have less control over their lives, including decisions involving their fertility" (Diana M. Brown, "Population Growth and Human Rights" in *Humanist in Canada* 30.1). Go ahead! Say it! They're more likely to be raped! That's what they were bought for!

"Son preference is strong when females are undervalued, so parents go on increasing their family until they have the desired number of sons" (Brown). *Parents?* Don't go all gender-inclusive on me *now*! *Men* are the ones with the obsession for progeny, *their* progeny, *male* progeny.

And also look! Iraq and Gaza top the chart with birth rates of 6.7 and 8.0 respectively. I wonder what the figures were for Bosnia, Croatia, Serbia — really, do you think that after a hard day of castrating the enemy and raping its women, the Man of the House is going to come home to bed and *ask* first? I don't think so. And don't forget, this is war! *We* have to outnumber *them*! (Why does the Pope come to mind just now?)

"We know from research in many countries that if women were allowed to choose for themselves and had unfettered access to suitable family planning methods, fertility would be

129

falling much faster than it is" (Brown). Go ahead, say it! The population growth problem is due to *men* — who *rape*.

So the solution is not female literacy or the availability of contraceptives. Government intervention? Yes. But not for a one-child policy. Rather, for an anti-rape policy, husbands included.

Hank

A while ago, I decided to afford an addition to my cabin. (Side note: A man would say he decided to build an addition, but I didn't build it, the people I hired did — so I don't say *I* did. I first understood this difference when a man asked how long ago I put on the new roof. I replied that I *didn't* put on the roof, I'd hired someone else to do it — but I built the gazebo and the lean-to myself — and I did so two years ago. He looked at me as if I had made a joke. I then understood that for men, he who pays for it takes credit for doing it. This is not a trivial insight.)

Anyway, a while ago I decided to afford an addition. So I asked around a little bit, looked in the yellow pages, then selected and called five contractors to come out, see what I wanted done, and give me an estimate. One didn't bother returning my call. And in this time and place, it's probably *not* the case that he didn't need the work. A second spoke with me over the phone at some length, arranged a time to come out, but then didn't show — and I never heard from him again. The other three did come: they all got the tour and a full explanation of what I wanted done. Of these three, only two submitted a quote. The third, once more, I never heard from again. By now, I'm wondering about this lack of interest, this not-being-taken-seriously. Were they disconcerted by the absence of a husband, a man in charge, a breadwinner — did the third contractor think I couldn't pay for what I wanted done? (Side note: Getting the money from the bank was a pleasure. The loan officer, a woman, didn't even ask about my marital status, let alone request a husband's signature. She asked only about the state of my *financial* affairs — current employment, salary, mortgage, debts, etc. And when I briefly outlined my projected budget/plan for repaying the loan, she never questioned my ability to stick to the plan. In fact, she reduced the interest in response to the low risk I presented.)

So, while I'd hoped my options wouldn't be quite so narrow, I decided between the remaining two contractors: I chose the one with the lower-by-$3,000 estimate and who was just a little less formal and business-like; I wanted to retain input into small decisions along the way, and I assumed this would be more likely with the contractor who engaged in conversation with me.

Things were generally fine — I say generally because I was a little peeved at the sudden slowdown come September. Work got done at full speed during the summer but as soon as the walls were up and the roof on, Hank (the contractor) started on another job. I agreed that the interior stuff at my place could wait a bit — construction's seasonal, you gotta take what you can get, winter's coming, I know it's not pleasant to be putting up walls when it's so cold your face hurts — but 'a bit' turned into four months and I ended up having to prod to get the crawlspace insulated before the snow fell. (Side note: I was also a little peeved that I was paying this builder $20/hour and he was paying his men $18.50/hour, while I, with three degrees, only two of which are required for my job, the only job I could get, am paid $17.10/hour.)

Anyway, things were generally fine until the new pump that Hank installed didn't work properly. First, he spread his four house calls, his four attempts to fix the problem, over three weeks. Clearly, other clients were getting priority — despite the urgency (most people would consider being without running water to be somewhat of an urgency). And despite the $33,000 I'd already paid him (I'd decided to add a second floor, at the cost of another $7,000, and I hired him to do some upgrading

132

in the existing cabin, which would cost another few thousand) — it's not like I was some small-change customer.

This seemingly second-class treatment was true too of the plumber I eventually called (four tries by Hank in three weeks and I still had no water): it took him two days to make his first appearance and another two days to make the second. (And he charged $25/hour.) It felt very much like they were coming only when they had the time — *as if they were doing me a favour.* (Is it because they're so used to doing favours for women they can't see us as paying customers? Where does that come from — the chivalry tradition? The history of women not having money of their own, with which to pay people? The man's blatant misunderstanding, like doing the dishes is *doing a favour* for his wife?) This is just speculation, but I think that if I were a man, I wouldn't've been put on the back burner like that.

More annoying was that each of Hank's house calls seemed to last just a little longer than the previous one. I tried not to be rude, but I really didn't want to chat with him all evening. He'd linger, not taking the hint of me sitting at my desk with work spread out in front of me (it's not like I was just sitting on the couch, let alone offering him a cup of coffee).

Then one evening, he asked, rather out of the blue in the course of a conversation I was trying politely to end ("...so I'll call you tomorrow then if it's still not working."), if I'd heard about the Gwen Jacobs decision and what did I think. I was a little surprised at this (Hank broaching a philosophical issue), but I thought, it's a small community and he knows the guy who lives and fishes on this lake, who knows I don't bother with a bathing suit, everyone knows, it's no big deal, so maybe *that's* why he asked. Part of me really didn't want to get into a discussion about this with someone who was bound to need a lot of explanation before he really understood the points I'd make ("I'm wondering about sexual assault," he'd said, with a grin) (*with a grin*) — but the other part of me wanted to kill that grin. So I spent a minute outlining what I thought.

It wasn't until later that I connected the dots: he had, on a previous visit, suggested that I put something (the pump line he thought was frozen?) wherever it was warmest — "What's the hottest place in your cabin — your bed?" I had responded that ten years of celibacy does not a hot bed make, hoping to indicate that I was not a sexual possibility. Did he take my response as a sexual challenge? Or worse, did he not even consider that my celibacy might be my choice — did he think my comment was therefore a veiled 'asking for it'? Amazing. On another occasion, after a few inconsequential elbow or knee brushes, he actually did the bum-pat thing.

After the second protracted evening visit, I called him to update him on the situation (pump still not working) when I thought his wife would answer. *If* something was going on in his mind, I wanted *not* to encourage it; so I preferred to leave a message with his wife rather than get into yet another conversation with him. I swear I heard ice in her voice. Did she think — Unbelievable. I thoroughly included her in the loop then, explaining in great detail the plumbing situation. I even told her to tell Hank that the next house call could wait until Saturday, if he was available then, because I didn't want another evening's work disturbed that week.

Well. Saturday he arrived. He hadn't called to confirm that he was coming, so I didn't exactly expect him. I certainly didn't expect him to just open my door and walk in at eight o'clock in the morning. My bed is right by the door; I was still in it.

I was, of course, enraged. The nerve, the assumption of familiarity, the proprietariness — this is *my* house, you *knock* before you enter, and you *wait* until I answer the door; even friends do that, and we are *not* friends, you are my contractor, I *hired* you, you *work* for me!

Did I say any of that? Of course not. When you're a woman, in a male-dominant society, and you find yourself still in bed, just awake, and a man is standing a mere two feet away, probably with a pipe wrench in his hand (hopefully he has come to fix the pump), you don't tell him off. (Not then. But, alas, not later either. And that's what makes me really angry — I'll never be able to set him straight. Because telling him what I really think would no doubt make him angry. And angry men are to be feared. He knows where I live. One 'accidental' shot at Chessie from the hunting rifle he no doubt owns and she'll be dead. So I let it go. I smile it off. And he carries on, oblivious to the damage he's done, the danger he is.)

Now the question is this: would he have done this if I'd been a man? I think not. He certainly wouldn't've walked in like that if I were a man, or if he thought I'd be in bed with my husband. In fact, I suspect *none* of this would've happened if I'd been a man or a married woman — the casual touches, the sexual innuendo talk, even the extended house calls. Not to mention the second-class client treatment. Nor perhaps all the clean-up work he left — piles of sawdust for me to sweep up, handprints on the walls for me to wash off, etc. (Is that women's work?)

Things *really* made sense when my neighbour told me that when I'd hired a someone to fix the bathroom floor and put in a shower stall several years prior, his wife had called this neighbour to ask about me — did she have cause for concern? I was flabbergasted to find out about this. As with Hank, I had asked Jim to do the work, if possible, on the days I wasn't there (I really don't like the solitude of my days off to be invaded, so I usually arrange to be there the first time, to make sure Chessie is okay with the guy, and then schedule subsequent visits for the days I have to work).

Both wives seemed to think that a woman living alone would automatically be sexually encouraging. And Hank seemed to think a woman living alone might be sexually available. (Perhaps he thought my friendliness was an invitation. Sad, isn't it — you can't even talk to a man without him thinking you're coming on to him. Why is that? Because men don't chat with each other? Because in the man's world, chatting is not considered part of normal friendly interaction, so when chatting does occur, it's taken to indicate *extra*ordinary friendliness?) (No maybe that's not what was happening at all. That's a woman's take on the situation. At one point in one conversation, I realized that he was giving me advice, about how to get business — I'm a disc jockey too — and I thought 'Wait a minute, did I ask you for advice?' I had merely said that business was poor. Why is it that when you say something's difficult, women will empathize but men will advise? So maybe what was happening was that he was seeing himself more and more in a 'superior' position and seeing me more and more as a subordinate and *that's* what led to the sexual stuff, sex being connected to power for men. Downplaying my degrees as I did, in order not to appear elitist (or rich) and in order not to make him feel insecure [damn my mother!], wouldn't've helped in this regard.) At the very least, Hank and the others considered my sex to be primary instead of irrelevant.

I just wanted to hire someone to fix my bathroom, to build an addition, to fix my pump. But being female got in the way: it restricted my choices, it affected the quality of the work I got, it limited my actions. It made ordinary shit difficult.

Making Enemies

Why is it that men make enemies more easily than women? One man will tell another to fuck off at the drop of a hat. A woman will bite her tongue and walk away.

Is it that men don't feel as vulnerable as women? And yet they are. To speeding cars, bullets — poison.

Is she afraid to get in a fight? Perhaps. Because she fears for her kids. Doesn't the man have kids? Surely he would refrain from doing anything that might put them at risk. Yes, but there seems to be some male code of honour such that one man pissed off at another man takes it out directly on the man — not his kids (to do so would be unmanly). Making an enemy puts *himself* at risk, not those he loves.

Okay, so what's the code of honour when a man is pissed off at a woman? There is none. Men don't fight with women. (At least not with women not their wives.) That's why women fear for their kids. And their windows, their tires ... It's safer, and/or cheaper, to keep the peace, to be civil.

Why Do Men Spit?
(and women don't?)

Is it physiological? Do males produce a larger amount of saliva? Even so, why the need to spit it out? Why not just swallow it?

Would that remind them of swallowing semen? Which is female, effeminate, gay? (I'll ignore for the moment the assumption that all, or even most, women swallow semen.)

But no, that can't be right: it seems too ... too reasoned. Spitting seems to be more of a reflex, a habit, a that's-the-way-I-was-raised sort of thing, a cultural thing, a *sub*cultural thing, ah: to spit is to be manly. Little boys spit to appear grown up. Grown up *men*. So what's the connection between spitting and masculinity?

Consider the way men spit. It's not a chin-dribbling drooling kind of getting rid of saliva. It's a forceful ejac — is that it? Is spitting a little pseudo sex act? Every time a man spits, does he experience a sort of orgasmic release? Both do involve a forceful expulsion of bodily fluids.

Hm — the pissing contest now comes to mind. What *is* it about expelling one's bodily fluids with some degree of force that proves one's manhood?

Is it just the forcefulness? Whether it's throwing a ball or — this may explain the unnecessarily loud, kleenex-devastating way men blow their noses. Bodily fluids there too. But then why don't men wail when they cry?

There must be something more to spitting. There seems to be a certain contempt in the gesture. Certainly to spit *on* *someone*, like pissing on them, (and ejaculating on them?), is to defile, is to degrade, them.

But what about the man just walking down the street who hacks up a gob and spits every few seconds? Is that, then, just a continuous display of contempt — for everything? *I am male: I am better than everything.* That rings true. (As does the corollary: *I am so insecure I have to display my superiority every few seconds.*)

Perhaps men see saliva, like mucous, as germ-filled and rightly expelled from the body. But then why don't they spit into a handkerchief or a kleenex? Spitting, according to this interpretation, *increases* the contemptuousness, the utter disregard for the other, the one who shares the sidewalk.

Men used to spit into spittoons, back when tobacco chewing was all the rage. So perhaps modern-day spitting is like any tradition: a practice whose rationale has long since disappeared, but whose emotional value lingers, on a barely conscious level — maybe there's some Marlboro-man feel about it…

Or it could just be that men are slobs. But, again, what's the connection? Why do men associate lack of hygiene with masculinity? I recall a woman auto mechanic explaining that the perpetually greasy hands thing was totally unnecessary, it was just a macho thing. Why are clean hands unmanly? Surely few women would want to be touched, inside or out, by greasy, dirty fingers. (And isn't touching women proof of one's manhood?) Maybe it's just that it's so opposite to women: *women are clean, so if I am a man, I am dirty.*

For surely there's something about the liquidity of saliva. Liquids are soft; soft is feminine. So they must dissociate themselves from it, get rid of it. Hm. Do men think hard stools are more masculine than soft stools — do real men brag about hard it is to shit?

The Other Sex

Men, I mean. After all, they're the ones who define themselves in relation to us: to be a man is to be whatever is *not* to be a woman.

If women are graceful, then to be graceful is feminine. A graceful man is effeminate. A real man is not graceful. He's not necessarily *clumsy*, he's just *not-graceful*.

If women like flowers, then men do not.

If women like pink and orange and mauve, then men do not.

And when women change their abilities, their desires, the men also change. For example, as soon women became clerks, men did not.

I pity a whole sex that is so dependent. Living in a rut of reaction, they are simply incapable of such a proactive move as defining themselves for themselves. They didn't even know they didn't like quiche until we said *we* liked it.

Frankly, I fear for their future. At the rate women are doing, well, whatever they please, men will soon be — *not*.

The Part-time Ghetto

What's the difference between people with part-time jobs and people with full-time jobs? If you're part-time, you don't get sick days (so when you're sick for a day, you lose a day's pay); you don't get time and a half for overtime (time and a half starts after 44 hours, not after whatever numbers of hours you've been hired to work); you don't get seniority (it simply doesn't apply to part-timers); you have to pay for your own dentist appointments, your prescription drugs, and your glasses (so you don't make dentist appointments just for check-ups, you don't buy prescription drugs unless they're absolutely essential, and your glasses are for your eyes of five years ago); and your only pension plan is the CPP and whatever you save on your own (which is not a lot if you're only part-time).

But more significant than these monetary differences are the differences in your perceived value: your input is less often solicited, whether regarding shift schedules or company policy; your work is thought to be less important, no matter what you're doing (your paycheque is thought to be less important too, so you often have to wait longer for it); you're automatically considered a beginner who needs more supervision, who's expected to prove herself; in short, if you're part-time, you don't get treated or taken seriously. And don't kid yourself, the differences exist along the whole job spectrum: the differences between the part-time and full-time waitresses are the same as the differences between the part-time and full-time professors.

So let me ask again, what's the difference between part-time and full-time? Usually, about ten hours. Why is this such a big deal? (Apart from 'It's a man-made world and men are obsessed with quantitative differences.) There's no difference between the cleaning done by the part-time custodian and that done by the full-time custodian; there's no difference between the lawyering done by the attorney who's part-time with the firm and that done by the one who's full-time.

Quite simply, an elementary but serious error in logic is made by those who perpetuate this two-class system: the assumption of a causal relationship between quantity and quality. (Again, *who* is it who keeps connecting quantity with quality, who keeps believing bigger is better?) The assumption is made that those working fewer than 40 hours/week are not doing as good a job as those working more than 40 hours/week.

Good as in as committed? But it's often not a person's choice to be part-time instead of full-time; they'd be full-time if they could. And in fact, the desire to *become* full-time often leads to *more*, not less, commitment to one's duties.

Good as in competent? The part-time worker is *not* necessarily less qualified or less experienced. In fact, given the glutted job market, the younger employees who must settle for part-time work are often *more* qualified than the older, full-time workers. (And again, they have good reason to try harder, to *be* more competent.)

Good as in enthusiastic? Wouldn't it make more sense to assume that the *more* hours one works, the more tired and burned out, i.e., the *less* enthusiastic, one is? In fact, how can one be a healthy individual, how can one live a balanced life, when 80% of one's waking hours are spent in the same place, doing the same thing?

It doesn't make sense. That's all there is to it. Why should the number of hours per week determine whether you are a first-class employee or a second-class employee? What's so magical about the number 40? And will the magic disappear if

142

and when we scale down to a 30-hour work week as the standard?

And here's the real kicker: most part-time jobs, the second-class group, are filled by women. Which begs the question, which came first: was part-time work devalued because women did it or were women put in the part-time positions because such positions were devalued?

Message to Amy Farrah Fowler:
LEAVE HIM NOW.

Is anyone else really *really* disturbed by Amy Farrah Fowler's character on *The Big Bang Theory*? She is so intelligent, has a Ph.D., is a neurobiologist, and yet she stays in a relationship with Sheldon Cooper, the most infantile, the most arrogant, the most selfish person ever. That in itself is boggling. But — the relationship. It's not. How low does her self-esteem have to be for her to think she can't do better?

Maybe, though, she's right. Eliminate the 99% who aren't as smart as her. Of those, eliminate the ones who are already married. Then eliminate the ones she's not likely to ever meet. *Is* there anyone left?

But wait. Why does the guy have to be as smart as her? How bad does the world have to be for it to be true that no man less intelligent than her will have the maturity to want her, to love her? Maybe her choices really are Zack, Sheldon, or no one.

Well, given that — it's a no-brainer, Amy! A life lived alone is far, *far* better than a life intertwined with someone who ignores you, who belittles your interests (neurobiology is not nearly as important as theoretical physics), who belittles your achievements (remember the time she was published in a major journal?), who knows what you want (because you've come right out and told him) and still does not give it to you (romance, sex).

I've actually started fast-forwarding through the Sheldon-and-Amy scenes because they've become just too sickening to watch. 'Emotionally abusive' is the phrase I'm looking for. (And *who* is it who thinks that's entertaining?)

Men's and Women's Sports:
A Modest Comparison

One good thing about television stations' mega-coverage of the Olympics is that women's events are shown a lot. Often within close temporal proximity to men's events. Comparison is inevitable. And interesting.

Consider volleyball. The women, when they dive for the ball, do this really neat shoulder roll: it's smooth, efficient, and really cool to see — you hardly know they went down, they're back on their feet in a flash. The men's technique? A belly flop. Really, it's sort of a chest first body slam. Some follow through with a give-me-ten marines push-up, but most just kind of lie there for a second, face in the floor. I suppose they think the move looks dramatic, extra-heroic. I think it looks stupid.

And men's basketball — that's not even a sport anymore. The guys are simply too big. Give me a ball small enough to hold upside-down with one hand, and I'll be doing some pretty fancy dribbling too. Give me a net so low to the ground I can just reach up and touch it, and I'll slam dunk *every* time. And give me a court I can cover in five strides, hell, I'll play a whole game without even breaking into a sweat.

And yet even with these size advantages, men's play pales in comparison to women's play. For example, men pass the ball a lot less often — even though it's easier to do so (one hand to throw/catch it, the other to screen the throw/catch). And even though they barely need to jump to make a basket, their timing and coordination is so poor, they hit the basket on their way down, often grabbing on to it for dear life so they can at least land on their feet. (A couple hundred pounds hanging onto the rim — I don't know about you, but we used to yell at anyone who bent the rim and then kick them out of the game!)

And gymnastics — okay, the differences between women's and men's gymnastics have always been rather obvious. For men, one of the big balance moves is a front scale: look at me, I can stand on one foot. For the women, the display of balance occurs on a 4" wide beam, 3-4' off the ground, and they *land* in a front scale — after an aerial-back-handspring-something-or-other. And the high bar. One bar. Oooooh. Try flipping around two of them. Set at *different* heights. And the men's floor. Homophobia at its best. First rule, no music. That would be too much like dancing. (Even though men have been known to dance on occasion.) (Some even have a sense of rhythm.) Second rule, no curves. Ever notice the getting-into-the-corner move? What is that? It looks like a Nazi goose step with a half-turn and a double 'Heil Hitler' salute.

Lastly, consider track. Have you ever wondered why the triple jump didn't become a women's event until some fifteen years after it became a men's event? It's because we're grown up now, so hopscotch isn't a challenge for us. Y'know what event I'd like to see? Men's double-dutch. Now *that* would be entertaining.

Men who need Mom
to clean up after them

I spend a lot of time walking on the dirt roads near my place, as well as on the old logging roads through the forest. Twice a year, I take a large garbage bag with me to pick up the litter — mostly beer cans and fast food containers, but often whole plastic bags of garbage that have been tossed in among the trees. (Lately, I've had to take two large garbage bags.) I typically wait until the fall, because it seems the summer people litter more than those of us who live here, and I typically wait until after the spring hunt, because it seems the hunters leave quite a bit of trash.

I have always suspected that men litter more than women, and I've come across a statistic supporting my hunch: males do 72% of deliberate littering and are responsible for 96% of accidental littering (greenecoservices. com/myths-and-facts-litter).

Why is this so? I think it's because 'cleaning up after' is seen as a woman's task. (This thought occurred to me when, while I was on one of my litter pick-up walks, one guy slowed down as he passed me in his truck and called out, "Good girl! Good to see you're good for something!") After all, wasn't it Mom who cleaned up after them when they were kids? (Mom did the cleaning; Dad did the fixing.) Of course the generalization from Mom to all women is a mistake: "Mom cleaned up after me, Mom is a woman, so women should clean up after me" is the same as "Princess is a kitten, Princess is white, so white things are/should be kittens". But I doubt these morons can think in a — well, I doubt these morons can think.

147

Of course a mistake is made too in thinking that when you're old enough to drink beer and buy your own fast food, you're still a kid who needs Mom, or any woman, to clean up after you. (No, wait, I'm making the mistake there — I'm confusing chronological age with developmental age.)

Sterilization:
The Personal and the Political

Ever since I have been old enough to ask myself 'Do I want children?', my answer has been 'No' — a rather emphatic 'No!' I consider parenting to be a career, and a very demanding one at that: twenty-four hours a day for at least fourteen years, you are responsible for the physical, emotional, and intellectual development of another human being. Quite simply, it wasn't a career I wanted.

So, I went on the pill three or four months before I started having sex, and eventually chose permanent contraception instead. I have explained this to quite a few people over the last ten years, and I continue to be amazed at those who are amazed. When I ask 'Why did you choose to become a parent?' (a fair enough question to someone who has just asked me the opposite), they sort of give me a patronizing smile and say something like 'It wasn't exactly a choice.' Yes it was. YES IT WAS. Unless you were raped or the contraception didn't work, it was a choice: you don't accidentally happen to catch some ejaculate in your vagina!

And not giving that choice much thought is nothing to smile about. Tell me, between the one who without really thinking about it, without really wanting it, becomes a parent, and the one who deliberately does *not* become a parent — who is the more responsible? I ask this question because of the response by both my own physician and the surgeon to whom he referred me (who then referred me to another surgeon). One of them actually snickered and said 'So you want the benefits of sex without the responsibilities?' I didn't respond, realizing only later that I was confused because he had asked the question incorrectly: yes I wanted sex, and no I didn't want the responsibility — of *children*, not of *sex*; I *was* willing to accept the responsibility of sex, that's *why* I was sitting in his office asking to be sterilized. I believe I was also asked why I didn't want children. When a woman comes to you pregnant, I said, do you ask her, before agreeing to deliver, why she wants the child? And would you be asking these questions if I looked older? If I already had two children, at least one of whom was a male? If I were a man seeking a vasectomy?

Not surprisingly, the appointments reminded me of a Therapeutic Abortion Committee (TAC) hearing. Are you married? Are you employed? Any congenital disease in your family? Substance abuse? Psychiatric hospitalization? The 'problem' is that I am competent and qualified to be a mother. In every way. Except one. I don't *want* to be. On that basis alone, a TAC should grant me an abortion. On that basis alone, a surgeon should perform the sterilization. But as always, the woman's *wants*, her *choices*, are irrelevant. (Do you believe we're incapable of *having* wants, of *making* choices?) They should be establishing my competence, not my incompetence. And if I am competent, then my decision should be accepted, my request should be granted. It's as simple as that. (Of course, if I'm incompetent to be a good parent, my request, for sterilization or an abortion, should be granted as well. Which begs the question, why are there TACs in the first place?) ('Course, if I were incompetent, irresponsible, I probably wouldn't be there seeking an abortion, I probably wouldn't have thought carefully about the situation, the future. Can you say 'Catch 22'?)

The other question I remember clearly is that of the third doctor: 'Do you want a tubal ligation or a cauterization?' That's really about the only question that should have been asked. I asked him to explain the advantages and disadvantages of each; he did so; I answered his question. (As for 'When would you like the surgery?', how about Mothers' Day?)

150

No, I don't regret it. I never have, not for one second of one minute of any day. Sure there's a possibility that one day I'll want children. There's also a possibility that one day I'll want a full-time office job. And anyway, I could always adopt. (But it wouldn't be your own! Sure it would; it just wouldn't have my genes.) (And if that's so important, you don't want a kid — you want a smaller ego.)

It gave me control over my life, my destiny. In fact, it has been one of the best decisions I've made, and I wish more people would *make* it (whether they decide 'yes' or 'no' is less important than *deciding* — considering and deciding and not just letting it happen).

In fact, I wish being sterile were our default state: one should have to *do* something quite intentional in order to *become* reproductive (like take a pill, with not insignificant side-effects, every day at exactly the same time for six months — men too), rather than the other way around.

In the meantime, I hope those women who do choose permanent contraception can get it without the bit of hassle I went through. I am thankful, however, that I live in a time and place in which sterilization, especially for a young woman without children, is at least legal. Had it not been, I may have chosen sexual abstinence. (If I had to think each time I had intercourse 'This could change — read, mess up — the next fifteen years of my life', I wouldn't have enjoyed it anyway.)

I am against sexism of any kind; I think that in a perfect world, one's sex would be as relevant as one's shoe size. I don't like any titles, but I like least of all, therefore, 'Ms.' and 'Mr.' because they differentiate on the basis of sex; being a woman, a Ms., has always been near the bottom of my identity list (I'm a person, a dog-lover, a writer, a composer, and I am all of these way before I am a woman). So I love being neutered — it's a bit of freedom from being sexed.

Why Aren't There Any
Great Women Xs?

A new (for me) answer to the classic question, Why aren't there any great women Xs, occurred to me when I saw a website for a small company of composers specializing in music for dance troupes (all four composers were male) shortly after a male friend of mine confessed that if he wasn't getting paid to do it (write a book — he's an academic with a university position), he probably wouldn't, and another male friend confessed confusion at the idea of composing something just out of his soul (everything he'd written had been for pay — soundtracks for video games and what have you). Until then, the answer to that age-old question seemed to go to merit and/or opportunity. Now I'm thinking it goes to money.

How many of those great-man achievements would have occurred if they had to have been done 'on spec'— that is, without any pay for the doing? How many men, indeed how many people, make important discoveries, for example, on their own time at home? When my (male) friend writes a book, it's just part of his job. All those great men, who we know to be great because of the prizes they win, the fame they garner — they get those prizes and that fame for just *doing their job, for doing whatever it is they do 'at work'*.

In addition to the motivation factor, there's also the legitimizing factor: payment for your work is the stamp of quality — consider the dual meanings of 'amateur' and 'professional'. So even if you do make a great discovery or write a great book on your own time at home, no one will recognize it as such; getting paid for it is prerequisite for its identification as great.

And it doesn't hurt that when you're in a paid position, you have access to resources, such as a lab or a studio, that you probably otherwise wouldn't have.

And here's the thing: men have, in far greater proportion than women, held paying jobs and received commissions; they're the ones who have been getting paid. They're the ones with the jobs at which they (potentially, have the opportunity to) *do* something great.

And why is that so? One could say that women don't get the jobs or the commissions because they're not as good — it could come back to merit after all. But we know that's simply not true.

It might come back to opportunity though: the people who get the jobs and the commissions are the ones in the boy's club — being male (still) increases the opportunities to land the money, status, and resources of a job/commission (the people who are in a position to pay, the people with money, are men, not women, and men are more apt to hire other men than they are to hire women, unless they're after some political correct currency).

But even the individual entrepreneurs, the guys who set up their own company to provide music for dance groups, for example — why is it that men, so much more often than women, have not just jobs, but careers? Because that's been their role. They're supposed to make a living. Women are supposed to make a home. They're supposed to support their family. Women are supposed to make that family.

Also, I think somehow men find out how to turn jobs into careers. I don't know how they do, but they do. Perhaps it's simply because their social network is more apt to include someone who has done just that, or perhaps it's because they get informal mentoring more often than women. But show me two composers, one a man and the other a woman, and I'll bet it's only the man who thinks to get some buddies together and form a company, and somehow knows how to do it.

Men, Noise, and
A Simple Request, Really

I finally figured it out — why the men in my neighborhood react with such escalated lack of consideration whenever I ask them, politely, to limit their noise. I've asked snowmobilers who are out racing around the lake and having a good time going VROOM VROOM to please just turn around a few seconds before they get to the end of the lake, which is where I live; I've asked dirt bikers to please ride up and down and up and down and up and down on a section of road that doesn't have a bunch of people living there; I've asked men who are building new houses to please put the compressor behind the house (so the house acts as a berm) rather than on the lake side (which means, of course, that the noise not only skids across the lake with wonderful efficiency, but it then bounces off the hills, echoing amplified all over the place); and I'd like to ask them if they really, seriously, need to use a leafblower — we live in the forest, for godsake.

And almost every single time, not only has the man *not* acceded to my request he's increased his noise-making and/or responded with confrontational aggression.

Do I live in a neighborhood with an unrepresentative number of inconsiderate assholes?

No. Here's what's happening. (As I say, I've finally figured it out.) Partly it's because I'm a woman asking a man to do something. Most men do not want to be seen taking orders from a woman; even to accede to a woman's request is apparently too much for their egos. My male neighbour has made similar requests and the responses have been along the lines of 'Sure, no problem.'

And partly, it's because making noise is perceived to be an integral part of being a man. I've long known 'My car is my penis' but I never realized that that was partly because of the *noise* the car makes. I didn't know that men routinely modify the mufflers on their dirt bikes in order to make them *louder*. And then I happened to catch a Canadian Tire advertisement on television (I seldom watch television) and was absolutely amazed at the blatant association of masculinity with power tools, the (shouted) promise that 'You'll be more of a man when you use this million-horsepower table saw' or whatever.

So my requests are resisted, to put it mildly, because I'm essentially asking that they castrate themselves.

A Little Less Evolved

Sometimes I wonder whether men have a defective chromosome: whether the Y was supposed to be an X, but somehow it ended up missing something — a case of stunted growth or arrested development. This defective chromosome, uniquely characteristic of the human male, causes them to be a little lower on the evolutionary scale, a little less evolved.

Consider their fascination with movement. They always have to be doing something, moving around, busy at this or that. They can't sit still. This importance of movement is characteristic of many lower animals; something doesn't even register in the frog's visual field unless it moves. Certainly movement is required for flight and fight. (And no other options occur to lower animals.) And for many, movement is a form of posturing — which explains the way men walk, and stand, and sit. On the other hand, such excessive physical activity may simply suggest that the organism's mental activity does not provide enough stimulation.

Not only must they be doing something, they must be doing it loudly. They even speak more loudly than women. And when they're not speaking, they must be making noise. They derive endless delight from engines, jackhammers, chainsaws... This propensity is suggestive of the lion's roar — the louder the noise, the greater the threat.

Because, usually, the larger the animal. And of course size is another male obsession. Girth which in a woman would be considered obese and disgusting is carried by men as if it *increases* their legitimacy, their authority: they thrust out their gut just as they thrust out their chest. It brings to mind animals that inflate themselves to achieve greater size (the balloonfish can actually double its size). Men are concerned not only with physical size, in general and in particular, but also with the size of their paycheques, their houses, their corporations. The bigger, the better.

Closely related to the size thing is the territory thing. Men occupy a lot of space — again, look at the way they stand and sit. They take up, they occupy, more space than they need — they lean over counters, spill out of chairs, take over small countries. They engage in turf wars, at every level.

Consider also men's obsession with speed. Cars, trains, planes. Sex. Speed is, of course, important for flight, one of the forementioned behaviours favoured by so many lower animals.

Like their sexual response, men's emotional response is, well, uncomplicated. They are easy to please. This lack of complexity is further indication that they are simply less evolved.

Some say that language is the mark of higher life forms. And, of course, any grade school teacher will tell you that boys lag behind girls in verbal development. They're just not very good at communicating. I believe the word I'm looking for is 'inarticulate'.

By way of summary, consider dick flicks. Also called action movies, there is indeed lots of action. And lots of noise. The heroes are usually big. And they have big things — big guns, usually. The central conflict of a dick flick is almost always territorial. There is little in the way of plot or character development, but there's always at least one high-speed chase scene. And, understandably, the dialogue in a dick flick consists mostly of short and often incomplete sentences.

When does the magical metamorphosis happen?

Our brothers were bossy know-it-alls, and they did cruel things to us and to animals.

The boys in our class taunted us and always got into fights with each other. They were rude and forever demanding to be the center of attention.

In high school, they became socially awkward, struggled with the material, and became fascinated by sports.

In university, they used pick-up lines (i.e., lies) to impregnate us, seemingly unaware of the immense consequences to us. In the lecture hall, they were always so full of self-importance, so full of themselves.

So how is it that they become our supervisors, our MPs, our CEOs? How is it they get in to be in charge of things? How is it they come to have power?

Why do we think they magically become competent, mature, responsible— When they graduate? When they put on a suit?

Because apparently we do think that. I saw that magic happen with my own eyes. My brother graduated, put on a suit, bought an attaché case, and suddenly the world was his. His entitlement.

When did that metamorphosis happen? When did he become so qualified? So worthy? Until then, he was worse than me, at everything.

We commonly joke that 'B students' become our bosses, because they're the ones that go in to business, whereas the 'A students' go into the humanities and the sciences.

We've got it wrong. The 'C students' go into business. The 'B students' go into the humanities and the sciences. The 'A students' were girls. And they're nowhere to be seen now.

I'm too drunk. No I'm not.

According to the Canadian Criminal Code, (self-induced) intoxication is no defence against charges of assault (33.1): if you're drunk, you're still able to form the general intent to commit said assault.

And yet, with regard to the sub-category of sexual assault, belief that someone is consenting is cancelled if that someone is intoxicated (273.1(2)): if you're drunk, you can't consent to sex.

So if you're drunk, you're capable of intending to assault, but you're not capable of intending to have sex? Given that it's mostly men who do the assaulting, and it's mostly women who do the consenting (and given, it's my guess, that the lawmakers had men in mind for 33.1 and women in mind for 273.1(2)), is this some sort of 'protect the weaker sex' double standard?

If we expect men to foresee the effects of alcohol and to be responsible for their behaviour while under its influence, shouldn't we expect the same of women? Yes, it may be morally scuzzy to have sex with someone who's drunk (and got that way of her own free will), climbing all over you and moaning 'do me', and you suspect that if she were sober she wouldn't be quite so willing — but you're not her legal guardian. 'Yes' means 'yes' and if she regrets it the morning after, that's *her* headache. Doing something really stupid is the risk you take when you get drunk (unless you've got a dependable designated sober friend with you).

If while drunk she says I can borrow her car, and I do so, am I really justly accused of theft? Am I my sister's keeper? She said I could. Do I have to second guess her? She may well say I can borrow her car when she's sober too. Or not. Am I supposed to know?

God: The Quintessential Deadbeat Dad

He left almost 2,000 years ago. Said he'd be back real soon. Yeah. He never writes. He never calls. He left us these notes though. But half are so cryptic, the rest so contradictory, he must've been sloshed at the time. 'Wait 'till your father gets home.' That got tired real quick.

Child support? It's not just that so many of us don't have enough to eat. A lot of us are starving to death. We have no roof over our heads. And we could use new clothes. 'Cheque's in the mail.' Right.

They say the typical dad interacts with his kids for just two minutes each day. Half of us would weep with gratitude just to hear his voice for two minutes.

Role model? 'Like father, like son' is an understatement. Lots of us have a temper, and we're a vengeful lot. We kill, we torture, we loot, we lie. We're racist. And women, well, they're just not very important.

Bottom line is he's guilty of neglect and abuse. His kids wouldn't recognize him even if he did show up. As for duty and responsibility, let alone love and affection, he may as well not even exist.

Permitting Abortion and Prohibiting Prenatal Harm

I think abortion should be allowed. And I think prenatal harm (especially that caused by ingesting various legal and illegal substances while pregnant) should not be allowed. Some accuse me of hypocrisy or, more accurately, maintaining a contradictory position: either women have the right to control what happens to their bodies or they don't, make up your mind.

I have made up my mind. Women, and men, have that right *except* when it causes harm to someone else: I can move my arms any way I want except straight into your face.

Ah, you may jump up and down, you said 'someone else!' So the fetus is a person! That's why you're saying prenatal harm is wrong! So that makes abortion wrong too! You can't have it both ways!

Yes I can. The fetus can be a person, and it may still be okay to abort. Killing in self-defence is permissible; killing in mercy is permissible. So if the pregnancy or birth poses a risk to me, I can kill the fetus. Or if the fetus is discovered to have some awful excruciatingly painful genetic disease, I can kill it. (In that case, I *should* kill it.)

Not only does being a person not mean I can't kill it; *not* being a person doesn't mean I can harm it. It's wrong to hurt a chipmunk, barring extenuating circumstances, because it can feel pain.

And in any case, I would argue that personhood is not all-or-nothing. Sentience, brain activity, the ability to communicate, the capacity for rational thought, consciousness, interests — all of these attributes, typically proposed to determine personhood, exist in degrees. So creatures can be persons in varying degrees.

And since personhood is typically established in order to establish rights, it makes sense then to assign fewer rights to 'lesser' persons. While there is cause for concern about the impact of such an argument on 'disabled' people, I believe this slippery slope should and can be avoided. For example, if a mentally disabled adult lacks the cognitive competence to vote, that right is justifiably denied. But it doesn't follow that other rights, such as the right to a livelihood, also be denied.

In fact, we already assign rights according to various capacities and competencies: children, because of their lesser capacity for rational thought, and perhaps also because of their lesser interests, do not have voting rights; only a few adults, because of their superior knowledge and fine motor skills, are awarded operating room rights. The acceptability of aborting a being with minimal personhood would not then contradict the unacceptability of harming a being with considerably more personhood.

In fact, going back to the matter of the right to control one's body, it might be reasonable to consider, in the case of pregnancy, the boundaries of one's body to be somewhat elastic. While the woman generally has the right to control what happens to her body, what is considered 'her body' changes through the pregnancy parallel to the changes in the personhood of the zygote/embryo/fetus: the less it is a person, the more it is her body; the more it is a person, the less it is (just) her body. Thus aborting the zygote, when 'her body' is very much just her body, may be acceptable, whereas harming the fetus, when it is not, may not be.

In addition to rights and personhood (though personhood 'reduces' to rights), there is another, perhaps better, consideration: consequences. Barring the capacity to feel pain, as long as there isn't going to be a human being who will at some future time suffer from any prenatal harm — that is, if the woman decides to abort the pregnancy — such harm, whether caused by the woman or some third party, isn't a wrong. In fact, assuming no such capacity, and given that it is has no interests or desires (which might justify pain, as in the case of vaccination), it's weird to even call it harm. (Do I harm a virus when I take cold medication? Or cancer cells when I receive chemotherapy?)

However, if there *is* going to be such a human being — that is, if the woman decides to continue the pregnancy and give birth — there *will* be an infant, a child, an adult who will suffer the consequences, which, depending on the harm done, can range from vomiting, inability to sleep, reluctance to feed, diarrhea leading to shock and death, severe anemia, and excruciating pain, in the newborn, to more permanent growth retardation, mental retardation, central nervous system abnormalities, and malformations of the kidneys, intestines, head, and spinal cord (Madam Justice Proudfoot, "Judgement Respecting Female Infant 'D.J.'," Madam Justice Proudfoot). Add to this the consequences to others, and the wrongdoing increases: the healthcare system (the rest of us) may have to pay (dearly) for newborn intensive care (Mathieu, in *Preventing Prenatal Harm: Should the State Intervene?*, estimates the average cost of prenatal intensive care to be about $2,000/day); the education system may have to deal with one more 'special ed' student; chances are the welfare system will be involved (Oberman, in "Sex, Drugs, Pregnancy, and the Law: Rethinking the Problems of Pregnant Women Who Use Drugs," estimates the cost of lifelong care for fetal alcohol syndrome to range from $600,000 to $2.6 million); and so on. Thus there is no contradiction in holding that abortion is morally acceptable and prenatal harm is not: generally speaking, abortion does not lead to morally unacceptable consequences, whereas prenatal harm does.

163

Of course, consequences to the woman must also be considered. For example eating a well-balanced diet is little to ask to ensure a healthy newborn, and giving up alcohol for nine months is well 'worth' a newborn free of mental retardation. But staying in bed for nine months may be too much to ask just to ensure the birth is not a week premature, and giving up life-saving treatment may not be worth the mere possibility of a healthy fetus.

Transgendered Courage

Transgendered people are often seen as courageous; they have the guts to take radical steps to become the people they really are. But I don't see them as any different from people, mostly women, who get nip-and-tuck surgeries, botox injections, and breast enlargements. After all, they too take radical steps to become the people they feel they really are — youthful and sexually attractive.

I understand the mismatch between what's inside and what's outside. Really I do. I look like a middle-aged woman. But I don't feel like a middle-aged woman. I feel like a young gun, still burning at both ends. Mixed metaphor and all.

Furthermore, transgendered people aren't snubbing sex stereotypes; they're reinforcing them. You're in a woman's body but you don't feel like a woman? You don't want to wear make-up, high heels, and a dress? You're not into gossip and giggles? You'd rather play football and fix the car? So do it. You don't need to get a male body.

You're in a male body but you'd really like to wear lavender chiffon and spend the day baking cupcakes and arranging flowers? So do it. You don't need a female body.

If we had more people with the courage to just do what they wanted to do, regardless of what others think they should do based on an indefensible notion of a sexual dichotomy based, in turn, on physical appearance, if we had more people who were willing to stand up to the consequent taunts and ostracization, maybe eventually the taunts and ostracization would disappear.

You wouldn't know by looking at her

When he was acting as a sports announcer, Toller Cranston once said, as Janet Lynn took the ice, "You wouldn't know by looking at her that she's a housewife and mother of three." What? WHAT?? Would he have said of Kurt Browning, "You wouldn't know by looking at him that he does stuff around the house and is a father of three"?? I think not.

Clearly Cranston thinks that — well, I don't know what the hell he thinks. That doing stuff around the house is somehow incompatible with — skating? I'll grant that being a parent could deplete one's energy to the point that maintaining an elite level of athletic performance is unlikely, but that would apply only if the kids were a certain age and only if one didn't have any assistance — and it would apply to men as well as women.

I suspect he has some stereotype of housewife and mother in his mind that Lynn didn't fit. Perhaps that of a ditsy simpleton or maybe an unkempt troll. (He should look in the mirror.)

Show a Little Initiative!

If you just do as you're told, you don't get promoted, you don't get advanced up the ladder, because you're not showing initiative.

Right. Every time I showed some initiative, I got fired. Or at least reprimanded.

Then I realized that that's because there are different rules of advancement for men and women. Initiative in a woman is insubordination, especially if her boss is a man.

Then I realized later, much later, that there *are* no rules of advancement for women: do X, don't do X; do X, do Y; it doesn't matter — either way you're not advanced.

Quite apart from the likelihood that the positions you get aren't even *on* a ladder of advancement.

'You can't get there from here' comes to mind.

Sanitary Receptacles

"For your convenience, a sanitary receptacle is provided in this cubicle. You are requested to co-operate and use it for the purpose intended."

"For *your* convenience." For *our* convenience? Given that the alternative to the requested behaviour would result in a bunch of clogged toilets (*your* toilets) and/or bloodied napkins strewn all over the washroom floor (*your* washroom floor), I suggest that it's as much for *your* convenience as for ours.

"For your *convenience*." Convenience? Is the trash can by the paper towel dispenser also for *convenience*? I suppose the toilet paper is a convenience too. *And* the toilet.

"A sanitary receptacle." The receptacle may well *be* sanitary, but I think you mean 'a sanitary *napkin* receptacle.' And actually, the napkins put into the receptacle are *not* very sanitary at that point, are they? '*Menstrual* napkin receptacle' would be more accurate. But men do have trouble with such words — menstrual, menstruation, menstruating. Though they seem to be able to handle 'cunt' easily enough.

"You are requested to co-operate." And *you* have been watching too many late-night movie interrogation room scenes. Really, I think a 'please' would've sufficed. Actually, I don't even think we need a 'please'. I doubt we even need to be asked. In fact, we don't even need the sign: most of us can figure out what it's for, and if there's any doubt, just label the thing and be done with it!

Really, why shouldn't we co-operate? Most women are inclined to keep things clean — this is the *Women's* Room, not the Men's Room. Furthermore, we know that the poor soul who has to clean up any mess we leave is a cleaning *lady*. Who's probably sick to death of cleaning up her own washroom after her husband uses it.

"For the purpose intended." What else might we use it for, a lunchbox? A weapon? ("And now for tonight's top story: as we speak, gangs of women are roaming the streets armed with sanitary receptacles...")

Ah, but this is a *government* building. That explains it then. At some point (it seems like only yesterday, the way they're carrying on), it was for Men Only. That explains the heavy-handedness (men don't know how to *ask*, they *threaten*) and the supposition of a predisposition to *un*cleanliness.

And, or, maybe the sign is intended to say "Look at us, we've gone out of our way to provide you ladies with women's things, not only a washroom all for yourselves, but one with little sanitary receptacles even, a *luxury* washroom; we want you to know this and be eternally grateful, we want you to be constantly reminded that your very presence in this building is exceptional." *Now* I understand the threatening tone: if we don't comply with their request, they'll take our little receptacles away, maybe they'll even kick us out, hell, maybe they'll go so far as to take back the vote.

Figure Skating:
A Very Gendered Thing

Many call figure skating a sissy sport, a feminine thing. To the contrary, and to my unrelenting irritation, it is a very gender-inclusive sport, a sport of *both* sexes, a sport where men must be men and women must be — girls.

Consider the costumes. The men usually wear ordinary long pants and a more or less ordinary shirt. The women, on the other hand, with such consistency I suspect an actual rule, show their legs — their *whole* legs — and as much of their upper body as they can get away with. And they always wear that cutesy short little girl skirt. What is it with that? Or they wear a negligée. (Ah. It's the standard bipolar turn-on for sick men: sexy-child.) (Why is child-like sexy to men? Because being a child *guarantees* power over. And that's what sex is to men — power, not pleasure. Or rather, the power *is* the pleasure. Probably because they don't recognize the responsibility of power.) (So even in a sport *without* frequent legs-wide-apart positions, the woman's costume would be questionable. But I believe it is actually a rule — the female skaters must show leg. Like most rules women are expected to follow, this one surely was made by men, for men. As if women exist for men's viewing pleasure.)

(Too, no doubt there's some compensation going on: the stronger women get, the more feminine, i.e., the weaker, they're told to be. Men can't accept women's superior fitness, physical ability, endurance, and agility; so the women are encouraged to compensate by being child-like (I'm really young, small, and no threat at all) and by being sexy (I'll still please you).)

In no other sport — I think of track, basketball, volleyball — do the men and women wear such different outfits. And in fact, not even in figure skating, at least not in *practice*, do they wear such different outfits: most skaters, whatever their sex, wear some sort of spandex bodysuit, perhaps with sweats, when they work on the ice. Often, you can't even tell them apart: there's no difference in speed, in line, in movement. (Ah. *That's* the problem: that we won't be able to tell them apart. Men define themselves as not-women; the greater the difference, the stronger their identity.) (And yet, as one male student of mine once explained, 'It's natural to pick a fight with whatever's different.' Men are so confused.) (Then again, maybe not — maybe they just like to fight. Hence the need to ensure there's always something different nearby.) (Men are so confused.)[1] Consider, too, the pairs. Always male and female. There are same-sex pairs in other sports (for example, tennis) — why the obsession with mixed-sex pairs in figure skating? And yes, there are mixed doubles in other sports, but only in this one is the strong boy/weak girl thing so prevalent, only in this one does the man routinely (seem to) support the woman: he is the subject who throws, pulls, pushes, lifts, and carries her, the object. It's the perfect metaphor for our deluded masculist world: the man lifts the woman, displaying his strength as he puts her on a pedestal. Deluded, because, of course, the woman, despite her incredible physical strength and skill, appears to be a mere object moved by

---

[1] This need to differentiate would explain the prevalence of the military theme, the warrior figure, in the men's solos: I'm not a sissy, I'm a real man, I'm physically strong and emotionally flat, I like to fight. (And kill. So it suddenly occurred to me, when I happened to watch a figure skating competition right after a newscast during the Serbia/Croatia 'conflict', what poor taste it was — to act out, on the ice, killing someone, with such pride, such celebration. Especially if there's a nationalistic edge to the performance, as there often is because of the accompanying music.) (Well, duh. Of course. From toy guns to action movies, it's not just poor taste, it's sick — to portray, and to consider as entertaining, hurting and killing.)

Consider too the male habit of thrusting (!) his fist into the air after a successful performance (in any sport), showing this unsettling association of victory with violence, pleasure with power.

the man when, in fact, the success of the move depends as much on her: her strength, her balance, her timing.

Given that, why aren't they called 'aerial balances' instead of 'lifts'? Or better yet, more fair, 'lifted balances'? The very name, 'lifts', describes only what the *man* does. As if the woman does nothing, as if she's completely passive. *You* try holding your body horizontal in mid-air and see how much sheer strength it takes, along with amazing balance. Go ahead: climb a tree; now hang over a branch; okay, now straighten your body and hold it; now add a couple pounds of skate to one end; and now lift both ends not just even with the branch but *higher* than the branch, that's it, arch; okay now let's make the tree move; now smile.

And now get down. But you can't just jump down. You have to land in the man's arms. Without slicing his balls off with your blades. That takes some skill. (And yeah, okay, some concern.)

And why aren't they called 'throwns' instead of 'throws'? Or better yet, more active, 'soars'? Contrary to popular belief, the woman doesn't need the man to throw her high into the air in order to do a couple twists before she lands. The side-by-side triple jumps show that she is quite capable of throwing herself. And, in fact, wouldn't it be *harder* to land when you've been thrown by someone else?

The answer to these questions about the names of the moves is that figure skating, like so much else, is defined by men. The quad is deemed to be the most difficult move; it is the benchmark of superior ability; it is more noteworthy than a spin or a spiral. This is not surprising. The quad is a short-burst feat of speed and strength. These are male obsessions. Perhaps because they are more easily mastered by the male body.[2] The

---

[2] Consider the fact that women leave the sport (or have to re-learn it) once they reach puberty — i.e., once they actually develop female bodies. As is the case with gymnastics. And track. There have got to be moves that a woman's body can do, for

spin, less lauded, is a feat of balance (as well as speed and strength). And more easily mastered by the female body. (Unless, of course, you're Surya Bonaly — she can do both a quad and a spin.) (Sometimes even while wearing a cute little skirt.) The spiral, less lauded still, a feat of flexibility (as well as balance and strength). The quad covers more ground, conquers more territory. The spin stays in one place. The spiral also covers a lot of ground, more, in fact, than the quad, but it's static, and beautiful, and is therefore demoted. The quad is also subject to quantification — it's *more than* a triple. The spin is also subject to quantification, moreso, in fact, than the quad, but as I said, it stays in one spot, and it's very small. That there is more comment about women not doing quads (or rather, more presumption that because they can do only triples, they're not as good as the men) than there is about men not doing the Biellmann spin, a difficult cross between a spin and a spiral (let alone the presumption that they're not as good as the women because they can't do it) indicates that the measure of ability, the standard, the norm of reference in figure skating, is male.

Perhaps the polarization, in costume as well as in movement, is perpetuated not by men in general, but by insecure men who are reacting to the 'real men don't figure skate' view. So they emphasize a 'masculine' physicality.

---

which hips and breasts and a certain amount of body fat aren't debilitating. Why haven't we made sports out of those? Well, we have. But the media, and society, in which men call the shots, don't put a lot of attention, time, energy, or money into distance swimming. (There, our fat is good — the buoyancy makes it easier. There, our anaerobic superiority is good — we last longer, we finish.) Or synchronized swimming. (Which men simply couldn't do.) (Or at least couldn't do very well.) (Or, most importantly, couldn't do better than women. They don't have that anaerobic efficiency. They'd drown. And they certainly couldn't get their legs very high out of the water — what with their poor buoyancy and their top heaviness, they'd be, well, pathetic. And few — only the young ones, the boys — could split them to the horizontal. And anyway, that complete relinquishing of the ego — absolutely no grandstanding, no upstaging, allowed — and that continuous adjustment which requires a sensitivity to others, is beyond them.)

There are, of course, thankfully, exceptions. The "Marbles" piece of Gary Beacom and Gia Guddat is one example: skating on their hands as well as their feet, in identical striped three-quarter bodysuits, they emphasize not sex, but technique and humour. The Duchesnays provide another example: in one piece, they each wear the same simple blue pants-and-shirt outfit, and the choreography has no heterosexual romantic undertone whatsoever, they are simply two skaters on the ice, each as apt to support the other; the piece is about, again, not sex, but art and athletics.

"Office Help"

You can tell, when a job ad is titled that way, that they expect, or want, a woman. Women *help*. They don't actually do a job, they just *help* someone else do a job. So the someone else gets the credit. And the big bucks and the benefits. After all, you're just *helping out*, you're just doing a favor. Because you're nice. That's what women are. You don't see "Maintenance Help" or "Engineering Help" ads.

Another give-away is when the job's for something like "10:00 to 2:00". A man wouldn't take a part-time job. They need a full-time job. Even if they haven't made a couple kids they now need to support. (Do I get paid more to support *my* choices? Don't think so.)

And they'll get it too. The full-time job. Men are good at talking about their needs. Because having needs makes you important if you're a man. If you're a woman, needing something makes you weak, dependent.

'Course everything makes you weak if you're a woman. Even ethics. It's called 'sentiment'. In a man, it's called 'integrity'.

Bambi's Cousin's
Gonna Tear You Apart

Well, it's autumn. That time of year when the breeze gets brisk, the leaves start to fall, and good men from all walks of life wear something besides blue, brown, grey, and black: they wear orange. Hunter orange. Yes this is the time of year when good men from all walks of life go into the forest to perform that masculine bloodwinner ritual involving beer, bullets, and Bubba. I don't understand hunting. I don't understand the desire to kill.

'Oh no,' the hunters say, 'it's not that, it's the excitement, it's the thrill of stalking an animal that's big and wild, and can tear you apart!' Yeah right. Like Bambi's cousin is going to tear you apart.

'And it's the challenge! Deer are smart, you know!' I'd say the average deer has an IQ of what, four? So I have to ask, smart compared to who?

The challenge. Give me a break. You hunt in a group, so already it's what, six against one? And you use dogs, and ATVs, you even use helicopters, to scare the animals out of the bush. And then you've got some geezer sittin' in a truck parked at the side of the road just waiting to pick off the first fear-frenzied creature that runs across. Oh, the challenge. (Then again, since he's probably been chugging brew all afternoon, I guess that *would* be a challenge.)

'It's not just all that — we like the meat.' Then why don't you go to a deer farm and just shoot one that's out grazing in the field? (Or a cow farm. Hey, I know! Get a job in a slaughterhouse!)

'Cuz it's gotta be wild.' Okay, how about a skunk?

Ah, but it's gotta be *big* and wild. Well, this 'bigger is better' thing is completely illogical. Anyone can shoot a moose that's just standing there. If you really want to brag, hang a pair of chipmunk ears on your wall.

Speaking of which, why do fishermen mount the whole fish but hunters mount only the head? If it *is* size that counts, then let's hang the whole moose on the wall. (Or cow, as the case may be.)

Face it, hunting is just another big business. And like most big businesses, it feeds off and into pretty sick impulses. I was looking through a hardware store flyer one hunting season, amazed at all the essential hunting paraphernalia.

First, you've got your 'Super Premium 200 Proof Doe-in-a-Can' — the scent of a doe in heat. This stuff is *very* special: it's "collected at the peak of the doe's hottest second estrous cycle". How do they know she's at her peak? And who does the collecting? And how? (And "hottest"? Seriously?)

Then you've got your "shoulder length dressing gloves". I'm thinking sexy over-the-elbow black satin. Try "heavy duty poly gloves" — to "protect against mess, stains, and infectious diseases while dressing game". The picture shows a man with his arm up a deer's ass — he's "dressing game".

And you've got your 'Rusty Duck Lubricant'. Any guesses?

And then you've got your calls — your duck calls and your deer calls and your moose calls. I understand that there were a lot of hunting injuries the year the "CM3 Moose Call" came onto the market. Well, what do you expect when some moron stands in the middle of the forest during mating season and yells out in moose language "Come fuck me now!"

I was talking to one guy, a duck hunter, and I asked why he preferred to go hunting with a friend. I thought maybe hunting was just a cover for friendship between men who were too homophobic to just be with each other. But the guy said 'for security.' Given the moose call affair, I thought, good point. I mean last year alone, *how* many hunters were killed by ducks?

Not enough.

The Political is Personal

Back in the 60s or 70s, one of the insights feminism gave us was that the personal is political. It's been a valuable insight. Many of us now routinely interpret personal interaction politically: we try to understand the influence of race, class, and gender; we try to determine the nature of the power differentials.

I suggest that the converse is an equally valuable insight: the political is personal.

I think we often imagine politics, broadly defined as decision-making by those in power, to proceed according to carefully considered principles and policies. Decisions are thought to be well-informed, conscious choices. We may not agree with the decisions, but we recognize them as decisions nonetheless.

I'd like to suggest, however, that the outcomes are seldom by decision; most of the time, they're by default. From the local shop hiring a secretary to the corporation hiring an advertising firm to the government appointing a Supreme Court judge — it may appear that resumes and recommendations are carefully considered and compared, but I think more often it's just a matter of 'you go for who you like'. It's 'the personal' that makes the difference.

That's why interviews are so important. They're personal. Oh sure, the masquerade is that the questions asked during an interview enable a finer appraisal of merit, but those questions could be given to shortlisted applicants with the request that a written response be submitted. The truth is that the interviewers are trying to figure out if they like you, if they can get along with you, if they want you to be in the office with them every day. It's personal, through and through.

They may not know it; I dare say most people in positions of power are not that conscious. In fact, they'll probably justify their choice on grounds of merit. Perhaps the more honest will simply admit they've 'got a good feeling about this one'. Which is why it's less a decision, a deliberated choice, than it is a default, a failure to act, a failure to deliberate.

Perhaps men in particular, having relegated the private, the personal, the subjective, to women, cannot and will not see, let alone consider, its role in their own behaviour. And if they deny the psychological (the individual), they must also deny the social (individuals in groups). So they are ignorant of, and often derisive of, any mention of psychological factors — that's too personal. They deny the self, the ego, the pride that motivates them to obey orders without question, to stand firm and never retract. This in particular has serious consequences: to live without the possibility of revision — no wonder they seldom get it right.

Consider also the importance of networking — making friends, by any other name. People know that's the way in — to offers, to opportunities. People ask 'someone they know' — they don't advertise. And if you aren't someone people know, you won't be asked. Knocking on the door won't work — no one's there to hear you. Having a key won't work — there's no lock. The door only opens from the inside. They call you and when you show up, they'll be there to open the door for you.

If you think about it, this notion of 'the political is personal' makes sense of a lot. The tennis court, the golf course, and the after work pub — we all know that's where the deals are made. Not literally, of course: the contract to be signed is back at the office. And often not even directly: the contract may not even be discussed; it may not even exist yet. But if and when it does, it'll go to good ole' Jack. We like Jack. We're personal with Jack.

179

That's why Joan won't get the contract. She's not excluded from the Board room. She's not even excluded from the clubs anymore. But still, a man and a woman can't 'just' be friends. *They can't get personal.* (Well, they can, but only in a way that would exclude her altogether.)

The Provocation Defence —
Condoning Testosterone Tantrums
(and other masculinities)

According to the Canadian Criminal Code (and probably a lot of other criminal codes), murder can be reduced to manslaughter if the person was provoked. Provocation is defined as "a wrongful act or an insult that is of such a nature as to be sufficient to deprive an ordinary person of the power of self-control is provocation for the purposes of this section if the accused acted on it on the sudden and before there was time for his passion to cool" (CCC 232.(2)).

It is unfortunate that "an ordinary person" is used as the standard for judgment rather than "a reasonable person". The ordinary person, in my experience, is not particularly reasonable. The ordinary person is a walking mess of unacknowledged emotions and unexamined opinions, most of which are decidedly *un*reasonable.

Furthermore, in our society, an ordinary person is gendered, and given the specific use of "his" in 232(2), it seems that it is men who are (mostly) in mind for use of this defence.

The ordinary man doesn't have a very high opinion of women. In particular, in our society, our heterosexist masculist society, men consider women to be almost solely sexual. And they consider them to be sexual property. The ordinary man also considers himself to be almost solely sexual. His physical strength and other supposed attributes of power (from his income to his hair) are also important, but mostly only as indicators of his sexual prowess or attractiveness (go figure). This means that an insult to his sexual prowess, or to any of the stand-ins, especially if uttered by a woman, who is, it goes without saying, a subordinate, may provide grounds for invoking the provocation defence.

Perhaps the typical scenario in which the defence is invoked is that of a married man who discovers his wife having sex with another man and in a "crime of passion" kills either his wife or the other man or both. We call the murder a crime of *passion*, but really it's just an outrage of proprietorship. O. R. Sullivan ("Anger and Excuse: Reassessing Provocation" in *Oxford Journal of Legal Studies* 13, 1993) calls it an outrage at a failure to dominate, which also makes sense, given the subordination of women and the defence's applicability to men.

So passion, in an ordinary man, is 'just' rage — it's a testosterone tantrum. We're legitimizing man's anger. ('I was angry.' 'Oh well then. That's okay. The *man* was *angry*.') (No wonder they get angry so often. It's a free, 'get out of jail' ticket.)

In fact, somehow, in our society, an angry man is more of a man than a calm man, let alone a fearful man, a grieving man, and so on. Real men must control their emotions, or, better, not have any (well, except anger). (It's just a little ironic to allow a defence of emotion to those who pride themselves on not being emotional.)

If we open the door to *this* unreasoned and unreasonable action, this knee-jerk response, shouldn't we open the door to all knee-jerk responses? What makes this one so different it excuses murder? If it's okay to kill someone because you think you own her, shouldn't it be okay to kill someone because, oh, I don't know, you think she's a spy for the aliens? Or because she called you stupid?

A further indication that this defence is primarily intended for men is that if a sexually unattractive man makes a move on a woman (an insult to *our* sexual prowess), even an illegal move such as sexual touching without consent, we generally don't kill the guy. And yet, apparently, an unsolicited homosexual advance

182

can provoke a man to kill. After all, such an unwelcome sexual advance is enough to make you lose control. (Oh yeah? Hm. Let me get my gun. There's a construction crew outside and a bunch of assholes down at the bar. And another bunch at work.)

I'm also not impressed that with this defence, the act must be done "on the sudden and before there was time for his passion to cool." This means we're condoning a lack of control. It has always puzzled me that premeditated murder is considered worse, not better, than *un*premeditated murder. Robert Latimer, for example, did not kill Tracy on the spur of the moment, out of anger; he thought about it, long and hard, literally for years, after trying every alternative to end the pain. Doing something after some consideration should surely be better than doing something thoughtlessly, without stopping to think about it at all — even if the reasons for the behaviour turn out to be unacceptable ones. (And we should definitely teach kids the difference between acceptable reasons and unacceptable reasons.)

And funny how men seem to lose control only when a perceived-to-be subordinate frustrates their desires. When they lash out at a bigger guy, it's just a fight. Better to be stupid than shamed? So the provocation defence is just a way out of the shame of 'picking on' someone *not* your own size? (Because if it really is the case that you can't control yourself, we can fix that: we can lock you up and keep you away from others or we can give you drugs that reduce that pesky testosterone.)

Furthermore, how can such loss of control be both a justification (as when the provocation defence is invoked — in which case what you did isn't as wrong) and an excuse (as when temporary insanity is invoked — in which case what you did isn't really your fault)?

Of course, yet another problem with allowing a provocation defence is that it puts at least part of the blame on the provoker. 'It was *her* fault. She provoked me.' I can see this for some situations; blame is often justly shared in a physical altercation. But in a murder? It's *her* fault he *killed* her? Please. She nags? She mocks you? She makes fun of your sperm count? She complains about your failure to get a job, a real job, a good job? She talks to other men? She has sex with them? So call her a bitch and leave. And don't look back. Send money for your kids or apply for custody if you want to look after them. Or put up with it until they're sixteen and *then* leave. But geez louise d'ya have to *kill* her?

It is not irrelevant that short of the formal provocation defence, provocation is often invoked in sexual assault crimes as well. It's a way to dodge blame. Not only do we allow this plea of provocation by men, we encourage, we expect, the provocation by women: women are expected to be sexually attractive all the time — to wear sexualizing make-up and attire, even at work. (Though given that men also rape asexualized women — we've all read about the 60-70-year-old victims — apparently it's our fault just for being a woman. Can you say 'Eve'?) It's a neat little trick: encourage the provocative behavior, then allow the provocation defence. And yet, as Lucy Reed Harris points out ("Towards a Consent Standard in the Law of Rape" in *University of Chicago Law Review* 43, 1976), "although a flagrant display of cash in public may very predictably precipitate a robbery, the law does not hold an alleged robbery victim responsible for his own foolishness in making such a display." (Unless it were a woman being so foolish?)

When will we insist our boys grow up? If there's a legitimate reason they lag behind girls in social development (and therefore have relatively little control) and language skills (which provide a much better response to an insult), then let's just say it — *they're* the inferior ones. And then let's follow through, and restrict their access to weapons, for example. (A higher age limit for drinking, and driving, would also be a good idea. And a curfew for two or more men under thirty gathered together.)

Power or Responsibility?

Several years ago, a local arts centre ran an ad for the position of General Manager. It caught my eye — for a second, I must've thought of applying. But then my conscious self must've recognized it as being out of my league and I read on.

But then I thought, wait a minute! I'm 37 years old, I'm a multidisciplinary artist who has published books, produced and marketed cassettes, and run music and dance studios, I've been Chief Negotiator for a union, I'm intelligent, I'm efficient — surely I'm capable! Even though I've had no experience specifically as a General Manager, surely I have the skills "to be a team leader, to balance the arts and business, to be sensitive to multiple art forms, to be a host at ease with the community and the industry...."

So why then was I reluctant to apply? Well, I thought, it's a lot of work, it's a lot of responsibility (the ad said the centre was "a $1 million venue") — and that daunted me.

But — and this is the point I want to examine — a man with half my background, and probably ten years less experience, wouldn't've thought twice about applying. *Why is that?*

Perhaps it's that women see responsibility where men see power. Women see burdens where men see benefits. Women see work where men see privilege.

And why is that? One, women haven't had a lot of power — so they're not used to looking for it, seeing it, using it. Two, women *have* had a lot of responsibility — so *that's* what they're used to noticing.

Wait a minute — men haven't had a lot of responsibility? But they run the government, big business — Yeah. Ironic, isn't it.

What I mean is, consider this. As girls, we get jobs as babysitters: that's a lot of responsibility — what if the house catches fire, what if the baby starts choking? On the other hand, as boys, men get jobs as 'paper boys': they were responsible for getting a newspaper onto someone's porch.

The trend continues in adolescence: women become camp counsellors and recreation leaders, while men work on maintenance crews; women are entrusted with the physical, social, emotional, and artistic development of children, while men are entrusted with shrubbery.

Then, or later, in matters of sex, it's the woman who has the *responsibility* — for deciding yes or no and for contraception. Men have the *power* — to rape.

It goes on. Which parent is primarily responsible for the child? The woman. Sure, the man is responsible too, but his responsibility is usually limited to financial matters (and even then, more to getting the money than to managing it). It's the woman who is primarily responsible for emotional matters — for providing attention, affection, love; for physical matters — for seeing that the child doesn't get hit by a car, doesn't put its finger in a socket; and for intellectual matters — for seeing that the homework gets done, planning and making trips to the library. The men's responsibility can be fulfilled in 8 hours each day; the women are responsible 24 hours each day. And yet, should he decide to make his car payment instead of his child support payment, he affects, in a big way, the quality of life for at least two others besides himself. That's power.

So it's no wonder we see responsibility where men see power.

And it's no wonder we don't apply for the positions higher up.

The Good Wife

The Good Wife, The Trophy Wife, The First Wives Club ... why in the 21st century do women continue to be so frequently identified as wives? That is, identified in relation to men?

We don't see a similar proliferation of tv shows and movies with "husband" in the title. The word is emasculating. It would be especially so if it were in the context of "The Good Husband" or "Julia's Husband" or some such.

Why don't people see that "wife" is just as bad, just as subordinating?

(They do. That's why the male writers, directors, and producers use it so often.)

Being Josh

It's Monday night basketball, an all-comers pick-up game, supposed to be fun and a good sweat. But week after week I steel myself against the anger, the frustration of not knowing how to correct the problem, and the despair of not being able to even begin to do just that. Eventually it happens: this time it's Josh who yells at me to switch, to guard the new grade niner who's just come onto the court to sub for the guy who'd been guarding Josh and Josh would guard the guy I'd been guarding.

I am distracted, as always, by the insult, the unwarranted assumption that I'm always the worst player there, and by the faulty logic that weak offensive players are weak defensive players and should therefore guard other weak offensive players.

Nevertheless, I manage to focus on yet another problematic aspect of the shouted order: that it *was* an order, and it was given with the full expectation of compliance. How is it, I thus have occasion to wonder yet again, that a kid, a 17-year-old less than half my age, believes he can tell me what to do, believes he knows better than me? The answer is simple: he's male. And I'm female. If I were a man over twice his age, he'd keep his thoughts to himself. And if he were a girl, he wouldn't even have such thoughts.

When Chodorow wrote "Being and Doing", a groundbreaking analysis of sexism in terms of passivity (of being, of women) and activity (of doing, of men), she got it right — but she also got it wrong. Josh is so easy in his authority over me simply because he's male, simply because he *is* — male. He hasn't had to *do* anything to gain that authority, or the respect I feel myself giving him just before I catch myself acting like

188

Pavlov's dog. The confidence, the assurance, the arrogance that he must have to even think he can just tell me what to do — he has it just because he's male. And he probably started developing it as soon as he realized he was indeed male: I've heard 5-year-old boys speak with the same kind of authority.

Women, on the other hand, have to *do* — we have to earn respect, we don't just get it automatically. And I'm not sure we ever achieve any authority, no matter what we do. And of course it's not just respect and authority men feel entitled to just because they're men: they also feel entitled to money (pay, and higher pay) and power (supervisory positions). In short, *they feel entitled to dominance*, just because of who, of what, they *are* (not because of what they *do*).

Testicular Battery and Tranquilizer Guns (what the world needs now is)

Given the relative vulnerability of men to sexual assault (all it takes is a swift forceful kick, or, at closer quarters, a good grab, pull, twist — almost anything, really) (whereas for women to be raped, they have to be partially undressed and then immobilized), it's surprising that we hear far more often about rape than — well, we don't even have a special name for it. Testicular battery?

Since most women are physically capable of such an assault, the reason must be some psychological social inhibition. And, of course, this is so. Girls are not permitted, encouraged, or taught to fight; boys are. All three. Women are socialized to see men as their protectors, not their enemies. Men are — well, this is the interesting bit: men used to be socialized to see women as in need of protection, and so would never dream of raping them (well, okay, they'd dream of it — perhaps often and in technicolour — but there was a strong social stigma against assaulting the fair sex: boys were shamed if they ever hit a girl, and if you ever hit your wife, let alone another woman, well, what kind of man are you?), but feminism got rid of such patronizing chivalry. And rightly so. Unfortunately, it has yet to make its replacement, self-defence, as commonplace.

There's another problem. We're afraid that if we hurt them, they'll come back (when they can walk again) and kill us. Which is why women's self-defence should include a small tranquilizer gun.

('Course they might still come back and kill us. After all, to be decommissioned by a woman! It'd be a new kind of honour killing ...)

190

Why Aren't Women Funny?

Well, they are, of course. It's just that many men don't find them funny. Which is why many stand-up clubs (those managed by men) (that is, almost all of them) actually have a rule: only so many stand-ups on any given night can be women. Too many and they kill the night.

But, of course, that's so only in clubs where most of the audience is male. Because, as I've said, men don't find women funny. Partly, this could be because men find farts and burps funny. (Except, of course, when women fart and burp. For some reason, they find that horrifying.)

The other mainstay of comedy (for both sexes) is (heterosexual) relationship humour — so men laugh at the caricatures of women presented by men (and only women laugh at the caricatures of men presented by women).

But my guess is that even with sex-neutral comedy, women comedians fare more poorly than men. A woman tells a socio-political joke, and people (men) just sort of stare at her (as if they're seeing a dog walking on its hind legs?). Give a man the same material, and the audience will respond. Ironically (given my topic), I think this is so because men don't take women seriously. To laugh at someone's joke is to accord them some sort of authority, if only the authority to make some sort of comment through humour.

Either that or they're just not interested in women (except as sexual possibilities). I'm reminded of a brilliant skit I once saw on *A Bit of Fry and Laurie*: a woman was giving a business presentation and everyone present, mostly men, was paying such close and supportive attention, I was, frankly, surprised (that had certainly never happened to me); then the woman casually mentioned that she'd come up with her proposal on the weekend when she was out with her boyfriend, and their attention turned off as quickly and as completely as a spotlight blowing a fuse — a woman is either a sexual possibility or she doesn't exist.

This would explain why, for example, Susan Juby didn't win the Leacock Medal of Humour with *I'm Alice, I think*. It's a hilarious coming of age story. But it's about *a girl*. So while generations of girls have had to read about boys coming of age (*A Separate Peace, Lord of the Flies, The Apprentice of Duddy Kravitz, Catcher in the Rye, The Outsiders, The Adventures of Huckleberry Finn, Tom Sawyer*, and on and on), boys have only had to read about *Anne Frank* (no doubt, it was 'saved' by the wartime setting) (oh well, put guns in it and ...). When a boy comes of age, that's important, because he's becoming *a man*. But when a girl comes of age, she becomes a woman. Not so important. In fact, the Medal has been won by a woman only twice in 30 years. I wonder if the panel of 17 judges consists mostly of men (the judges aren't named on their site, but the President and Vice-President are, and they're both men, whereas the two secretaries and person in charge of the dinner? They're women).

What's Wrong with Being a Slut?

slut, n. Slovenly woman, slattern
slovenly, a. Personally untidy or dirty, careless and lazy, or
unmethodical
slattern, n. Sluttish woman

Surely not what my mother meant when she called me a slut. For whatever else I am, I am tidy, clean, careful, industrious, and methodical. Quite methodical. So just what did she mean? I don't know. I really don't. I asked her, but she refused to discuss it. (She couldn't even look at me. And said as much.)

1. Maybe people call you a slut if you have sex before you're married. This poses a bit of a problem if you don't intend to get married. Did my mother expect me to remain a virgin all of my life? Surely not. (Perhaps.) Besides, that would reduce marriage to a license for sex, and I'm sure she (and many others) would object to that interpretation.

However, even if I did intend to get married, what's wrong with having sex before I sign on the dotted line? A little knowledge and experience might make for more realistic attitudes — less disappointment, frustration, and anger. Not to mention regret. Call it informed consent.

And actually, if Jane *did* have a little sex with Dick before she married him, I don't think my mother would call her a slut. She might be pissed off that Jane didn't follow the rules and wait, like everyone else — like *she* — did. And if she could get beyond herself, she might be angry with Jane for exposing the lie that marriage — i.e., religious and civil law — has a monopoly on love and/or that love must be recognized by law before it can be expressed physically. (Though we certainly allow its psychological expression before marriage. Interesting implication then about which is considered to be more important.) But she wouldn't call Jane a slut for having a little sex with Dick —

2. Maybe people call you a slut if you have a lot of sex. Certainly after marriage, that's okay. Though my mother may tsk tsk a bit, she wouldn't call Jane a slut.

What about a lot of sex with Dick before their marriage? I think my mother would tsk tsk a little more loudly, but I don't think she'd cry 'Slut!'

Okay, what if Jane had sex with not only Dick, but also with Tom and Harry? Aha. I think we've got it.

3. People call you a slut if you have sex with a lot of different people. Before marriage *or* after marriage. Why is this such a problem? Multiple partners increase the risk of disease, yes, but my mother's tone for 'Slut!' wasn't quite the same one she used for 'Take your umbrella!' (Not that umbrellas prevent disease.)

a. Insofar as one has sex in order to reproduce, multiple partners may make paternity harder to establish. Or it may not: if Tom is Black, and Dick is White, and Harry is Asian — or if Tom had a vasectomy, and Dick used a condom ...

Nevertheless, why is uncertain paternity a problem? Why does it introduce an element of immorality? Given that the amount of quality time a man spends with offspring known to be his is only negligibly more than that which he spends with offspring *not* known to be his, the not knowing wouldn't seem to result in much of a deprivation.

194

However, given that financial support and inheritance is determined by genetic lineage, uncertain paternity opens the door to — what? Not exactly fraud, but misappropriation of funds? So I'm a slut because my behaviour may put some guy's money into the wrong kid's hands? Is *that* what it's all about? There has to be a less ridiculous explanation.

(And if sex for reproductive reasons is considered the only 'legitimate' sex, then not only must one call lesbians sluts, but one must call all married people who have sex more than once every nine months sluts.) (And if consistency in thought matters at all, then women who use different samples from a sperm bank are also sluts. Though a few minutes with a turkey baster might not qualify as 'having sex'. Despite the similarities.)

b. Insofar as one has sex for pleasure, multiple partners is immoral because … it's a sin to have too much pleasure?

Actually, that may not be too far off the mark. My mother also disapproves of my being semi-retired at twenty-two. Apparently I'm supposed to work 40 hours/week for 40 years before having the time to read and go for long walks every day.

In fact, I suspect the force of the insult reflects the perceived injustice, the underlying envy: 'Slut!' means 'That's not fair — you're breaking the rules — *I* had to limit myself to one man!'

But I think there's an even better explanation.

c. Insofar as having sex is making love, someone who has sex with many people shatters the romantic myth of Mr. Right. It says either that there's more than one Mr. Right or that sex isn't just making love (see 3.b above). And of course both proclamations are to my mind more realistic and more rational, indeed more mature, than the alternative.

First, isn't it a bit weird to consider *that* — sexual intercourse — to be the ultimate expression of love? It seems as arbitrary as touching one's big toe to another one's nostril (except that there can be, sometimes, presumably, a little more physical pleasure involved). It seems to me that a lot of other things — continued support in one's chosen field, for example — are far greater expressions of love than the mere provision of a few minutes of physical pleasure.

Second, if the objection is that I'm making love with someone I don't love, then half the married women in the world are sluts. How many people stay married even though they don't love each other any more? And how many of those people still 'make love'?

Third, though one may well want to give pleasure to the person one loves, why stop there? Why should we be ungenerous? Should we not want to give pleasure to other people as well, people we like? And why not also to people we don't know — what's wrong with doing something nice to strangers? And all of this applies equally to getting pleasure.

Fourth, even if one does restrict sexual pleasure to the beloved, do you really believe you will or can or should love only one person, consecutively or simultaneously, in your entire lifetime? If not, maybe loving two or three doesn't make one a slut; how many is too many?

4. Maybe people call you a slut if you have sex *with someone you just met*. I suppose the argument could be that Mr. Right is less of a risk than Mr. Goodbar. But in two-thirds of all marriages,

Mr. Right will beat his wife at least once. That sort of takes care of that argument. Furthermore, my mother didn't seem concerned about my safety so much as my morality. (And, actually, now that I think of it, she seemed concerned not so much about my morality as about her own).

Of course, if it's sex for reproduction, then it seems to make sense to know something about the biological father. But who can judge how long it takes to find out all the important things?

If it's sex for pleasure, does it matter whether you've just met? I can have lots of fun with a motorcycle I just met.

And if it's sex as love, I concede that if it's someone you just met, the definition of love is stretched a bit. But then again, aren't those who believe in Mr. Right the same people who believe in love *at first sight*?

My guess is, however, that 'someone you just met' is taken to mean 'with anyone'. Which is, in turn, taken to mean 'with everyone' —

5. People call you a slut if you have sex with anyone and everyone. This is interesting because I think that under this definition, there are very few sluts indeed. It is rare, very rare, for someone to have sex with anyone, to have *no* criteria for choice, to be *totally* indiscriminate. First, almost everyone discriminates on the basis of sex — that is to say, almost everyone is either heterosexual or homosexual. Second, most women discriminate on the basis of attraction; those women who don't, such as prostitutes, discriminate on another basis: ability to pay. Third, I don't think I'm alone in not having sex with a person I suspect of having an STD. Fourth, I don't have sex with someone if I think they might be physically violent. And fifth, I don't have sex with a person who wants to impregnate me. So far from being indiscriminate, my behaviour is *very* discriminate.

It's important to note that my discussion so far has not included men. Why? Because the word 'slut' applies to women only. There is no equivalent for men. 'Stud' is perhaps the closest in denotation, but it is exactly opposite in connotation: positive rather than negative, complimentary rather than insulting. This is, of course, very interesting because it reveals a double standard. And I could dismiss the entire question of what's wrong with being a slut by merely drawing attention to that duplicity. But I wanted to examine the standard that justifies the insult by itself, independent of any other standard. Besides, there is no doubt that the standard by which men are judged is equally deficient and therefore of dubious value in proving a point.

Nevertheless, a comparison at this point might be rather interesting. My behaviour, I'll argue, is not only as discriminate as that of most men, it's far *more* discriminate. One, men do not seem to restrict themselves to women they find sexually attractive: sex for men is not just a sexual thing, it's a power thing; so they'll have sex in order to display dominance, in order to conquer — and sexual attractiveness, therefore, becomes irrelevant. Two, I don't think men are very concerned about having sex with women who have STDs: not one that I have been with has ever *insisted* on a condom; indeed, most didn't want to use one, even when supplied by me. Three, they are no more discriminate concerning the next criterion: men don't seem to consider possible physical violence (yet how easy it would be to reach over for a knife in the back when he's about to come ...). Lastly, the possibility of pregnancy does not seem to matter either: apart from the sad absence of condoms, no man has ever asked if I'm using contraception, indicating either a confusion or an indifference as to purpose. So it appears that men are far less discriminate. Indeed, of all the men I've ever asked, only one said 'no'. Does that make *them* sluts?

Men's Precision Teams

Have you ever wondered why, in the sport of figure skating, there are no *men's* precision teams?

Sure, precision skating requires attention to detail and a highly developed spatial sense. But both are surely male capabilities; in fact, aren't they male superiorities? Isn't that why (so we're told) men dominate science and engineering?

And of course, it requires skating skill. But countless men — Alexei Yagudin, Elvis Stojko, Kurt Browning, Brian Boitano, to name a few — have proven this to be Y-chromosome-compatible.

Perhaps it's the degree of cooperation required that's simply beyond men. Yes, men are capable of cooperation — that's what *team* sports are all about. But in hockey, football, basketball, and the like, there's always room to be a star; there's always room for grandstanding, for upstaging. In a precision skating team, there's no room for even the teeniest of egos. (Synchronized swimming — there's another sport men simply couldn't handle. There'd be way too many deaths by drowning.)

And yes, men are capable of the timing that cooperation entails. Quarterbacks and their receivers demonstrate this all the time. But the perfect synchrony of a precision team performance is not achieved by such *discrete* instances of cooperation. It's a matter of *continuous* cooperation. The sport requires continuous adjustment to others, which requires awareness of and sensitivity to others, not to mention patience, and persistence, with the practice. Furthermore, it's not only about relationships — to the ice, to the music, to each other: it's about *maintaining* those relationships. (Hey, this sport should be mandatory for boys 13 to 18.)

But no, this can't be right. Consider marching bands and drill displays. They have as much precision and uniformity as a skating team. (Oh, well, give a man a gun —)

Maybe it's because so few boys go into figure skating that after the channelling into solo, pairs, and dance, there aren't enough left over for precision teams. There are no *male* corps de ballet either. Is it really just a matter of supply and demand?

Perhaps. Or maybe it's just that members of a precision team have to put their arms around each other.

Reporting What Women Do

What if for just one year, the media reported 90% of the time what *women* were doing instead of, as is now the case, what men are doing?

Not because what women do is better, or more newsworthy, but just to see how it would change our outlook, our world view.

The news might be more boring. But then, hey, what does that say?

It would likely involve a lot less death and destruction. Ditto.

It probably would have less to do with money. Again ...

"And son? Take care of your mom while I'm gone."

Excuse me? I don't need a child to take care of me. I know, he might reply, I'm just trying to — trying to what? Teach him to be a man? Teach him that grown women need looking after? And that *he*, as the one with the penis, is just the person to do it?

For six months while we're pregnant — if we get pregnant — we're vulnerable, yeah. And while we have kids, okay, yeah, if we're attacked, one of us should protect, hide, get the kids to safety. We could both fight, but the kids need one of us alive. Though of course who does what need not be determined by sex. If I'm closer to the gun and you're closer to the kids — be reasonable! But otherwise — that is, for the other 594 months of our lives ...

So whatever it is you think you're trying to teach the boy, it's at my expense. He grows up to think — hell, already at thirteen, he thinks he's more capable, more competent than me. Than a thirty-five-year-old — *woman*. And since everything tells him to, he generalizes: he comes to think he's more capable, more competent, than *all* women. And the patriarchy lives on.

It's interesting that when there are two boys in the family, it's the older one who's told "Look after your mom and your sisters and your younger brother." Then, age is the critical factor. But when there are boys and girls, sex trumps age.

Which is why I love Sarah Connor (*Terminator: The Sarah Connor Chronicles*). Even when her son is sixteen, *she's* the one protecting, looking after, him. And why not? She's twice his age. And he's no less 'a man' for it — John still manages to be capable, competent, interesting, sexy-in-progress. True, they've added the 'He's more important, she's more dispensable' factor, perhaps because without that, male viewers would consider John emasculated by her protection. But still.

("Tell me again why are the boys in here and the girls are in there?" "'Cause one of the boys is still wanted for murder and one of the girls is harder than nuclear nails." "And the other one's a cyborg.")

Imagine that ...

... all males had to have their DNA on file with the government

... all newborns had to have their paternity established by law

... all males discovered to be fathers had their wages garnished at the source to support the mother of the child for six years (assuming she would be the one to be with the child 24/7 for the first six years and could not therefore obtain employment and thus financial self-support) and the child for 18 years (half-support from the 7th year, the mother, at that point able to obtain employment, to provide the other half)

... and condoms and vasectomies were illegal.

Chefs and Cooks:
What's the difference?

Used to be women did the cooking and the baking. Then men starting getting into it. And in theory, I have no problem with that. In fact, I'm all *for* making *everything* gender-*un*aligned. But now that men are in the kitchen, suddenly it's *important*. So important it's being *televised*.

And my god, the drama! (And they call *us* drama queens.) The tension, the conflict ... Chefs (yes, men are chefs; women were just cooks) scream with self-righteous anger at their minions, they rush around with great urgency making sure every sprinkle of cinnamon is just right, because, goddammit, it's so frickin' important.

The phenomenon defies logic. Drama, therefore importance? No, because then the toddler screaming about his toy truck in the shopping mall would rank right up there with nuclear disarmament.

If anything, the reasoning goes the other way around: important, therefore drama. (Although that's not necessarily true either. I tend to present my case calmly and rationally, without drama, but one time, the vet's wife failed to recognize an emergency, dying or dead fawn in my arms notwithstanding, because I wasn't screaming. Another time, the local township council didn't put up a requested road sign until I called a council member and screamed at her, since minutes earlier, I'd almost been turned into a paraplegic by a speeding vehicle — my previous half dozen requests, accompanied as they were with just sound arguments, were ignored.)

Or is it that the drama, the tension and conflict, are the consequences of the endeavour now being *competitive*.

And why is that? Because men are involved? Apparently. Men see everything as a competition (except those who resist their primal brain, their testosterone, and/or their Y chromosome). Women freely share their favourite recipes.

But it's not just the cooking shows. Song and dance, even travelogue shows, they're all bloody competitions now. And why is that? Have we been turned into competition addicts (by male producers) (seeking male sponsors)?

I'm thinking men, therefore important. Look at what happened to bank tellers: when men were bank tellers, it was important; once women started being bank tellers, it became much less important. Similarly, but in reverse, when women did the cooking and baking, it was no big deal: some were very good at it, some not; sometimes it was a chore, sometimes a joy; it was an art and a skill, yes, but women didn't make a show — a *show* — of it.

Actually, food preparation was important before too; doing it the wrong way can be fatal. Literally. Which makes it even more irritating that the recognition of importance didn't occur until *men* started doing it.

And the bizarre thing is they've made the *trivial* aspects of it important; people don't die if the cinnamon sprinkle isn't just so.

Which suggests something else: since they *aren't* focusing on the legitimately important aspects, the aspects with *intrinsic* importance, they have to *manufacture* importance; and making something into a competition is a way to do just that, a way to make what they're doing *seem* important. Explains a lot of things.

Made for Men
(and so made harder for women)

Because chest-waders are made for men, I have to buy a size medium so the thighs fit. Which means the shoulder straps, even at their smallest, keep slipping off. And, okay, after suffering the frustration of that a couple times — either struggling against them as they restrict my movement hanging halfway down my arms or constantly putting them back onto my shoulders — I rigged up a tie-back. But, worse, it also means the boots are clown-size. Do you have any idea how bloody difficult it is to do anything, let alone something like fix a dock wading on slimy rocks in muck, with clown-size boots on?

Because kayaks are also apparently made for men, the footpegs even at their closest setting mean I have to paddle with my legs almost straight, instead of, as is more comfortable, and more efficient, with my legs bent.

And I'm not talking about just relentless inconvenience and reduced quality of performance on a personal level. It's my understanding that, for example, the hoses at firehalls are stored at a height that makes it easy for men, but extremely difficult for women, to get them off the wall. So in an application-for-employment test, women are more apt to fail as they stumble and fall, too-top-heavy, given the height of the hoses, their own height, and their center of gravity. In a real fire-fighting situation, should be not fail and consequently be hired, they may hold up the rest of the crew as they take extra care *not* to stumble and fall.

Do you see the problem?

And do you see a solution other than 'Stay the fuck in the kitchen where you belong?'

Combining Family and a Career

People say that women can't have, can't combine, a family and a career, that it's having family responsibilities that keeps them from advancement — the inability to work late or on weekends, the tendency to need time off to tend to kids ...

I'm not so sure. I've never had such competing obligations, and *I* don't have a career. I think the family thing is a red herring. Women just don't get hired into career-track jobs nearly as often as men, and when they do, they don't get advanced. (And not because their family responsibilities get in the way.)

In fact, it might be an advantage to be a mother, because you're seen as more adult then, you're seen as an authority. Certainly one carries oneself with more authority, I notice that a lot: as soon as someone becomes a parent, the authority they are to their kids spills over, and they start acting like they know everything with *everyone*, like they have a right to tell *everyone* what to do. It's especially obvious with women, perhaps because it's the first time they have, or are seen to have, authority. Women without kids aren't grown up yet, they aren't granted *any* sort of authority, certainly no position of responsibility. It's as if becoming a parent proves you can be responsible.

(Though of course it does no such thing: witness the very many irresponsible parents; indeed, becoming a parent in the first place is, for many, due to *ir*responsibility. And, of course, there are many other ways of demonstrating responsibility.)

Trust — the movie

I'm so bloody sick and tired of men who assume center stage is for them. The way *Trust* ends, and the way most of it plays out, it's about the dad, about how he can't deal with his failure to protect his daughter.

Mom's not quite so important, apparently, despite her greater empathy with the whole experience: not only is she too beating herself up over her failure as a parent, for, after all, she is as much the girl's parent, but also she must surely be saying to herself 'It could've been me — at 13.'

And *that's* what the movie's really about. The real story, the far more important story, is about Annie, at 13. *She's* the one who misplaced her trust. *She's* the one who pays for it, with her life almost. She even says as much, but apparently the director didn't hear the writers (assuming he chose the last scene and determined how it was shot — who got the close-up, who got their big face in the camera last ...).

This movie should've been an examination of not only trust (what is trust and how do we know who to trust), but also an examination of love: with all the shit we force-feed our kids (including the shit ads the dad makes), it's perfectly reasonable and perfectly predictable that what happened happened (and I refer here both to what Charlie does and what Annie does).

Shame on Schwimmer for making it about *the man*.

The Little Birdies

So I'm out walking today, and as I pass a neighbour tending his bird feeder, I wave. And the guy calls out to me "I'm feeding some seed to the little birdies!"

The little birdies? What am I, twelve?

No, I'm female. (I have a hard time believing that he would've said the same thing to a middle-aged man.) And (many) men talk to women differently than they do to men. They talk to us like we're children. Idiot children.

Here's something else that would never happen to a man

So this guy in our neighborhood has early Alzheimer's and dizzy spells. He's looking for a babysitter (his word) and someone to cook for him and do his cleaning so he doesn't have to go into a home. And he asked me.

I have no experience babysitting. And absolutely no aptitude for it. Yes, I do my own cooking and cleaning, but I have no interest in it, at all, and do as little as possible.

So why did he ask me? Because I'm a middle-aged woman. Apparently that's what middle-aged women do, that's what we are, that's what we're for.

Yes, I've been friendly with him, stopping to chat or at least wave when I walk by (as a result of which he once asked me if I like sex and whether I'm any good at it — apparently that's another thing women do, are, are for), but I doubt that friendliness on the part of a man would have indicated that he's available for babysitting, cooking, or cleaning. (Or sex.)

I have three degrees, I used to be a philosophy instructor, I've published several books, and I'm currently a freelancer. Would a man with such credentials be asked to be someone's babysitter, and do their cooking and cleaning?

Ah, but this guy doesn't know I'm all that. And that's also telling. If I were man who has lived in this neighborhood (small, rural) for twenty-five years, everyone would likely know all of that about me. But I don't go around announcing these things, and no one's ever asked. Because they just assume I'm — well, none of that. After all, I'm just a middle-aged woman.

Failing to Compete

It's not that women compete and lose. It's that we don't compete. We don't know how. (We know how to work hard. But apparently that's irrelevant.)

Men, on the other hand, have been competing since infancy. They see everything in terms of competition, in terms of win/lose. Every action, every gesture, every word is measured in terms of 'Does it put me one up or one down?'

Women don't think that way. In fact, since infancy, *we've* been *co-operating*. We see everything in terms of helping others. 'How does it affect my status?' simply isn't a question we ever ask. Because women are exempt from status ranking. To put it bluntly, we don't count.

So even if we *did* compete, we wouldn't stand a chance. Not against men who've been doing it since birth.

Consider my choice of university. I chose Wilfrid Laurier University over Harvard. But of course I didn't see it that way. It wasn't Wilfrid Laurier 'over' Harvard. I didn't even consider Harvard though I realize now that as the top girl student in a graduating high school class of 150 (okay, so we do get ranked — separately) (which means we don't compete with men) (which thus guarantees that very thing) with a 93% average, an outstanding record of athletic achievements and community service activity, and GRE scores almost 2100 (which puts me, roughly speaking, in the upper 10% of graduate school applicants), I may have been accepted at Harvard had I applied. I chose Wilfrid Laurier because it was small and I get lost a lot. I chose Wilfrid Laurier because it was in my home town, which meant I wouldn't have to work 30 hours a week to pay for rent and food (I already had to work 20 hours a week to pay for tuition and books). I didn't even *consider* status. I didn't even *consider* whether going to Wilfrid Laurier put me one up or one down. I didn't know that which university you went to could *do* that.

And then I enrolled in Eng220, the first year EngLit course for general students, instead of Eng190, the first year EngLit course for honours students. The double honours English Literature and Philosophy program required a second language course, and I didn't want yet another year of French, having done five at high school, and the only other language offered was Latin, and it was at the same time as Eng190. I was told by the Dean of Arts that I could move into the honours Eng stream in second year. No problem. I didn't realize, didn't even consider the possibility, that I'd be thought of as a general student making the step up to honours in second year, a ranking stigma that I realize now, twenty years later, probably affected how people saw and evaluated me. The English faculty didn't know I'd gotten 90s in English all through high school, they didn't know I'd gotten a first-year scholarship to get into Wilfrid Laurier, they didn't know I intended, had intended all my life, to be a writer, they didn't know I'd already been published in several magazines and won a few literary prizes. The professor teaching Eng190 didn't see me in his class, and the one teaching Eng220 did; ergo I was a general student. Not destined for great things.

And then I decided not to go on to pursue an M.A. or a Ph.D. I didn't want to spend years studying the use of the semi-colon in T. S. Eliot's poetry, or some such ridiculously narrow subject. And my Philosophy options were epistemology, metaphysics, history of philosophy, or logic. Environmental ethics, biomedical ethics, social philosophy, and feminist philosophy hadn't been developed yet. At least not at Wilfrid Laurier. The stuff I really wanted to think about wasn't listed in the table of contents of any of my Philosophy textbooks.

And certainly no one took me aside to explain, explore, encourage. No one explained that in feminist philosophy or social philosophy, which were certainly offered at other universities, I could think about gender and how it determines your life. Seeing my passion for even the epistemology and metaphysics courses, one of my professors actually suggested I take six years to do the B.A. instead of four. Why didn't he tell me instead that I was clearly born to distinguish myself in the graduate/post-grad/post-doc world?

Even in high school, did anyone suggest I apply for a scholarship to Harvard? No. In fact, I was discouraged from even studying Philosophy at Wilfrid Laurier, because philosophy was "hard". (I'll bet the top *boy* student wouldn't've been told that.)

Besides, I wanted to write. And I wanted to write what *I* wanted to write. I wanted no more assignments to keep me from my first novel. No one explained that in an M.F.A. program, my first novel could *be* my assignment.

Years later, trying to correct the course I'd taken, I *did* enrol in an M.A. program. At some point, a professor asked whether I wanted to co-author something he was working on. I said no, I wasn't that interested in his subject, and I knew I could certainly write papers on my own. I completely didn't see it as a status thing. I didn't know that being a co-author on some known philosopher's paper conferred status. I figured doing it *on your own* meant getting more credit, because you had done it all without help.

I could go on. And on. Studies show that people with mentors advance in their careers further than those without mentors. I didn't have a mentor. It's possible no one really stepped forward, but it's just as possible someone did and I didn't recognize it (perhaps someone asked me to lunch one day, and I declined because I wasn't hungry).

But then didn't I distinguish myself out in the real world? Didn't I finally gain the status I deserved? Well, no. I mainly sought part-time jobs so I'd have time to write. I didn't realize that part-time jobs aren't on *any* ladder of advancement, they aren't in any competitive arena, no matter what the job. If you work less than 40 hours a week at something, you aren't taken seriously. Status? You're nothing. Furthermore, I worked at a great variety of jobs. I thought I was obtaining lots of experience. But breadth counts for nothing; status is gained by specialization.

Maybe my ignorance has been a generation thing, or maybe it's been a class thing, or maybe it's been both, but it's also definitely been a gender thing: how many women have gone through life sabotaging their success by not seeing the competitive subtext to all the decisions, all the choices, we make — by understanding them instead either at face value or within a completely different subtext?

Mainstream and Alternative

So I was browsing the movie collection at an online DVD rental site and feeling so very tired and bored with movies by men, about men, for men. My request list had dwindled to almost zero, and I wasn't finding anything I was interested in. So I decided to check out the "Alternative" section for at least an off-beat movie (by men, about men, for men) and WOH. *There* they were! The movies by women. About women. For women. Lots and lots of movies with women front and center. Strong, interesting women.

So I'm thinking, what a labelling mistake. They should just call the mainstream 'male' and the alternative 'female'. (Oh. Right.)

The Academy Awards

Why is the acting category of the Academy Awards sex-segregated (Best Actor in a Lead/Supporting Role, Best Actress in a Leading/Supporting Role)? We don't have separate awards for male and female directors. Or screenwriters, cinematographers, costume designers, film editors, soundtrack composers, or make up persons.

Is one's sex really relevant to one's acting ability? In a way that justifies separate awards? Of course not.

My guess is that it's because the award isn't really for the actor/actress, but for the character portrayed. Probably partly because most people can't distinguish the two. I'll bet George Clooney still gets asked what to do by moms whose kid has a fever.

Even so, why do we have separate categories? Because if we didn't, women would never win. Not because they're worse actors (remember the award isn't for acting ability), but because we award the heroes. And women never get to play the hero.

Men and Words

As a result of a recent exchange on a blog in which I felt insulted enough by the patronizing tone taken by the moderator that I'd decided not to participate any further, while another commenter (a male) responded with a mere "LOL", I asked yet another commenter (also a male) about why he thought our reactions were so different. "Don't men know when they're being insulted?" I asked.

His response? "We know, we just don't care. At the end of the day, it's just words on a screen. Most of us don't expect to convince anyone else, this is a social event of sorts for people who like to talk about stuff."

He went on to say "We don't expect to change anything, we're just engaging in venting, observation, and entertainment. If we learn something new, all the better."

I find this horrifying. Words have meaning! Meaning is important! At first I thought maybe that's just a philosopher/non-philosopher thing, but then I recalled conversations with male philosophers in which I similarly felt like I wasn't being taken seriously, in which I felt like, the man nailed it, entertainment.

I don't feel like that when I speak with women on these matters. So it's a sexist thing, not a philosopher thing. But it's not that men don't take women seriously, it's that they don't take each other seriously either. Suddenly their attitude toward debate—it's a game—made sense. As for the convincing, changing, maybe that's a teacher/social activist thing, but again, if it's a 'man' thing, then again, it's horrifying. No wonder the world isn't getting better and better: the people in power aren't talking, thinking, acting to make it so. Their discussions on policy are just "venting, observation, and entertainment"!

I wonder if at its root, it's part of the male relationship to words. Women are better with language, so it's said, whether because of neurology or gendered upbringing; men are better with action, so it's said, again whether by neurology or gendered upbringing. So that would explain why women consider words to be important, and men don't.

(And yet, for all that, men seem to have an awful lot of euphemisms. Though, upon examination, many of them serve to frame something as a competition or to aggrandize the speaker.)

Walking Alone in a Park at Night

In a rape trial, that the woman was walking *alone in a park at night* has been considered relevant — presumably it's a mitigating circumstance: the accused can be excused for thinking she wanted it if she was walking alone in a park at night.

What!? Why? Why is it that a woman walking alone in a park at night is understood — by men — to be implying consent to sexual intercourse with any and all men?

Are parks designated sex zones? I suppose in a sense they are. Lovers often meet there for clandestine encounters. Yeah, for *consensual* clandestine encounters.

Okay, but parks at night are also popular mugging zones, perhaps because of the poor lighting which makes escape easier. And yet a woman walking alone in a park at night is more at risk for rape than for purse-snatching.

So why is a woman walking *alone* — ah, is *that* it? A woman *unaccompanied by a man* is unowned? Up for grabs? Literally?

Solo Women's
Invisible Economic Expenses

It really hit home when my father gave me twenty bucks for a pizza, his treat. As if I were a teenager. Instead of a 50-year-old woman with a mortgage to pay, property taxes, and monthly bills for oil, electricity, phone, internet, tv, house insurance, car insurance … Amazing. He was sitting in my living room at the time. (*My* living room.) A carpenter I'd hired to do some renovations on my house (my *house*) was outside working at the time. And yet, he seemed to think I didn't need, or couldn't use, any *real* money. He couldn't see me as an adult negotiating my way in the real world, the one with jobs, paycheques, mortgages, and bills.

How did he think I came to own my own house? Who did he think would be paying the carpenter? Who does he think bought the car sitting in my driveway? And pays for its repairs?

I don't doubt for a minute that my parents have given my brother and my married sister *a lot more* than twenty bucks over the years (I divorced them thirty years ago, so I don't really know) (and for that reason, I don't feel entitled to anything from them, but that's not my point), starting with the hundred-dollar (thousand-dollar?) gifts they gave them to start their households. Said gifts were ostensibly wedding gifts, but hey, I had a household to start too. Why do they get a new fridge and I get a hand-me-down blender?

And it's not just my parents, of course. The twenty-bucks-for-pizza wasn't by any means the first time my economic expenses have been apparently invisible. A neighbour (a kept woman) explained to me once that she and her husband were happy to have given a certain real estate agent, a woman, the commission (instead of selling the property without involving her, which they could have done) because her husband had recently died, so she was on her own now. No similar sympathy has *ever* been directed my way. And I've been on my own since I was twenty-one.

Why is this? What can explain this phenomenon, a phenomenon that is surely causally related to women's lower salaries? The belief, clearly mistaken if anyone cared to open their eyes, that every woman is married? (And every married woman is completely supported by her husband?) The insistent belief that women are, or should be, considered children? (And children don't have adult needs, adult financial responsibilities...)

In 2005, 51% of American women were living alone; in 2011, 53% of British women were living alone; in 2013, about 27% of Canadian women live alone. So what do people like my parents think? That banks waive our mortgage payments, and landlords never charge us rent; that insurance companies waive our premiums; that oil and propane companies fill our tanks, but never send us a bill; that we get our cars and bus passes for free; that we don't have to pay for gas; that grocery stores let us walk out with all the food we want, for free; that our dentists and optometrists don't charge us for check-ups; and that little elves come in the middle of the night and leave heaps of money so we can pay for whatever else we need.

Men? Your turn.

Men, if you are truly for equal opportunity, truly against the gender roles that subordinate women to men, you'd start wearing make-up, dresses, and high heels. Not just for an hour, or a day, but until we live in a post-sexist world.

We are, and have been for a while, enlisting as soldiers and working at other high-risk jobs,[1] and, thereby, subjecting ourselves to even greater risk than that due to the actual duties of the job (our male co-workers withhold cooperation, sabotage our equipment, and so on). We are, and have been for a while, working as sole providers, for ourselves and often for our kids. We are, and have been for a while, refusing to perform femininity, refusing to simper and giggle, refusing to shave our legs and get breast implants, and, therefore, experiencing even further marginalization and mockery.

That is to say, many of us have already crossed over, we are already subverting sexist gender roles, have been doing so for years.

(And if you're reluctant to do so, if you refuse to wear make-up, dresses, and high heels, *ask yourselves why*.)

---

[1] That is to say, *traditionally male* high-risk jobs — we've been working forever at traditionally female high-risk jobs, such as that of nursing, which involves handling infectious blood, vomit, and shit, and the possibility of serious back injury (thanks Femonade).

Boy Books

Boy books. You're thinking *The Boys' Book of Trains* and *The Hardy Boys*, right? I'm thinking most of the books I took in high school English.

Consider Knowles' *A Separate Peace*. Separate indeed. It's set at a boys' boarding school. The boys are obsessed with jumping out of a tree. This involves considerable risk of crippling injury. And yet they do it, for no other reason than 'to prove themselves'. My question is, 'What are they proving themselves to be — other than complete idiots?' We don't get it.

They are also obsessed with going off to war. While this again involves risk of injury, it could, at least, be done for some lofty and heroic reason. But the reasons for the war aren't discussed. Not once. So it seems to be just another peer pressured ego thing: 'My dick's as big as yours.' Again, we don't get it.

Consider also Golding's *Lord of the Flies* and Conrad's *Heart of Darkness*. In all three, a major theme is the loss of innocence — not through the discovery of evil in the world, but through the discovery of evil within. The boys discover their heart of darkness, their capacity for cruelty. Well, we can't identify with that — after all, *we* didn't spend our childhoods tearing the legs off harmless flies and putting fish hooks through live frogs.

We especially can't identify with the feelings of *pride*, which lie just beneath the pretensions of horror, that accompany this discovery. For make no mistake, in forests and on farms, and on foreign battlefields, killing is still the rite of passage, the test of *maturity*, for boys to men. Hands up, does anyone else see this as sick?

Let's go back to *Lord of the Flies* for a minute. Again, all boys. Plane-crashed on an island, their task is simple: co-exist. They must figure out how to live with each other. They can't do this. Instead, they figure out how to kill each other.

Would girls have done any better? Well, yes, I think they would have. Would they have splintered into rival groups? Probably. Would they have picked on the fat ugly girl? Sigh. Probably. But they would not have killed the pig, especially like that, laughing about its squeals of pain. (Especially not with all that fruit around.) And the little 'uns would've had lots of mommies to look after them. And at the end, they would *not* have been discovered smeared with blood and war paint. Instead, they probably would've been found on the beach singing and doing the Macarena. (And the really horrible thing is that many men reading this won't see that as *unquestionably* better.)

So don't tell me these novels are universal. They're not. They're boy books. By boys about boys. And I'm a girl. Was a girl. I can't tell you the effect *Lord of the Flies* had on me. First of all, *I had to change sex to even be a part of the world.* Read that sentence again. Then I saw myself as seven parts Simon, two parts Ralph, and one part Piggy. And I saw my options: insanity or death. Quite the education.

But even when the theme *is* universal, we get boy books. Consider Richler's *The Apprenticeship of Duddy Kravitz.* Duddy wants to buy some land. As a *person*, I can identify with that. Unlike much of the previously-mentioned novels, this is not a boy thing. But still, Duddy is a boy. Very much a boy. So there's not much else I can identify with.

However, also unlike the previously-mentioned novels, this one has a few female characters in it. Actually, so does *A Separate Peace*: one is Leper's mother and she is *just* that — Leper's mother; the other is Hazel Brewster — the 'town belle', a mere object to be observed and perhaps used by the boys. Yvette, in *Duddy Kravitz*, is seen, by both Richler and Duddy, as either sexual or secretarial. Am I supposed to identify with that?

Consider Bradbury's *Fahrenheit 451*. I can *really* identify with saving books, with perpetuating the intellectual heritage of civilization. But the five men Montag meets at the end who are doing just that *are* just that — five *men*. So are the *thousands* of others: "Each *man* had a book he wanted to remember..." Where am *I*? What was *I* supposed to be wanting? (Another television wall — recall Mildred, Montag's wife.)

So I'm very thankful for Lee's *To Kill a Mockingbird*. For Scout. She's one of the two main kid characters. She's a girl. A spunky girl. A girl who runs, and thinks, and feels. *There* I am!

But, alas, she doesn't have a mom. She has a father and a brother; if she had a mom, if there were an adult woman like her, like her dad, and that would even it up a bit — Scout wouldn't be the female minority in her world. But that would be too much, I guess. Equal representation is going too far.

And I'm thankful for Laurence's *The Stone Angel*. It's about a woman. An old woman. A feisty, sarcastic old woman who embraces her inner bitch. I wanna be Hagar when I grow old.

But what do I want to be when I grow up? There's a huge void between Scout and Hagar. Why? What the hell happens to girls when they turn thirteen? I'm an adolescent, was an adolescent, presumably discovering and creating my identity. If I stay within the boundaries of the familiar, the apparently possible, I — Where are the girl books? Where are the books set at girls' boarding schools? Where are the books about 'girls only' islands?

And what would happen if boys read them? What would happen if adolescent boys experienced Gilman's *Herland* and

226

Tepper's *The Gate to Woman's Country* (and Fitzhugh's *Harriet the Spy*, and Newman's *A Share of the World* and McCarthy's *The Group* and...) instead of Golding's *Lord of the Flies*?

Maybe, eventually, instead of boys and girls, we could have kids, and then people; kids, and people, would read kids' books, and people's books.

Introduction to the 2nd Edition

Although the pieces from this point on are additions to the first edition, not all of them were written since the first edition (in fact, some of them date back to the '80s), and I don't know why I didn't include them in the first edition. But they're here now!

Regarding the pieces that *were* written since the first edition, well, apparently there hasn't been any decrease in the sexist shit that's out there. In fact, I'd say there's been an increase. Sigh.

Speaking Up

Women's problem is that they never speak up. They never ask for what they want. We've been told all our lives to be quiet. But if you don't tell people what you want, how do you expect to get it? Are they supposed to read your mind? You'll spend your whole life waiting for someone to offer you, to invite you to, whatever it is. I know.

Men's problem is that they *do* tell people what they want. Because they expect others to give it to them. And the mere expectation—well, you've heard of 'self-fulfilling prophecy'?

The Waiting-for-the-Elevator Thing

So I'm sure this has happened at least once to every woman. You're standing in front of an elevator, waiting for it, and a man comes up and presses the button.

> Oh is *that* what that's for? I saw the button, with an upward-pointing arrow, and I understand that elevators go up, but you know, *I just never put the two together!!*

> I was just waiting for it to *know* that I was standing there.

> I thought I might try to push the button, but then I thought, no, I'm just not strong enough.

> So I was just standing there.

> Or maybe I did push the button (you know, I just don't know?), but the system doesn't recognize buttons pushed by people with uteruses. Which is why *you* had to push the button. *You've* got a *penis!*

> So good thing you happened to come by! I could *still* be standing there!

Responding to Wolf-Whistles

Many men will wolf-whistle at *any* woman.[1] So it's not a special insult toward the woman in question (yes, men, wolf-whistles are insulting when they occur in everyday contexts, because they emphasize our sexuality when we're trying to be seen for our personhood and our various competencies; it thus *reduces* us to sexual objects) (a wolf-whistle in the bedroom directed toward your consenting sexual partner is, can be, a completely different matter).

Instead, such blanket expressions are indications of the man's insecurity about his manhood: he feels the need to assure himself and/or others—since his behaviour is *public*—that he's a *man*. Apparently, to such men, finding women sexually attractive is proof of manhood. *Heterosexual* manhood. So really the wolf-whistle is an indication of homophobia.

So rather than focus on the inherent misogyny (the implication that women are, above all, sexual objects, and the implication that men have the right to make a public assessment of our appearance), we should focus on the man's insecurity. And, therefore, we should respond with something like "Don't use me to deal with your insecurity about 'being a man'!"

Granted, most men won't understand that, so you'll have to simplify and expand with something like "I understand that you're afraid that your friends think you're gay, but don't use me to deal with that fear. Just talk to your friends; tell them you're not gay." (Right. Like that's ever gonna happen.)

---

[1] And once women realize that, perhaps they'll give up the make-up, the dress, the body obsession: *to men, it really doesn't matter how you look.*

And those who *are* smart enough *to* understand our initial response will be so resistant they won't process it. Because introspection, self-awareness—these are not part of the definition of manhood. (My father *hated* it whenever I tried to get him to examine his behaviour; 'Are you trying to psychoanalyze me?' he'd shout. As if I was proposing castration.) (I suspect that like most men, he was afraid I'd discover there's nothing much there; men spend so much time thinking about strategy, at heart, a sort of duplicitous insincerity, they haven't developed any genuine core.) (Sigh.)

The 100

If you haven't yet discovered it, check out *The 100* (available on Netflix).[1] There are so many female leaders and principals! Clarke, her mother, Raven, Octavia, the three grounder leaders …

And in one episode, not only does Clarke do something really difficult and really important (with Finn—trying not to spoil), the camera ends with a close-up of *her*, not him. How often does *that* happen? (Men *always* get the last shot, the last word! Their reaction is *always* the most important, the definitive one!) And that wasn't an anomaly. Scenes often end with a close-up of Clarke's mother and Raven instead of the other guy and Bellamy.

---

[1] Also enjoying *Madam Secretary* at the moment! And *hating* what's happening on *Code Black* now that Rob Lowe's been added to the cast. Don't know whether to blame the actor, the writers, or the directors, but my god is he taking over. As white men do. Sigh.

The Trouble with Trans

To the extent that a transsexual is someone who experiences body dysphoria, someone who feels they're in the 'wrong' body, someone who feels their body is the 'wrong' sex—how do they know? What is it like to *feel female* (or male)? I was *born* female, and *I* don't know. So how can *they* know? It's Nagel's 'What is it like to be a bat?' problem.[1] I know what it is to feel healthy only because I have also been sick. I don't know what it is to feel female because I haven't been male. Anything that I feel that I can know *for sure* is due to being female, rather than due to simply being human, is related to having a uterus (which can ache and hurt during menstruation) and breasts (which can feel heavy). Other things subjectively felt are certainly due to my body—to its levels of estrogen and progesterone, for example, but *also* to its levels of dopamine and vasopressin, for example. Given the overlapping range of levels of these biochemicals in males and females (many of which are *not* differentiated for males and females), again, how can one say 'I feel this—*because I'm female*'?

Furthermore, to the extent that sex is brain-based, and so MtFs feel like they have a female brain in a male body, it's the brain that produces hormones. So if they *do* have a female brain, it would be producing estrogen, and there would be no need for hormone treatments.

I'm not saying body dysphoria isn't 'real'. In fact, I experience every day a kind of mismatch between my exterior and my interior: I look like a middle-aged woman, but I don't feel like a middle-aged woman. Then again, I do. I must. This must

---

[1] faculty.arts.ubc.ca/maydede/mind/Nagel_Whatisitliketobeabat.pdf

be what a middle-aged woman can feel like. (Similarly, if you're in a male body, what you feel *must* be male. Maybe it's not the male you see on billboards and television, but it is male nevertheless.) (Welcome to our world.) When I say I don't feel like a middle-aged woman, I'm using my personal and thus limited experience (my interaction with other middle-aged women) and I'm using stereotypes, pushed at me primarily by profit-seeking marketing departments.

But even so, in this case, I *can* know that my interior doesn't match my exterior: at forty, for example, I know what I felt at twenty, so when I say I still feel twenty, I know what I'm talking about. I could mean, for example, that my skin feels the same, even though when I look in the mirror, I see that it's lost its elasticity. Usually, though, I mean something like I still feel energetic and impassioned, not bland and resigned. But this takes us back to my point about referencing limited experience and stereotypes.

What we need are thorough and carefully conducted studies of MtFs and FtMs. Only they know what it felt like when they were male or female and what it feels like *after* they add or subtract certain body parts. (To the extent that those parts aren't connected to the whole in the same way, though, any change in subjective experience won't be very useful.)

More importantly, only they know what it felt like when they were, for example, flooded with testosterone and what it feels like to be flooded with estrogen. Sadly, those studies aren't being done, as far as I can tell (which may mean they're just not being publicized). And even if they were, their reliability would be compromised by the nature of subjective report and a self-selected sample, both of which are likely to be further confounded by the subject's conflation of sex and gender.

Next. To the extent that a transgendered person is someone who adopts the gender that is traditionally aligned with the other sex, there are several problems. If gender is socially constructed, then it's not dependent on sex—so one need not change one's sex in order to change one's gender. In fact, transgendered people don't even need their own label. Every woman who refuses to wear make-up and shave her legs is as much a transgendered person as the man who insists on wearing make-up and shaving his legs. (Assuming that not wearing make-up is not just not-feminine, but is masculine. If it's just not-feminine, then perhaps it's more accurate to call such a woman non-gendered. So would a woman who wears pants instead of a dress be transgendered? Still no. It turns out that aspects of appearance commonly associated with men are more acceptable for women than vice versa. Perhaps that's why there are more men than women seeking to cross the gender divide. Women already can, at least on superficial matters.) And if it *isn't* socially constructed—that is, if gender *is* dependent on sex, how do we explain effeminate men and 'tomboys'? How is it that many males use their voice and their hands in a very expressive fashion? How is it that many females are strong and aggressive?

Next. Are MtFs female? The answer to this question requires an informed understanding of biology, chemistry, and biochemistry that I don't have. It also requires a definition: how much of how many (and which) primary and secondary sexual characteristics is required to be a member of that sex category? Is a female who has undergone a hysterectomy and a bilateral mastectomy still female? Is a post-menopausal and thus low-estrogen female still female? (I suspect that sex is solely determined by chromosomes, in which case MtFs are not, and can never be, female.)

Next. Are MtFs women? To the extent that being a woman is a matter of sex, see the preceding paragraph. To the extent that being a woman is a matter of gender, maybe. Again, we need a definition: which elements of gender are necessary or sufficient, how many of those elements, how much ...

Of course it *is* possible, by observation and comparison, to identify what it's like to be *treated as* a female/woman. I was born female, raised as a girl, and all of my adult life, I have been treated, by most people most of the time, as a woman. And what does *that* feel like? It feels like shit. To be patronized, marginalized, objectified ... So perhaps a more useful question is 'Should MtFs be treated as women?' Should we pay them less for work of equal value? Should we mock or at least ignore their contributions to society? If we want consistency, yes. If we want justice, no.

On that note, it needs to be said (apparently) that how you're treated affects the person you become. Kick a dog often enough, and it becomes a cowering, fearful mess. The same is true for humans: ignore a person often enough, and she stops speaking up; make her feel like all of her value is in her body, and she obsesses over it; and so on (and so on, and so on). There is a difference between being a FAAB (female assigned at birth) and being an MtF: a lifetime lived in a female body. That difference is not inconsequential. To understate. And if MtFs had any understanding at all of sexism, they'd know this. (But perhaps they've been too busy dealing with their dysphoria.) (Or they've just been, well, men.)

So answering the question of whether MtFs are women is a no-brainer for the people who've been women all their lives. MtFs make demands, not polite requests.[2] They are quick to resort to insult, threat, aggression. They compete. They dominate. They convey a sense of entitlement none of us has ever had. They don't take 'no' for an answer. They scream "WHO THE FUCK ARE YOU TO KEEP US OUT WE

---

[2] At least, those we hear from.

HAVE A FUCKING RIGHT TO BE HERE TO GO
WHEREVER THE FUCK WE WANT!"—a response to
exclusion from FAAB spaces that is "right up there,
ideologically, with demanding that girls and women be sexually
available visually and physically, for and with men" (Julian Real,
radicalprofeminist.blogspot.ca/2011/02/who-gets-to-define-
women-only-space.html.[3],[4] In short, it quacks like a duck.

In any case, perhaps the most important question is '*Why
does it matter?*'—whether one is male or female, a man or a
woman? It matters only to those who want to maintain a rigid
sex/gender dichotomy. And why would someone want to do
that? To support a sexist system/society.

So, I say to MtFs, who are apparently among those who
want to maintain such a system/society, if you want to be
considered a woman, act like one. Sit down and shut up.
Understand that your opinion doesn't count. Be sensitive to
everyone else's feelings, respect them, accommodate them.
Don't assume you know more than anyone else. In particular,
don't assume you know more about sex and gender than
second-generation feminists and radfems; they are Ph.D.s (in
fact, many of them *have* Ph.D.s) when it comes to sex and
gender, and no man *of any kind* comes close to their level of
understanding: "They lost many of [their] privileges when they
started identifying as women, but rather than recognising that
this is because of sexism, they decided it was because they are
trans. Why? Because, being male, they knew fuck all about

---

[3] Though one wonders if they're screaming so loudly because they're men or because
they're like frogs who have just jumped into a pot of boiling water. (The rest of us
women have had a lifetime of to get used to it.) (Poor MtFs, they thought they
were going to be special little princesses on a pedestal. What a shock real life must
have been.)

[4] And so once again, women (FAABs) either stay and fight or thus bullied, silenced,
and far too tired, sigh and leave.

sexism" (thebeardedlady, Nov17/09 at factcheckme.wordpress. com/ 2009/11/16/the-fallacy-of-cis-privilege).

It is no surprise to me that twice as many MtFs as FtMs commit suicide. I have not read many accounts of their transition, but in most of those I've read, I see a shocking naiveté with regard to sexism, gender politics, etc. It is as if these people had no idea that they were voluntarily becoming a member of the sexed subordinate class. So no wonder, on top of everything else, they can't handle, are broadsided by, the sudden and almost complete disenfranchisement ...

(So as for the dysphoria, like the person who rejects their leg because it doesn't feel right, because it doesn't feel like it's theirs, isn't it better to deal with the dysphoria than to go through life as an amputee?) (Because yes, being a woman in the patriarchy is, in many ways, like being an amputee. We are crippled. We are, relative to men, dis-abled.)

How to Make a Man Grow Up

I was recently surprised to discover that in the U.S., men are required by law to register for the "selective service system". *Only* men. I thought women were allowed in their military now. And *required*. I didn't think they had 'the draft' anymore.

When I expressed my surprise, hoping to engage someone in conversation, the guy in line behind me (I was in a U.S. post office, where the brochures reminding men of their duty were prominently displayed) said that he agreed that it should be mandatory to serve for two years: "It makes 'em 'grow up'."

Hm. How does teaching someone to kill make a person grow up? That is, what's mature about learning how to kill? What's mature about actually killing?

Of course, being in the military isn't just about killing. Arguably. But what's mature about being pressured to conform, to obey orders?

Sure, the forced routine, of physical exercise and psychological effort, might become a habit. And that's a good thing. A grown-up thing. But there are other, far better, ways to achieve that same result.

And sure, the presumed altruism—you're serving your country, life's not all about you— is good, is mature. But again, is killing someone really the best example of altruism we can put before young men? Young men who need to grow up?

It seems to me the selective service system is a bad way to fix a bunch of other bad ways.

The question we have to ask is how do boys *get* to eighteen *without* growing up? (And are women already grown up? Or is it that they don't need to become grown up?)

"If my wife will let me."

"If my wife will let me." That's what Richard Branson said when he was asked whether he'd go to Mars: "It may be a one-way trip …. So maybe I'll wait till the last ten years of my life, and then maybe go, if my wife will let me" (Klein, *This Changes Everything*, p.288). Does he really think no one will notice how inauthentic he was being? He's one of the most powerful men in the world. He doesn't need anyone's permission for anything.

On top of that, he doesn't want to take her with him?

And on top of *that*, she doesn't have a name? (I'm surprised he didn't say 'the wife' rather than 'my wife—to underscore his view that women are all just so interchangeable.)

It's tiresome. Wife/girlfriend as Mom. It enables the man to continue being a child, just one of the boys. Wife/girlfriend as authority. See, I'm not sexist, women have the *real* power.

Even from our most intelligent, most capable, men.

So very tiresome.

This is your brain.
This is your brain on oxytocin: Mom.

I think many women realize that their children make them vulnerable; their love for them holds them hostage. So many things they would do (leave?)—but for the children. I wonder how many realize that their imprisonment is partly (largely?) physiological. And, in most cases, as voluntary as that first hit of heroin, cocaine, whatever.

'But I *love* my children!' That's just the oxytocin talking. You think you love them because you're a good person, you're responsible, and dutiful, and, well, because they're so loveable, look at them! That's just the oxytocin talking.

All those women (most, according to at least one survey) who didn't really want to become pregnant, but did anyway (because contraception and abortion weren't easily available, and sex was defined as intercourse), and then claimed, smiling, that they wouldn't have it any other way, they love their children—just the oxytocin talking.

The assurance that the labour will be worth it, that you'll forget all about the pain as soon as you see your baby, as soon as you hold your baby—all true. Because of the oxytocin.

Which you'll get more of if you breastfeed.

And which you'll get more of if you have a vaginal birth. Which is why women who intend to give up their babies for adoption or who are surrogates should have caesareans. It'll reduce that drug-induced attachment, making it easier to follow through with their plans. (Why doesn't anyone in tell them that?)

"Roused by the high levels of estrogen during pregnancy, the number of oxytocin receptors in the expecting mother's brain multiplies dramatically near the end of her pregnancy. This makes the new mother highly responsive to the presence of oxytocin."[1] And, "Researchers have found that women's oxytocin levels during their first trimester of pregnancy predict their bonding behavior with their babies during the first month after birth. Additionally, mothers who had higher levels of oxytocin across the pregnancy as well as the postpartum month also reported more behaviors that create a close relationship, such as singing a special song to their baby, bathing and feeding them in a special way, or thinking about them more. Quite simply, the more oxytocin you have, the more loving and attentive you are to your baby."[2]

So those new mothers who *don't* fall in love with their babies? The ones who want to throw them out the window because they're fucking crying all the time? Their brains just didn't produce enough, or perhaps any, oxytocin. Post-partum depression? It's just oxytocin deficiency. (It certainly doesn't mean you're a bad person. I'd throw the kid out the window too.)

And here's the kicker: *oxytocin rewires your brain. Permanently.* "Under the early influence of oxytocin, nerve junctions in certain areas of mother's brain actually undergo reorganization, thereby making her maternal behaviors 'hard-wired.'"[3]

You become a mom. Permanently. Oxytocin makes you sensitive to others' needs (not just your baby's needs, not just your kids' needs). It makes you want to fulfill others' needs. (Not just your baby's needs, not just your kids' needs.) You

---

[1] attachmentparenting.org/support/articles/chemistry

[2] ahaparenting.com/ages-stages/pregnancy/oxytocin-pregnancy-birth-mother

[3] psychologicalscience.org/media/releases/2007/feldman.cfm

become nurturing, affectionate, caring. (You become a proper woman? A woman who knows her place?) *Oxytocin changes your personality. It changes you. As any drug does.*

The rest of us, those of us who live oxytocin-free? We don't give a damn. We're not into nurturing others — children *or men*. When we say we don't like kids? We mean it. And when you say 'Oh, just wait until you have some of your own, you'll change your mind!', you're right. Because we'll become doped up with oxytocin.

So if you don't want to turn into a Mom, if you don't want to dedicate your life to others, to meeting their needs and desires, *Just Say No.*

Just tell me what to say and I'll say it

"What do you want me to say?" your pre-Nigel, Nigel, or ex-Nigel says helplessly, having obviously said the wrong thing, again. "Just tell me what to say and I'll say it."

I want you to say what you think. And if I don't agree with it, then I'm outta here. It's that simple. (Because why would I want a relationship, a friendship, with someone with whom I don't agree? On the important things. Maybe even on the unimportant things.)

Why is it so hard for so many men to just say what they really think? Because they don't know. They are so supremely unaccustomed to introspection.

Because, in any case, the truth is irrelevant, useless. That's why it's so difficult for them to know what to say. "What do you want me to say?" means "What lies will work here?"

They think that their relationship with you is all, and only, about sexual access, recreational and reproductive. And they're willing to say whatever it takes to get that access. To seduce is to manipulate.[1]

And guys, if that's how you get a date, a girlfriend, a wife— by figuring out 'the right thing' to say — are you really surprised that it doesn't last? That one day she realizes you're bullshit through and through, have been since the beginning?

---

[1] Why doesn't it occur to men that if the woman really wanted them, they wouldn't have to seduce her, they wouldn't have to manipulate her?

Trying to figure out people's actions or thinking: Banned on Reddit? WTF.

So I posted the following on the AskMen subreddit:

Why do men rape?

That's my question. Seriously. Why do men rape? I just wrote a novel answering that question, *Impact*, but I'd like to hear from men. (And perhaps should've posted here BEFORE I wrote the novel. Didn't occur to me.)

I *immediately* received the message:

Sorry, this post has been removed by the moderators of r/AskMen. Moderators remove posts from feeds for a variety of reasons, including keeping communities safe, civil, and true to their purpose.

I assumed that it was an automatic removal, and I assumed that it was the word 'rape' that triggered the removal (which in itself would be telling—they anticipate getting, or do get, a lot of 'Which way do you like to rape cunts the best?' queries … ?). So I sent a note to the moderators, asking them to please read my post and reconsider. And received this response:

Your post has been flagged as trying to figure out a specific person's or group of people's actions or thinking.

Seriously? It's taboo to try to understand people's actions or thinking? WTF.

I decided to experiment and posted the same question on the AskWomen subreddit. It was also removed. Reasons:

> Graceless generalizations are not permitted
> – People are not a hive mind.
> – Speak only for yourself.
>
> Do not
> – generalize across all people of a gender, race, or ethnicity
> – ask for mind reading
> – ask for us to defend/justify other people's behaviors
> – assume that all people in a gender, race, or ethnicity do/think something
> – ask for 'male equivalent'/'female equivalent' as these would not exist for most things due to different cultural processes
> – exceptions: discussion of cultural norms; quotations

Woh. First, notice the difference. The women's response is SO much better. More detailed, more explanatory ... It is, in a nutshell, indicative of superior thinking.

And yes, I agree. The way I'd phrased the question *was* assuming a hive mind and generalizing across a sex. I could rephrase it: Why has rape become normalized in our culture? That would clearly fall into the exception of 'discussion of cultural norms' ...

Even so, I wonder at the 'Speak only for yourself' rule. Limiting oneself to anecdote is no way to acquire knowledge. Are we to assume no one knows anything but their own subjective experience? Could no one have referred me to, say, Smithyman's

1976 research, recently mentioned in *The New York Times*? Or the NFB film, *Why Men Rape*? Not to mention Neil Malamuth's work ...

And why is it a problem, as it was for the men, to ask for mind reading? Do people not know their own minds? Have we become so incapable of introspection? Or is it, in the second case, that I was asking women to read men's minds? Even so, can't we speculate? With good reason and evidence?

"The Adult Market"

What's adult about coercing someone to do something she doesn't really want to do?

What's adult about humiliating another person?

What's adult about hurting another person?

What's adult about doing sexual things to children?

We should call it what it is. The psychopathic sociopathic misogynist market.

SlutWalk:
What's the problem?

What exactly is the problem with SlutWalk? The event was reportedly initiated in response to a police officer's comment about not dressing like a slut if you don't want to get raped. The underlying assumption is that one's attire—specific items or style—sends a message. And indeed it does. High heels, fishnet stockings, and a heavily made-up face are considered invitations. So if a woman is wearing 'fuck me shoes', she can hardly complain if someone fucks her.

But *is* that the message the woman is sending? A message that she's sexually available to everyone? Maybe. Maybe not.[1]

---

[1] Given that the values and norms are different for men than for women and given that we are neither accustomed nor socialized to giving (or requesting) explicit consent for sex, it's essential to be clear about the signals of 'implied consent'. It's also almost impossible: the signals, ranging from mere presence to attire to a gesture to a look, are ambiguous and variably sent/received—some men assume mere presence in their apartment means 'yes', some do not; some women intend a certain outfit to mean 'yes', some do not. Even on the few occasions when consent may be given or withheld explicitly, men may understand 'no' to mean 'yes'. And indeed, given the socialization discussed earlier, a woman may mean 'yes' when she says 'no'. As Margaret Jane Radin puts it (in "The Pragmatist and the Feminist"), 'Just say no' as the standard for determining whether rape has occurred is both under- and over-inclusive. It is under-inclusive because women who haven't found their voices mean 'no' and are unable to say it; and it is over-inclusive because, like it or not, the way sexuality has been constituted in a culture of male dominance, the male understanding that 'no' means 'yes' was often, and may still sometimes be, correct.

However, as Susan Estrich points out (in "Rape"), "the 'no means yes' philosophy ... affords sexual enjoyment to those women who desire it but will not say so — at the cost of violating the integrity of all those women who say 'no' and mean it". This is the minefield when 'group membership' is 'mandatory' (when females are considered a group — women): if there is no room for individual subjectivity, serious errors will be made.

Frankly, given the ambiguity, and the nature of the outcome in the case of misunderstanding, I wonder why women take the risk.

It's much like wearing one's gang colours in the territory of a rival gang. Of course it's going to be provocative. Is any consequent assault legal? No. Is it deserved? No. Should it have been anticipated? Yes. So unless the intent was to make a point about the wrongness of gangs and violence, a point best made by arranging media presence *for* the incursion into the other gang's territory, well, *how stupid are you?*

Granted, most women who dress in a sexually attractive way don't go that far (fishnet stockings and heavy make-up), but why go any way at all? Why *does* a woman dress in a sexually attractive way? Why do women put on high heels, show their legs, wear bras that push up their breasts and tops that expose cleavage, redden their lips, and so on? What does she hope to *attract* exactly?

My first guess is that she hasn't thought about it. She dresses in a sexually attractive way because, well, that's what women in our society are expected to do.[2] In which case she's an idiot. Doesn't deserve to be raped, but really, she should think about what she does.

My second guess is that she dresses in a sexually attractive way because she wants to attract *offers of sex*.[3] But then, she

---

[2] There's a difference between attractive and *sexually* attractive. At least, there *should* be. Perhaps because men dominate art and advertising, the two have been equivocated. (No doubt because *everything* is sexual for them.) (Which may be to say, everything is about dominance for them.)

[3] Maybe part of her smiles to think of herself as a slut. She's a bad girl, she's dangerous, she's taking risks, she's a wild girl for once in her life. But that's exactly what they want. Sexual access. No-strings-attached sex. We fell for that in the 60s too. Free love, sure, we're not prudes, we're okay with our bodies, we're okay with sex, we're 'with it'. But they never took us seriously. They never considered us part of the movement. Behind our backs, they'd snicker and say the best position for a

shouldn't be angry when she *receives* such offers, either in the form of whistles and call-outs or in more direct ways. That she may respond with anger or offense suggests that she wants to attract only offers she's likely to accept, offers only from men she's attracted to. But, men may cry, how's a man to know? Um, try to make eye contact. If you can't do that, she's not interested. If you *do* make eye contact, smile. If she doesn't smile back, she's not interested. Surely that kind of body language isn't too subtle to grasp.

And yet, many men seem to have such an incapacity for subtlety that if you act like bait, they may simply reach out and grab you. Are they entitled to do that? No. Any unauthorized touching is a violation. Is clothing authorization? Well, sometimes. Consider uniforms.

So it would be far less ambiguous if a woman who wants sex just extended the offers herself. Why take the passive route of inviting offers from likely candidates? Why make men try to figure out whether they're a likely candidate? Why not just let them know and go from there?

Another problem with SlutWalk is that many people may not have been aware of the police officer's comment. So what are they to make of the event? What are they to understand is the point? (Prerequisite to deciding whether to support it or not.)

> (a) "It's okay to be a slut!" Given the 'sluttish' appearance that many women present during the walk, this understanding is understandable. But whether or not one wants to endorse that message depends on the definition of 'slut'.[4]

---

woman is prone (Stokely Carmichael). (Read your history, learn about our past.)

[4] See "What's Wrong with Being a Slut?".

254

(b) "We're proud to be sluts!" Ditto.

(c) "No woman deserves to be raped, regardless of her attire!" This is probably closest to the intended message, but in this case, better to have called it a 'Walk Against Rape'. Better, further, to advocate changes that would make rape more likely to be reported and rapists more likely to be sentenced commensurate to the injuries they've caused. Perhaps better still to advocate a male-only curfew.

Of course, 'SlutWalk' is far more provocative, far more attention-getting, than the ho-hum 'Walk Against Rape', but I don't think the organizers considered the difficulty of reclaiming an insulting word. And 'slut' is a very difficult insult to reclaim. Harder than 'bitch' and 'nigger' (sex trumps skin color; better to be a black man than a white woman) and even those reclamation efforts haven't been very successful. Mostly, success has been limited to conversations among women in the first case and conversations among blacks in the second. SlutWalk is not conducted in the presence of women only. So, really, did the organizers expect people in general to accept (let alone understand) their implied redefinition?

The organizers also didn't think through the male over-dependence on visual signals. The gawkers and hecklers who typically undermine the event should have been expected. The inability of men to process any verbal messages (even those that are just a few words long) in the presence of so-called 'fuck me' heels should be expected.

Consider that even Gwen Jacobs' action to make it legal for women to be shirtless wasn't immune to sexualization, despite the clearly non-sexual nature of her action; men (BOOBS!) hooted, men (BOOBS!) called out, and the media, no doubt reflecting a decision made by a man (BOOBS!), or perhaps a thoughtless woman, *continues* to use the sexualized "topless" instead of "shirtless" when reporting about the issue (BOOBS!). Imagine the response had Jacobs gone shirtless while also wearing short shorts exposing half buttocks. It would have been, to understate, a mixed message.

And that is, essentially, the problem with SlutWalk. High heels, exposed legs, pushed-up breasts, and a made-up faces sends a message that one is sexually available (which is why it's appalling to me that it has become convention for women to wear heels and make-up in public every day all day) (those who *accept* that convention accept the view that women *should* be, or at least should *seem* to be, sexually available every day all day).[5] And if it doesn't send a message that you're sexually available, what message *does* it send? That you're sexually *attractive*? Back to *what are you hoping to attract?* (And why are you trying to attract that when you're at work, working?)

> (d) "Women have a right to tease!" *That* seems to be the message SlutWalk conveys, given the likelihood that women who present themselves as sexually attractive *aren't* actually trying to be sexually attractive to everyone or, at least, aren't sexually *available* to everyone. And that's a message that many women would *not* endorse. Especially those who know about the provocation defence.[6]

---

[5] Of course there's the possibility that if/when women forego the heels, bared legs, accentuated breasts and butts, and make-up, men will consider a little ankle to be an open invitation. Which just means the issue isn't attire *at all*. It's being *female*. In a patriarchy. (Which still means SlutWalk is off-target.)

[6] See "The Provocation Defence".

There's nothing wrong with extending invitations to sex. Doing so in public in such a non-specific way—that's the problem. Especially given men's inability to pick up on subtle cues and/or their refusal to understand the difference between yes and no, let alone yes and maybe. Maybe when men can handle a sexually charged atmosphere without assaulting ... Maybe when other men penalize, one way or another, those who can't handle a sexually charged atmosphere without assaulting ...

In the meantime, we're living in an occupied country, a country occupied by morally-underdeveloped people with power who think women are just walking receptacles for their dicks. So women who make themselves generally available, or present themselves as being generally available, are, simply, putting themselves at great risk (and, yes, in a way, getting what they asked for): some STDs are fatal; others are incurable; most have painful symptoms. And pregnancy has a life-long price tag.[7]

---

[7] I hear the objections already: 'No, wearing high heels and make-up *doesn't* mean I'm sexually available! *That's* the point!' (And around and around we go.) Then why do you wear high heels and make-up? Seriously, think about it: high heels make the leg more shapely, attracting the male gaze, which follows your legs up ... ; make-up makes your face younger, hence more sexually attractive; lipstick attracts the male gaze to your lips, your mouth ... If you just want to be attractive, then what you do to your body wouldn't be sexualized: you'd wear funky gold glittered hiking boots, you'd paint an iridescent rainbow across your face, you'd do a hundred *other* aesthetically interesting things ...

Taking Tiddlywinks Seriously

Imagine a game of tiddlywinks being played by men. Imagine it televised. And broadcast to the whole world on any one of over a dozen Tiddlywinks Channels. Imagine a play-by-play description of the proximity and angle of orientation each tiddlywink, relative to the pot; of the exact positioning of each man's squidger, relative to each tiddlywink; of the precise force with which the players flip their tiddlywinks. Imagine after-the-game interviews with the players, eliciting earnest reflections about their every move.

If you're laughing, why don't you also laugh at football, hockey, baseball, basketball, and soccer games?

And if you're not laughing, behold the legitimizing force of serious-men-doing-it.

Baby Androids

It finally dawned on me after reading one too many 'failed android' stories. The problem. They always try to create an adult without a childhood.

Mary Shelley aside, I'm be tempted to put the blame on our sexist society: leave it to the men to 'forget' childhood, to forget that we don't come out of the womb fully formed, to forget that we are as much a product of our nurture as our nature. After all, most men aren't responsible for it, they don't participate in it, they don't work at daycares, they don't teach elementary school.

You want to create an android? An artificial life form that can think and feel, that can respond to questions, to situations, like an ordinary human being? Then create a baby android. One with the capacity to learn, to benefit from experience, to grow, to develop. In fifteen or twenty years, eureka!

The Futility of Teaching Business Ethics or Why Our World Will End

There are a few reasons why teaching ethics to business students is an exercise in futility.

1. The profit motive trumps everything. As long as this is the case, there's no point in teaching students the intricacies of determining right and wrong. Whether something is morally acceptable or not is simply irrelevant to them. It might come into play when two options yield the same profit, but how often does that happen? And even so, other concerns are likely to be tie-breakers.

But *is* this the case? *Does* the profit motive trump everything? Yes, according to their economics, marketing, and even human resources professors: profit is the bottom line. It's primary. It's the raison d'être of business. Good thing. Because business students enrol in business because they want to make a lot of money. I have yet to meet someone who's enrolled in business to make the world a better place. (Wait a minute. Don't shareholders matter? Doesn't what *they* want trump everything? In theory, yes. In practice, no. Most don't cast their vote. And anyway most shareholders also want to make a lot of money. As much as possible, in fact. I have yet to meet someone who becomes a shareholder, who invests, to make the world a better place.)

2. Ethics is for girls. (Apparently.) And business is dominated by boys. It's mom who teaches us right from wrong; she's the

moral compass. And anything mom does is to be held in contempt as soon as a boy hits twelve. In order to become a man, it's necessary. To hold in contempt all things female. Ethics presumes caring, and real men don't care. (Qualification: they don't care about others. They care about profit, their own place in the scheme of things, and because their sons are extensions of themselves, they care about *them*, *their* place in the scheme of things, but caring about strangers? Strangers are other; the other is the competition.) Ethics is something for priests to worry about and we all know priests aren't real men. They're celibate for god's sake. So, men avoid ethics—it's effeminate to be concerned about right and wrong.

3. Ethics is a grey area. It's complicated. There are often no clear-cut answers. Ironically, there's seldom a right and wrong answer to questions of right and wrong. Men prefer black and white. They gravitate toward the quantitative, the ill-(but sexually aptly-)named 'hard sciences' of engineering and chemistry, rather than the 'soft sciences' of psychology and sociology. They say such fields are not as legitimate, but really they're just harder to navigate because the reasoning and the evidence are 'stronger' and 'weaker' rather than 'right' and 'wrong'. (Which is why, when men *do* get involved with ethics, they prefer moral legalism, the approach that equates right and wrong with legal and illegal, which is black and white.)

So actually, there's just one reason why teaching business ethics to business students is an exercise in futility: business is dominated by men (point 2), and the masculist mode is quantitative (points 1 and 3). This explains, or is supported by, their obsession with size. Girth which in a woman would be considered disgusting is carried by men as if it *increases* their legitimacy, their authority: they thrust out their gut just as they thrust out their chest. It brings to mind animals that inflate themselves to achieve greater size (the balloonfish can actually double its size). Simply put, for men, the bigger, the better. I think this is because the male mind is more primitive, and at a very primitive level, the contest for survival is won by the bigger animal. (Actually, that's not true even at that level: small creatures with toxic stings and the capacity to remain hidden often survive. But unfortunately, men have evolved enough to create a system in which it *is* true.) (And anyway, even as they don't win, they'll take the rest of us down.)

Sticks and Stones

"Sticks and stones will break my bones, but words will never hurt me." What an awful lie. It makes me wonder who started it.

Someone for whom words have no meaning? Someone who, therefore, says whatever will achieve the desired effect, regardless of the truth of the matter?

Someone who has few words? Someone for whom, therefore, words have limited expressive value?

A man?

Artificial Intelligence Indeed

So I first heard of the movie *Ex Machina* when I read a review (by Chris DiCarlo) in *Humanist Perspectives*—and was so disgusted that I wrote a letter to the editor. Why? Because the reviewer had revealed his own misogyny by failing to address the obvious: the fact that the body the guy created for his AI was that of a female, a sexy female, a young female. Apparently, that was just coincidence. The picture chosen to accompany the review (no doubt, the one chosen to promote the movie) showed her bound. In fishnet.[1] Her pose was right out of a BDSM scene. Apparently, that too was just coincidence.

As I said in my letter, "That you failed to remark on any of this is disturbingly telling. It indicates just how much men have come to *expect* to see women as young and sexy. Apparently it's the norm, *it's normal*, to pornify women, to present their bodies as sexually available. Well, fuck you. (Have you heard of sexism? Feminism? Check it out, why don't you.)"

The letter was not published. The editor wrote back and said, "I don't know if this changes anything, but Chris had nothing to do with the selection of photos for the review. That was done by a woman who helps me with the onerous task of laying out the magazine."

Which is a comment that opens up a whole 'nother area worth investigation: how is it that people think that if a woman does X, it must be okay (that is, not sexist)? This notion informs

---

[1] Right, okay, it was actually metal mesh, I get that. And the similarity to fishnet is *also* mere coincidence? (If you think so, you are too naïve for words. Certainly too naïve to be writing movie reviews.)

the currently popular misconception of feminism as indiscriminate female solidarity. (As a commenter said recently in response to one of my posts on BlogHer, implying that I was not a feminist, "My feminist sisters support all woman in whatever choices they make ..." At the very least, that stance would be rife with internal contradictions.)

But onwards. Does it change anything? No. As long as the image is from the movie, then the movie is evidence of the normalized pornification of women, and DiCarlo still ignored that.

If the AI had been black-skinned and called 'boy' and given menial tasks and whipped, I suspect it would have been noticed. I suspect DiCarlo would have, at the very least, made passing mention to the implied racism.

But not only is 'Ava' a sexy woman-child (there's even a 'play dress up' scene in the movie), the guy who created it/her has a hall full of closets containing similar AIs. *He's not making AIs. He's making fucktoys.* He actually tells his (male) guest that the AIs have fully functioning holes. We see him using said holes for his apparent pleasure. The guest realizes that the guy has created Ava to match his (the guest's) porn file. (What the hell is a porn file? Oh.) All very unremarkable, apparently. Thought DiCarlo.

There was one promising line (in the movie, not DiCarlo's review): the guy insists that consciousness is gendered. But the claim isn't really challenged. And it becomes clear that he has come to that conclusion because his 'source material' (his 'blue book') for Ava comes from a net cast wide upon the world-as-is. That is, he's just grabbed all the sexist sociocultural conditioning in the world and built something from it. No wonder, Ava.

In short (and this is *my* review), *Ex Machina* is just another movie that objectifies women. It pretends to be about AI, but it's not even a little bit past Asimov's *I, Robot*.

Is it redeemed by the fact that Ava escapes, after killing the guy (and leaving the guest imprisoned, facing the same outcome)? Not really. Because she does so by sexual manipulation ("I want to be with you," she tells the guest in her soft, little-girl voice. "Do you want to be with me?")[2] Which is apparently what the script writer and director believe intelligence is—when female-bodied.

And she escapes into the forest wearing high heels. Fuck-me heels. Though, okay, that's probably all that was available to her, and we do see that she takes them off. But she doesn't throw them away. Once in the real world, does she choose instead Doc Martens, loose pants with pockets, a comfortable sweatshirt, and a jacket? No. She remains sexualized. *Artificial* intelligence indeed.[3]

---

[2] "Yes," I imagine the guest replying. "I'd like the girlfriend experience, please."

[3] You know we're laughing at you, right? (When we're not screaming at you.) You who investigate artificial *intelligence* but are too stupid to recognize your own immaturity, you who have conferences on "The Future of Humanity" with all-male panels, you who publish special issues called "Speaking of Humanism" featuring nothing but male faces ...

Women Discover Life on Mars

"Should we fund a mission to Mars? Sure. Give us a bit of time and we can make that planet uninhabitable too." (jassrichards.com)

That said, I *thoroughly* enjoyed watching *MARS*. Why? Because the three astronauts who walk out onto the planet's surface at the end to discover life on Mars are *all women*. Not a token one of three. Not even a remarkable two of three. But ALL THREE. OF THREE.

And the bureaucrat back on Earth who makes the announcement? Again, a woman.

And none of this was presented as in-your-face feminist. Not one line in the entire script made reference to their *being* women. There was no male resentment, no resistance, no snide comment about quotas or reverse discrimination. There was no undue praise, no celebration for having achieved the status of being the first humans to discover life on Mars.

They just were.

I can't tell you how gratifying it would be to *just be*. To be an astronaut if I wanted to be. To be the one to discover life on Mars. To be the head of a Mars mission program. Just because I was qualified to do so and lucky enough to make it through the selection process. And my sex had as little to do with it as my ear shape.

Furthermore, throughout the expedition, there was as much female presence as male. Sure, okay, one of the women became leader only because one of the men died, but when the second crew arrived, its leader was a woman. And if I'm mistaken about this, it's only because regardless of the actual hierarchy, women were as central, as important, as valuable, as active.

They were just living their lives.

And yet, seven of the eight writers are men. The director is a man. All ten executive producers are men. Even so, they had *three women* discover life on Mars. Three women, all by themselves. They didn't need a man to go with them to protect them. They didn't need a man to go with them in case they got lost.

Amazing. Truly amazing.

And so truly ... gratifying. To see this. To actually *see* this. Thank you.

Sports Competition, Sports Scholarships

In my novel *Gender Fraud: a fiction*, several people discuss the negative effect of gender recognition legislation on women's sports (in a nutshell, it allows men to compete in women's events and often they win ... sponsorships, scholarships ...) and one person suggests that sports should be categorized not by sex but, instead, by *directly* relevant factors, such as muscle mass (proportion and position), height, weight, even foot size (for swimming) ...

I'd go further and say let's just forget sports *competition* altogether, because, really, can we ever make it fair? Determining what we have is hard enough; determining what we've been born with (which creates an unfair advantage) and what we've developed (which is fair game for competition) is near impossible. Why not just have athletic *activity*? Why this obsessive desire to figure out who's *best*? Who *wins*? (And who's a LOSER ...) Enough with the 'You get a medal and all those advertising contracts because on a given day you ran a certain distance a tenth of a second faster than a bunch of other people.'

Sports *scholarships* in particular have *got* to go. On what grounds is *admission* to an institute of learning justified by *athletic* achievement? Because yes, universities are, should be, places for the intellect. They prepare scholars, architects, engineers, psychologists, mathematicians, biologists, physicists, chemists, doctors, lawyers ... What place do football players have there? (Who is it who insists they be there? Oh yeah.) It's not like they (the football players) don't cost a ridiculous amount of money to *be* there. Money that could be used for library resources, labs, etc. (All that money for sports scholar-ships could go to writing scholarships, math scholarships, science scholarships ...)

So in addition to, perhaps prior to, the elimination of sports scholarships to universities, I call for the elimination of sports at universities. (And so, too, the elimination of sports *competitions* between universities.) Sure, let's have gyms and fields. Physical activity often *enhances* mental activity. *Activity. Competition* is not required.

Football takes precedence ...

People are fleeing for their lives from Hurricane Florence, but there may not be enough rooms in Columbia hotels because—football. Apparently there's a (male) game scheduled for play and (mostly male) people have come to Columbia to watch.

Clear evidence of the male obsession with competition having a stranglehold—wait, the hurricane itself is clear evidence of that: a long but incontestable causal chain leads back from the increasing frequency and severity of storms to the desire of (overwhelmingly) male executives and stockholders (of, for example, oil companies) to become rich—i.e., to be #1, to win.

And as is their way, they give the hurricane a female name; as if we're to blame.

My god, is there no end to their psychopathology??

I'm ashamed to be male

I am ashamed to be male:

We turn everything into a weapon.

We are obsessed with competing, with being better than not our previous selves, but others.

We enjoy hurting. We tear the legs off flies, we put firecrackers into dogs' mouths, we attach electrodes to people's genitalia.

We are unable to experience pleasure without conquest.

We fell entitled, to everything.

We do not think of the consequences of our actions.

We expect others to clean up after us, to sweep up our messes, the wipe away our smudges, to pick up the things we just toss wherever we like, to fix the things we break ...

Half the human species is afraid of me.

They don't walk at night because of me.

They don't go out alone because of me.

So they can never enjoy the sunset, the night, the stars in solitude because of me.

They have to watch their drinks at bars because of me.

They are ever vigilant in public—on sidewalks, in subway stations—because of me.

And children are wary of every stranger's help, every stranger's generosity, every stranger's kindness because of me.

Transsexualism is a problem
only because sexism is a problem

Transsexualism is a problem only because sexism is a problem. (Transgenderism is no problem at all: females have been wearing pants and becoming doctors for ages, and there's nothing preventing males from wearing dresses and becoming nurses.)

If being female didn't put people at greater risk of sexual assault from males (though it's hard to say whether male violence is due to sexism, cultural pressures for males to differentiate themselves from females, or to their biology), it wouldn't matter whether male-bodied people were placed in women's shelters and women's prisons or allowed in women's washrooms and change rooms. In fact, there wouldn't need to *be* women's shelters and separate prisons, washrooms, and changerooms. (Although there could be, for reasons other than fear of violence: there could be male, female, and mixed sex facilities across the board.) There may not even be a need for sex-segregated services; we would need only sex-tailored services.

If being female-bodied didn't disadvantage athletes for most sports (as we have come to know them, which means male bodies have an advantage in most of them), it wouldn't matter whether they had to compete against male-bodied people. In fact, there wouldn't need to *be* sex-segregated sports.

If being female didn't mean unjustified subordinate treatment, there would be no need for compensatory programs or data collection to monitor such treatment. And so it wouldn't matter if male-bodied people skewed or eliminated such data collection (by making it illegal to record sex) or diminished the funding for such programs (should that be a consequence for refusing to serve male-bodied people).

In short, if there were no sexism, it wouldn't matter whether males said they were females and females said they were males. Just as it doesn't matter whether brown-haired people said they were red-haired (except maybe to a psychologist interested in delusion). (It *would* be a problem, however, if white-skinned people claimed to be black-skinned, because racism is a problem.)

But there *is* sexism, so it *does* matter. By identifying themselves as female, and demanding access to women-only services and activities, 'transwomen' are oblivious not only to biological reality, but also to sexism. Or perhaps they are simply insensitive to women's fears (which in itself suggests that they are *not* women, but are, in fact, still men). Because how can they not understand that someone with male levels of testosterone and male muscle mass is unwelcome in places where women would be vulnerable to their propensity to violence? Especially since there is much evidence showing that males prone to violence against women see nothing wrong with using deceit to gain access to women, and no evidence that males who are in various degrees of transformation are any less violent. (Of course 'transwomen' are also at risk of men's violence, just as effeminate men have always been, but that's a problem that *men*, not women, need to solve.)

So ... until sexism has been eradicated from our society, 'transwomen' will just have to abstain from sex-segregated sports and wax their own balls (or, here's an idea, go to waxing clinic that has personnel with experience waxing testicles—that is, a *men's* waxing clinic). Is that too much to ask?

As for public restrooms and change rooms, if 'transwomen' are afraid to continue using the men's rooms, they should lobby for trans' rooms, not the right to use women's rooms. As for prisons, I suppose 'transwomen' could lobby for separate trans facilities within men's prisons.

Further, to the extent that transsexualism involves transgenderism, it *depends on* sexism. If not for sexism, there would be no need to change sex in order to change gender. If not for sexism, there would be no gender: the various attributes that are grouped together and then aligned with one sex or the other would be just individual attributes, as likely to be present in, or desired by, any given male as any given female.

History, the News, Men, Women, Life, Death, Joy, Pain

History, many say, is nothing but violence, war, death ...
Yes, because men write it. If women wrote history, maybe
they'd put something else center stage. Maybe themselves.

And maybe if all that violence didn't make the front page,
there'd be less of it.

And maybe if men became unimportant, then what they
did would become unimportant.

But pain, death—it can't help but be important. Yes, but
there's been more birth than death. More joy than pain?
Perhaps. What I feel when I'm out paddling, the sparkles on
the lake, the music in my headphones, it'll never make the news.
For others, it's the delight of a child's giggle. For others still, it's
the spark of new knowledge, the glow of an antique restored.
These things do not make the news.

(But how powerful a new car is? That makes the news.
Every fucking day.)

Educating Women to Reduce Over-population.
(Right. *They're* the problem.)

So the other day I came across, yet again, mention of the idea that educating women would reduce over-population. I find that questionable. If education makes the difference, then why aren't we educating the men as well? And if the men are already educated, then clearly education isn't the solution: they're still impregnating/reproducing. (Perhaps advocates of such a solution are imagining that an educated woman is going to tell her uneducated husband or other would-be-impregnator to not stick his penis in her vagina, and the man will say 'Okay' and go do something else.)

I suggest that if we want to reduce over-population, we need to get rid of sexism. In a sexist society, men are valued more than women, so people want to have at least one son, so they keep reproducing until their goal is met. No sexism, no pressure to produce male babies, less reproduction.

In a sexist society, women have little control over their bodies, so contraception and abortion are often not easily available. No sexism, no mandatory pregnancy, less reproduction.

In a sexist society, men feel entitled to use women sexually without their consent. No sexism, no rape, less reproduction.

On getting paid. Or not.

So I was reading James Morrow's *The Wine of Violence* and when I got to "Will the *Journal of Evolution* publish it? Publish, it, hell, they'll make me an editor" (25), I stopped, puzzled for a moment. Then it hit me. To Francis, the character whose thoughts those are, becoming an editor means status and income. To me, it has just meant more work. That's how it is for women.

Case in point: for five years I served on the Ethics Committee of our local hospital. That meant I attended monthly meetings. I also offered to be on the Education sub-committee, which meant I prepared and delivered a special topics seminar each month; the Consultation sub-committee, which meant I'd meet with physicians who wanted assistance making decisions, and for which I researched and prepared an ethical-decision-making 'tree' (for which one of the physicians thanked me profusely, saying it has made such a difference, he was henceforth able to find a way through all the complexities and competing claims...); and the Research sub-committee, which meant I'd meet as needed to discuss research proposals put to the hospital, and for which I researched and prepared, again, a tool for decision-making (which has since been circulated among other hospitals who now use it). The nurses, doctors, and hospital administrators on the committee were paid because their participation was on 'hospital time'; the minister and lawyer on the committee were also paid for their participation by their parish and law company. As a sessional at the local university, I was paid per course; any community service I

279

decided to take on was 'on my own dime'—that is, on a purely volunteer, unpaid, basis.[1]

At one point, the committee arranged for the ethics officer of another hospital to come give a talk. He was paid to do so. He didn't say anything I couldn't say (and indeed hadn't already said in one form or another).

After five years, a new hospital was built with lots of bells and whistles; I thought it a good time to propose that I be hired as an on-site part-time ethics officer. The response to my proposal was 'no'. Just—no.

Women are expected to help, to assist; what they do is done as a favour. No one expects to pay them; it's why we ourselves don't expect to be paid.

Men, on the other hand, expect to be paid. And they are. They are the ones we help; they are the ones we assist. They do. We just help.

But take away any man's help, any man's assistants, and let's see how much he achieves, how many programs he develops and implements; how many books he writes; how many companies he creates and runs.

---

[1] No one questioned this. Hell, I didn't even question this. Because … for several years, I was on the editorial committee for a magazine, *Humanist in Canada*. I was not paid. I assumed no one else was either, but now I wonder about that.

I also offered to be on a committee preparing a website for the new high school Philosophy course. Again, I was not paid. Again, I assumed no one else was either, but, again, now I wonder about that.

On being wanted

Also while reading James Morrow's *The Wine of Violence*, I read " ... a world finally wanted his ideas" (119). That too stopped me. Because even academia, not just the world at large, has never wanted my ideas. Simply because they come from a female-embodied person.

Maybe that's why 'love' is so much more important to women than to men. And so too, marriage and kids. It's the only way they get wanted. (I bet when you read the title of this post, you were thinking about being wanted emotionally, sexually ... see?)

Why Men Like Fishing

I understand now why men like fishing.

First, there's the noise of the motor. Men like noise. They think *they're* the ones making it. So they think they sound like a lion or a bear. They think they're threatening. Instead of just bloody annoying.

Second, there's the stink of the exhaust fumes. Men like stink. Most of them are still farting at the dinner table and snickering about it.

Third, since they often go fishing with other men, they get to compete. Men like competing. Anywhere, anytime, with anyone, about anything. Consider the following typical scenario. First one of the men will stand, perhaps casually, explaining to his buddies that he can get a better cast. A mild discomfort will start to spread among the other guys, but not one of them will be able to explain it. Certainly it's not that they're afraid their buddy may fall out of the boat. Eventually a second guy will stand. And his discomfort will go away. Or at least recede a bit. Depending on how tall he is, relative to the first guy. The remaining two guys will become even more incomprehensibly uncomfortable, until eventually they too will stand. There. That's better. Despite the increasing precariousness of the whole. Then the first guy will stand up on one of the seats, and almost immediately another one will stand on the prow. Of course the lot of them will likely go overboard, but apparently that's not a foreseeable result.

Lastly, there's something very sexual, very masturbatory about reeling in, moving one's hand around and around at cock level. No wonder they wanna be a rock star strutting around on stage strumming an instrument slung low just right *there*. And no wonder men go fishing for hours.

Men, Women, and Fairness

It's not that men aren't fair. It's that they don't even think about fairness. When Linda Babcock and Sara Laschever (*Women Don't Ask*) asked people whether they deserved what they wanted, women typically responded with something like "... my training—what is really engrained in me—is that you're never quite deserving of what you might want" (58). Men, however, said things like "Um, sure, I deserve the things I want—yeah" (58) (he obviously hadn't really thought about it) and "Interesting question! ... The sense that I deserve something is not a sense that I carry with me, generally. Do I deserve this, or deserve that?" (59) (even more appalling). The authors summarized, "Where women are often preoccupied with ascertaining what exactly they deserve, it doesn't really cross Mike's [men's] mind to consider whether he deserves something or not—this approach isn't relevant to his thinking" (59).

Which explains this: "Because Linda hadn't asked to be promoted, the dean never even thought of her—she was off his radar" (64).

So, it's not that men aren't fair to women. It's that they really just don't think about it.

Babcock and Laschever also found that "only 7 percent of the female students had negotiated [for a higher initial salary] but 57 percent (eight times as many) of the men had asked for more money" (2). Why? I suggest it's because men think their wants are needs; it's because men think that what they want is *important*; it's because men think they're *entitled* to *get* what they want; and it's because men think they'll *get* what they ask for, and women don't. *And they're both right.* "'...[A]s a man I

283

have been raised with this sense of entitlement, that I should get what I want. And I almost think that societally women are conditioned that you don't always get what you want'" (74).

"...[M]odern Western culture—strongly discourages women from asking for what they want" (14). So true. women are taught to be give. Not to get. And then there's this:

"You might think that women also need to be assertive to negotiate successfully—able to present strong arguments, defend their interests and positions ... Unfortunately, research has revealed that assertive women are less well liked ... This means that an assertive woman, no matter how well she presents her arguments in a negotiation, risks decreasing her likeability and therefore her ability to influence the other side to agree with her point of view" (96). So damned if we do, damned if we don't. And this: Regarding an instance in which a man asked for more money out of a discretionary fund and the woman didn't, she says, 'This fund—I never knew of its existence ... It had never been publicized ... There is no application procedure...' (20). How is it the man knew about it and the woman didn't?

"'...[H]is father had taken them [the boys] out and ... taught them how to tip—basically, taught them how to slip the maître d' money for good tables or give some money to the guys who were in the band to play a good song ... how to circumvent the system to get what [they] wanted" (34). Yeah, my father didn't teach me that shit.

Stop Being Complicit
in your own Subordination

Although the cautionary 'Don't blame the victim' is important in the context of assault, especially sexual assault, especially in a sexist society in which women are typically blamed more than men (and why is that, exactly?), I think we have overgeneralized.

And although I would certainly put more blame on men than on women for our sexist society, because it is men who are in a position of dominance (with greater power comes greater responsibility), I do think women are often to blame. We have agency. We are not idiots. And often we are *not* coerced.

And yet, often, we are complicit in our own subordination. We speak in a higher register than is actually necessary and thus come across as child-like. We smile more often than we need to and thus cancel the importance of our words. We endorse the importance of our appearance by wearing make-up to cover blemishes and wrinkles and by constantly dieting. Worse, we emphasize the sexuality of our appearance—by reddening our lips, emphasizing our breasts,[1] exposing our legs—as a matter of *daily routine*.[2]

---

[1] A 'plunging' neckline points like an arrow to breasts that are likely padded and pushed up—is it any wonder you find yourself saying "My eyes are up here"? Talk about a mixed message.

[2] What if it were convention for men to wear their shirts with the sleeves rolled up and the top few buttons undone and to wear make-up that accentuated their jaw and cheek lines? Would they get chest hair implants and start obsessing about the muscularity of their forearms? Would they consider facial reconstruction surgery? And would women ever take them seriously?

No one coerces us to do any of that. Coercion is implicated when you allow yourself to be assaulted by your live-in partner because that's the only way to feed your kids, when you do not refuse because someone has drugged you, and when you shut the fuck up because otherwise he'll kill you. Coercion is *not* implicated when you wear make-up, high heels, and a sexualizing dress.

Cultural conditioning, social expectation, peer pressure— why go along with it all? Why not think for yourself? Consider the meanings, the implications, of what you do. For yourself. For others. And have the courage to refuse, to reject, whatever makes you into something you don't want to be.

I'm suspect of claims that one would be fired if one stopped performing femininity. (Try doing so in small increments.) (Try suing.) I imagine that yes, one might not be *hired* for some jobs if one doesn't perform femininity, but if possible, apply for a job somewhere else. And yes, since Hooters pays more than Walmart, I may be asking you to make a sacrifice. For the greater good.

Because only when men *don't* see us as hooters will the female sales associate at Walmart be considered for a managerial position. It seems to be all or nothing: if men see us as sexual, they see us as *only* sexual; if we have sexual power, we won't have any other kind of power, be it political, economic, or social. It's understandable to think otherwise, but most women realize, once they hit forty and whatever sexual attractiveness they had wanes, that any power they had to that point *was* in fact merely due to their sex, their sexuality. Not their knowledge, their ability, their competence. (And that realization requires a major rewrite of your life.)

So please, don't use your sex, or your sexuality, to get what you want. It makes it harder for the rest of us to be considered *persons*, with interests and abilities other than having sex and having kids.[3]

---

[3] I'll respond in advance to everyone who's thinking that I'm a prude, that I'm anti-

Yes, I know you *can* use your sexuality to get what you want. Men are idiot children when it comes to breasts, butts, and legs.

But make no mistake. They are in power. Over us. They own most of the property, they hold most of the managerial positions, they hold most of the political positions, they make more money than we do ... And they typically don't concern themselves with ethics[4] and that adds to their power: they will not hesitate to hurt us. Just take a look at contemporary porn, which is, thanks to the internet, viewed by most men, many of whom started when they were still kids. (You are, you become, what you expose yourself to.)

So please, just *don't* do it. Don't speak in your little girl voice. Don't smile at everything and everyone. Don't wear make-up and heels. Don't even expose your legs unless you're sure you're not being sexual about it (which means you don't shave). Present yourself as a person, not specifically a *female* person.

And don't expect a man to pay your way for anything. Only invalids and children need to have someone else pay their way. Don't even accept it because you think he's just being nice.

---

sex, that I don't like sex. You know what? You're right. I *am* anti-sex. I *don't* like sex. *Not as it typically occurs today.* Which is primarily *for men's pleasure*, often via women's pain (physical and psychological—anal penetration, vaginal penetration without sufficient lubrication, often accompanied by humiliation, degradation, insult ...). Sex *for women's pleasure* wouldn't even *involve* the penis! The clitoris (which is not in the vagina or the rectum) best responds to fingers.

While I'm at it, I'll also respond in advance to those women who reprimand me for abandoning the sisterhood. Excuse me? You are not my sister. We are accidentally the same sex. You have embraced the gender that society aligns with your sex. I have not. You're a woman. I am not. (And that you wonder, mocking, laughing, 'Well what *are* you?' indicates the depth of your internalization of the importance of sex. To everything. Including, most especially, your *identity*.)

[4] Even *speaking up* about doing the right thing gets them accused of being a wuss, of going soft. Which apparently is more than most men can bear.

He's not paying your way to be nice. He's paying your way to express his superiority (just watch how angry he gets when *you* insist on paying *his* way) and to underscore your need for him, your dependence on him.

Don't get married for the badge of maturity. It makes it that much harder for those of us who see marriage as the sexist trap it is: the unmarried are treated like children, perpetual teenagers who haven't yet grown up.

And unless you really like kids (did you want to become a nursery school teacher?), don't have them. It too is a badge of maturity and your endorsement of that irrationality makes it that much harder for those of us who choose to be child-free to be seen as adults. It too is a trap. In fact, in our society, there is no stronger, no more complete, trap into subordination. Because then you *will* need him. Then you *will* become dependent on him. Which will triple his power over you.[5] And kids make you vulnerable. Oh so vulnerable to threat, to blackmail, in all its subtle forms.

So just don't. Don't be complicit in your own subordination.

---

[5] Because look, you can't take your infant to work with you, so you *will* need someone to look after it while you're out earning rent, and that will cost, probably as much, or almost as much, as you make, so you *still* won't have rent … Better to form an alliance with another mother; you can work eight hours at your job while she looks after yours and hers, then she can work eight hours at her job while you look after hers and yours.

How many times?

Men are incredibly selfish and irresponsible. Every time they have sexual intercourse without a condom, they prove it. Because every time they have sex without a condom, they risk making someone else's life a living hell for twenty years (that's what it's like to be a parent against one's will).

And every time they have sex without a condom, they risk creating a new human being. One who will require food and water, and a computer and a car, and so on and so on. Our resources are not unlimited.

How many times does a man have sex without a condom? Studies show that only one-third use a condom. Sometimes.

I rest my case.

Men Need to Reclaim the Moral

Something I noticed when I taught Business Ethics, primarily to male students, is that men seem to think ethics is 'a girl thing'. What? *What?!* (My god, that can explain *everything!*)

Men routinely insult other men who express concern about doing the right thing: "What are you, a fucking boy scout?" Note that boy scouts are children.

Worse, men who raise ethical questions are accused of going *soft*, being *weak*, being a bleeding *heart*. Note that these qualities are associated with being female. It's thus *emasculating* to be concerned about right and wrong. *What?!*

Furthermore, ethics presumes caring, and real men don't care. They may protest that they can't 'afford' to care; they have to make real decisions about profit and war, and feelings just get in the way. As if ethics is all, only, about feelings. (Where did they get their education? Oh, they didn't. We don't actually *teach* ethics. Except in a few university courses.)

The problem with all this is that men run the world. And it's not going well.

So isn't it about time men reclaim the moral? If rising above the gendered worldview is too much, then just redefine your terms a bit. *Man up! Consider* (and then *do*) the right thing!

Rape: a men's issue

Men are the ones who rape, so why is rape a women's issue? Because men see nothing *wrong* with rape. Men: the sooner you recognize this, the sooner you'll see rape as a *men's* issue.

Picard ... Seriously?

So I watched *Star Trek: Picard*, wherein he saves the day, and the future, for the creation of synthetic life. A surprising move for someone so ... intelligent. Because with respect to the creation of organic life:

1. We have not been able to control how many we create. Our planet can comfortably sustain 2-3 billion people ('comfortably' defined as the current European standard of living) (which is about 60% of the current American standard). To date, there are 7.8 billion organic life forms in existence. And we're adding (that's net gain) 150 per minute.

2. Men often force women to create organic life (by raping them, when they aren't using, often because they don't have access to, effective contraception). Although statistics show that one-quarter (United States) to two-thirds (Africa) of all women are raped, we really don't know how often this is forced reproduction because, apparently, it's no big deal.

3. Men (primarily) also often force women to be incubators for organic life forms (by prohibiting abortion).

4. Once organic life is born, men (primarily) have been woefully irresponsible toward it, abandoning it in one way or another (financially, emotionally) or, worse, hurting it (up to 93% are beaten, and over a million are raped each year).

So, Jean-Luc, what is it that makes you think 'we' will be any more responsible when creating synthetic life?

Gwynne Dyer
(along with half the species)
misses an obvious point

I highly recommend Gwynne Dyer's *Climate Wars*, but I must say he misses an obvious point, especially evident when he says "There are almost seven billion of us, and it is almost impossible to imagine a way that we can stop the growth before there are eight and a half billion" (268)—because it's *very* possible to imagine a way: men just have to stop ejaculating into women's vaginas.

Just think: the devastating climate changes that have already begun to happen (i.e., the beginning of the now-inevitable end of life as we know it) could've been avoided if we'd kept our greenhouse gases to under 350 ppm—which would have been so easy if we'd kept our population to a certain level.

So it begs the question: why is *not* ejaculating into women's vaginas so unimaginable for men?

The APA is so Fucked Up

Why Are Some People Transgender? an APA pamphlet asks.[1]

Their answer? "Many experts believe that biological factors such as genetic influences and prenatal hormone levels, early experiences, and experiences later in adolescence or adulthood may all contribute to the development of transgender identities."

Um, no. People are transgender because they are intelligent and thoughtful enough to realize that gendered behaviours are typically constraining and that feminine behaviours in particular are subordinating. And so, they reject them; they refuse to conform to the gender expectations aligned to their sex.

How Does Someone Know They Are Transgender? the pamphlet then asks.

Their answer? "They may have vague feelings of "not fitting in" with people of their assigned sex or specific wishes to be something other than their assigned sex. Others become aware of their transgender identities or begin to explore and experience gender-nonconforming attitudes and behaviors during adolescence or much later in life."

Again, no. I know I'm a writer because when I write, I actually realize that that's what I'm doing when I do it. Similarly, when I refuse to wear make-up and high heels, I

---

[1] "What Does It Mean to Be Transgender?" from "Answers to Your Questions About Transgender People, Gender Identity, and Gender Expression" American Psychological Association 2011. apa.org/topics/lgbtq/transgender

know I'm doing it. I'm that aware. And I know it's transgressive. I'm also that aware. I *know* what the gender expectations are in our society, so I know when I'm refusing to meet them. That's how I know I'm transgender.

One doesn't "become aware" of one's gender identity. One *creates* it. One *chooses* it. Unlike sex,[2] sexual orientation, height, skin colour, eye colour ... *gender is not a biological given*. It's an arbitrary collection of preferences that our culture says should you should adopt: the so-called feminine collection is supposed to be adopted by female people, and the so-called masculine collection is supposed to be adopted by male people. Do you always do what you're supposed to do?

---

[2] Which is why it's particularly disturbing that professional psychologists believe that "Sex is assigned at birth ..." No, sex is *recognized* at birth (or before, if a conclusive ultrasound is obtained). Typically by external genitalia.

In a late-breaking story,
Caitlyn Jenner ...

In a late-breaking story, Caitlyn Jenner now says she's black.

"Deep down inside, I've always felt black," she confessed, smiling at the cameras despite recent surgery that has left her lips overly puffy. Her nose will be widened in a subsequent surgery, and she has already begun skin dye treatments. "I can't wait to get my afro, yo!" she added, doing something vaguely black with her hands.

An unnamed spokesperson from the NAACP applauded Jenner's honesty, adding that Latisha (formerly Caitlyn) (formerly Bruce) is a role model for blacks everywhere. "We may well be nominating her for the Black Woman of the Year Award!"

Why do men *seek* arousal?

So I'm reading Robert Jensen (*Getting Off: Pornography and the end of masculinity*), and he says porn is intended to provide sexual arousal. Sexual *arousal*? Not sexual *satisfaction*? If you're not aroused in the first place, why would you intentionally try to *get* aroused? Because then you'll just have to find a way to deal with it. If you don't happen to be itchy, you wouldn't intentionally go sit in a patch of poison ivy to *get* itchy. Because then you'll just be uncomfortable until you can scratch. If you're not hungry, you wouldn't intentionally fast in order to *feel* hungry. I don't get it. It makes sense only under three conditions.

One, the state of arousal is itself pleasing. This may be true, but since men seem to prefer ending the erection to maintaining it all day, I'm rejecting this possibility. The arousal is clearly just a means to an end.

Two, the satisfaction of sexual arousal is mind-blowing—a pleasure far *beyond* the satisfaction of an itch or hunger. If that's the case, and if men are therefore intentionally seeking arousal in order to achieve that pleasure, we're talking addiction. Which, actually, makes sense of a lot. Imagine that boys become naturally addicted to something (the endorphins released with orgasm) when they hit puberty and that they stay addicted well into their forties. Their gross misconduct (look around—this is *not* the best possible world)? Explained. Imagine that the best supply of the pleasure is a female body.[1] Their misogyny? Explained.

---

[1] Suspect. Unless the pleasure of emotional attachment (unlikely, given their behaviour) or conquest (more likely, given our sexist society) is added into the equation.

No doubt only cultural conditioning keeps them from seeking castration. Which takes us to three: the socialization we put males through from day one ensures that sexuality—arousal and satisfaction—is not just a physical phenomenon. It's inextricably bound with their identity, their self-esteem, their self-respect. Sex arousal and satisfaction are measures of masculinity. And masculinity is *the* measure of (a) man.

Misogyny: a clear case of projection

Misogyny is a simple and clear case of psychological projection, a defence mechanism whereby one denies the existence of a quality in oneself and instead attributes it to the other ('It's not me, it's you'). Men hate that they want us, that their thought, their behavior, is so overwhelmingly and relentlessly occupied with wanting us. Instead of identifying them*selves* as the source of the sexual attraction (and so the problem is that they, men, are sexually attracted), they identify *women* as the source (and so the problem is that they, women, are sexually attracting). And so they hate *us*, they hurt and kill *us*. When the rational thing would be to hate *themselves*, hurt and kill *themselves*.

Actually, no, the rational thing would be to simply take the drugs that *reduce* their desire so it's *not* overwhelming and relentless. But what do they do instead? Take drugs that *increase* their desire. (*Who* was it who said they were the rational ones?) Because the greater their sexual desire, the more manly they are. But the greater their sexual desire, the more they hate us. So, the more manly they are, the more they hate us. Despite the faulty logic, that rings true: only wusses actually *like* women. That is to say, it accurately reflects the psychopathic notion of manliness. (And *that* would be *another* rational thing to do: reject the notion of manliness.)

Why are cosmetics routinely sold in pharmacies?

Why are cosmetics routinely sold in pharmacies? Pharmacies are for health products. Products that contribute to and maintain *health*, mostly physical health, but also psychological health. Not only do cosmetics *not* contribute to or maintain physical health, they *compromise* physical health. They cause damage: cancer, endocrine disorders, developmental delays, neurological disorders, and more.

So … are they presumed to contribute and maintain *psychological* health? Perhaps. I've heard that many women can't leave the house without their face 'on'. But if that's the case, better they seek psychological counselling or a feminist consciousness-raising group. Because there's something seriously wrong with thinking you need to always appear beautiful and young. There's something seriously deficient with uncritically accepting such social norms.

How many men are addicted to porn?

How many men are addicted to porn? We don't know. There are no visible symptoms. No, that's not true. The visible symptoms are what we call normal behaviour.

She wanted it.

She was dressed all prim and proper = She wanted it
She was dressed like a slut = She wanted it

She was aggressive = She wanted it
She was submissive = She wanted it

She ran = She wanted it
She didn't run = She wanted it

She was afraid = She wanted it
She wasn't afraid = She wanted it

She screamed = She wanted it
She didn't scream = She wanted it

Where did all the good guys go?

Sometimes I feel like I haven't grown up at all: I didn't get married; I didn't have kids; I didn't fall into any kind of career path. Basically, I'm still doing what I did in my twenties: reading, writing, thinking, listening to music, and running/walking through the forest. In short, my passions haven't changed.

But then I listened to the 'best of' CDs that I made a few years ago from the hundreds of 45s and LPs I purchased in my teens and twenties.

And I discovered how much I *have* matured. Or at least changed. It's impossible to listen to *any* of the songs I once loved, often with an obsessive addiction (I make great use of the 'repeat' mode on my CD players) (great invention, that!), in quite the same way as I once did.

Was I ever that innocent? That naïve, that young? That *stupid*? Gallery's "It's so nice to be with you", James Taylor's "You've got a friend", Simon and Garfunkel's "Bridge over Troubled Water", England Dan and John Ford Coley, Seals and Croft, Chicago, Bread, The Commodores ...

Or were men really better people then?

If the latter, what the hell happened? Where did all the good guys go? How is it we're on the brink of extinction, what with our dependence on oil and meat, our irresponsible treatment of our water and our forests ... How is it that the internet has enabled the pornification of sex, the 'entitled male' ... All those good men are now in their 60s. So they would have been the CEOs and board members that have led us down this awful path ...

Consider …

"Knock three times on the ceiling if you want me, Twice on the pipe if the answer is no."

See? See how easy it is to ensure consent? Do you see how the guy doesn't just assume he's entitled to sex? And are you guessing that if she knocks twice on the pipe, he's *not* going to go kill her because—because she *doesn't* want him?

And "Tie a yellow ribbon 'round the old oak tree, it's been three long years, do you still want me …"

And "If you want my body and you think I'm sexy, come on sugar, let me know!"

See? He doesn't assume. He invites her to show some interest, some willingness …

("Give me a dime so I can phone my mother"? What? She doesn't have a dime on her? Well, okay, still. At least she's calling her mother to let her know.)

Though …

It's a good thing I didn't process the end of "1, 2, 3, Red Light"—"1, 2, 3, red light won't stop me …" All I heard was "1, 2, 3, red light" over and over (it's pretty much every second line in the song): a young woman is saying 'no' to what we would have called 'going all the way'.

"If her daddy's rich, take her out for a meal, if her daddy's poor, just do what you feel … "

So, what, rich women have to wined and dined first, but poor women are okay to rape?

"We're not bad people ... but we do as we please."

Um ... if you do as you please, without regard for other people, you *are* bad people. Sing along with *me*, dee-dee dee-dee dee.

And ...

"Don't ya love her madly, wanna be her daddy."

Don't ya wanna be in a position of authority over her, maybe engage in a little incest?

"Go away, little girl ..."

Little girl? Yes, let's double the diminutives, make *sure* she knows her place.

"I'm not supposed to be alone with you."

Then *you* go away! Don't foist the responsibility on *her*! (Especially if she really *is* a little girl.)

"Young girl, get out of my mind, my love for you is way out of line, better run, girl, you're much too young, girl ..."

Again, *you* better run.

"You're sixteen, you're beautiful, and you're mine."

Given that the man singing this isn't also sixteen, or even seventeen or eighteen ...

"You're my baby" emphasizes the point.

(Though women call their male lovers 'baby' too ... This has always disturbed me ... Why the need, the desire, to infantalize the loved one?)

"You're my pet."

Seriously? Seriously.

And oh my god, this: "Brown sugar how come you taste so good, now? ... Just like a young girl should, now ... Just like a black girl should."

Racist sexist pedophilist. And we made him a rock star.

And this: "She stood there laughing, I felt the knife in my hand and she laughed no more."

Atwood. Men are afraid women will laugh at them; women are afraid men will kill them.

And ...

"Brandy, you're a fine girl ... When he told his sailor stories, she could feel the ocean fall and rise, she saw its ragin' glory ..."

So why doesn't *she* become a sailor? Sounds like she's in love with the ocean at least as much as with the sailor who left. Sounds like she'd rather be out there than in some bar serving

306

whiskey and wine all night. (Unless she'd be raped by the crew every day …)

"We'll see the world through my Harley."

Why can't she get her own Harley?

"Having my baby."

My baby? MY baby??

"What a lovely way of saying how much you love me."

What? The woman's an idiot if that's why she's pregnant, if that's why she's going to go through labour then give up her life for twenty years to look after another human being. (And if her face *is* glowing, that's just the oxytocin.)

And yet, and yet …

So many songs from the 60s and 70s are sexy in a warm or sensual way: "Make It With You", "The Air that I Breathe", Barry White …

So many celebrate friendship, not sex: "I'll be There", "United We Stand", "You've Got a Friend", "You are the Sunshine of my Life" …

So many are just joyful: "Saturday in the Park", "Dancin' in the Moonlight", "Me and You and a Dog named Boo" …

Many are impressively honest: "Neither One of Us", "Don't Expect Me to Be Your Friend", "Rock me gently … I have never been loved like this before ..." (by a woman on top? or is he a virgin? either way ...), "Everybody plays the fool some time..." "Billy, don't be a hero ..." "All by myself" ...

Many are introspective, thoughtful, insightful: "I learned the truth at seventeen, that love was meant for beauty queens ...", "Taxi", "Father and Son" ...

And many are simply outstanding: "War", "I will survive" ...

Jeannie C. Riley's "Harper Valley, P. T. A." showed us that a woman, a mom, can be a bad-ass.

Steppenwolf's "Born to be Wild" surely influenced my decision to get a bike and head out on the highway ...

Elvis Presley's "In the Ghetto"—sure, okay, Presley himself probably never gave a cent to that kid in the ghetto, but still, that such a song was out there ...

Joe Cocker's "With a little help from my friends", Donovan, Cat Stevens, Harry Chapin, The Moody Blues, The Eagles ...

The Beatles— "You say you want a revolution, well, you know we all want to change the world ... But when you talk about destruction, don't you know that you can count me out" ...

How did we get from there to ... Eminem and XXXTentacion?

What happened?

When men are raped

When men are raped, as they often are in prison, does anyone ask them are they sure they didn't want it? Does anyone come even *close* to suggesting they asked for it, they are to be blamed for it? Is anyone quick to add 'alleged' to the report?

Crying Rape for Regret

Regarding the view that women 'cry rape' when they regret having had sex, let's concede for a moment that that's true. The concession begs the question: *why do so many women regret having sex?*

Even if it turned out to be a mediocre experience—if the man wasn't very good at it, due to lack of skill or lack of maturity (in terms of wanting the woman to have an orgasm too)—one would hardly cry *rape*.

Perhaps the woman got pregnant. If she didn't want to get pregnant, one would think she'd either be using contraception or she'd trust the man to wear a condom. So either the contraception didn't work or the man didn't wear a condom (or took it off part way through) or he promised to 'pull out' before ejaculation (not knowing that semen can get into a woman's vagina even before ejaculation).

However, my guess is that the woman thought they were going to make love, and it turned out he was just fucking her. Worse, she realized (once she realized it *was* just a fuck) that she'd get a bad rep, to put it mildly: her name would circulated, the guy would post humiliating comments, maybe even images, on social media, etc., etc., etc. It makes perfect sense: as long as women who consent to sex are considered sluts, they'll be tempted to cry rape—non-consent.

So men, you don't want to be charged with rape? Don't have sex the woman will regret: make it great sex; use a condom; and don't consider the woman a slut because she wanted it.

Making Fun of Rapists

1. Big words confuse them. They think 'No' means 'Yes'.

2. They have no sense of direction. They confuse running *away* with running *toward*.

3. They have a questionable understanding of basic biology. They think they *need* sexual intercourse. (Like, what, if they can't stick their dick into some woman's vagina, they'll die? Wouldn't that be nice.)

4. They also seem to think pregnancy is under a woman's voluntary control. (Wouldn't *that* be nice.)

5. They don't seem to understand the difference between fiction and reality: they think porn movies are documentaries.

6. And they're completely incapable of logical thinking. For example, if it's no big deal, as they assure us when we resist, why are they *forcing* us?

7. And they're so thin-skinned, aren't they? When someone politely expresses a lack of interest in having sex with them, they completely lose their shit.

It's not poverty, stupid.

Poverty is not the cause of crime. Because even when men have enough, they steal more, kill for more. Think of all those rich white CEOs. They couldn't possibly have *earned* their riches. There are not enough hours in the day. Assuming a fair wage. Think of all those men who manufacture, buy, and sell weapons. All those men who traffic girls and women. No, it's not poverty that makes them do it.

Hunting: only men

It's hunting season again—moose for a week, then deer for two weeks—and I have yet to hear an acceptable justification.

The animals are having enough trouble surviving because of what we've done, and what we're still doing, to the forests. And now you want to just go out and kill them.

Oh, but we kill only the old and the sick. We cull the herd and keep it healthy. First, liar. One of you shot a moose calf just the other day. Second, herd? Seriously? When's the last time you saw a *herd* of moose or deer? Third, if you were really killing them out of compassion, you'd tranquilize then euthanize them—not shoot them (I doubt one shot from your gun kills them instantly and painlessly).

And my favourite: we like the meat. *Only men would think that their liking, their wanting, something justifies the use of lethal force to get that something.*

On gender identity
and changing your sex

Let's say we *are* born with a gender identity. Either (1) it isn't a binary, in which case there's no need to change your sex to attain some sort of 'fit' or (2) it is binary, but it doesn't necessarily or always align with sex, in which case again there's no need to change your sex, or (3) it *is* binary and it *does* align with sex, in which case one couldn't possibly feel a mismatch— feeling a mismatch would just prove that (2) is the case.

I suppose one could say that for 99% of us, it is aligned, and those who feel a mismatch are anomalies, but look around at all the women who are *not* feminine. Are we *all* anomalies? If so, then we're not really anomalies, are we. (And even if we are, so what? How does that necessitate chemical or surgical transformation?)

The "M" Word on Primetime TV!

I'm delightfully surprised by the current (last) season of *Scandal.* I had trouble getting into the show, and actually, I'm surprised I'm still with it; catching a glimpse of a political debate between two women and Melly's bid for the presidency kept me involved, even though I don't really like her, or Olivia …

And this season, Olivia's arrogance is *really* off-putting, but my god, her 'Monument or Asterisk' speech to Melly—she actually used the word 'misogyny'! The "M" word! Spoken by a character on primetime TV!! Been waiting for that for almost fifty years.

And then in a subsequent episode, Marcus takes Fitz to task for his white privilege.

And for turning Olivia into a 'black ho'. Bring it on!

And that was *after* he lands that "Welcome to the plight of almost every successful woman in the history of mankind" remark. (Though pity he didn't say 'humankind'.)

Who *are* these writers? And why weren't they on the show since the beginning? (If I'm reading the IMDB site correctly, the writer has always been Shonda Rhimes. Hm.) (Perhaps that shouldn't surprise me: perhaps if she'd used the "M" word in the first episode, she wouldn't've gotten any further.)

(Though I have to say … I worry that Olivia will set feminism *back* fifty years if she continues with, well, murder and blackmail. People will say shit like 'See what happens when we let women in power?' conveniently forgetting that every man in power that has done the same …)

"Men need Sex" —
a story about a story

So I wrote a story, "Men Need Sex." I started with the mistaken, but wide-spread, belief that men need sex (PIV). Mistaken because, unlike food, water, and oxygen, without sex, you don't die. Then, 'inspired' by Roger Elliott, I thought, '*What if?*' What if men really *did* die if they didn't get sex. I postulated contagion, perhaps social. Then I postulated a shortening incubation period (between belief, not getting sex, and suicide). And I added the belief that men are entitled to get what they need, which ramped up rape and, consequently, women's self-quarantine (after begging, to no avail, for stricter gun laws and a curfew for men). I ended the story with something like 'And then the women just ... waited.'

The *SciPhi Journal* rejected it. Which was disappointing, because I thought the story was clearly sf with a philosophical element ("As its primary mission, *SPJ* wishes to provide a platform for idea-driven fiction, as opposed to the character-driven mode that has come to predominate speculative fiction"). *Future Fire* also rejected it, which was also disappointing, because they focus on feminist sf. But what I want to focus on is the first rejection because it came with the explanation that my story "reads as a fully seriously intended apology of gendercide."

How is what I described gendercide? The women didn't kill the men; they just waited for them to kill themselves. Yes, they withheld sex, but if you'll die without food and I refuse to give you food, am I killing you? *Perhaps.* The philosophical community has not yet come to a consensus on that; it's called the passive euthanasia vs. active euthanasia debate (and the *SciPhi* editor should have been well aware of that debate).

Framed another way, if you'll die without being able to hurt someone, and no one steps forward to be hurt, are we all killing you? Not at all clear. *That's* called the Good Samaritan debate (and again, the *SciPhi* editor should have been well aware of it), often illustrated by the scenario of a drowning child: if the passerby is a competent swimmer, then yes, she has a duty to rescue, but if the passerby cannot swim, and the rescue puts her own life at risk, then no, she has no duty to rescue. The essential question is 'On what grounds would one have a duty to sacrifice oneself for another?'

So the question is 'Does intercourse put a woman's life at risk?' If she has no contraception and no abortion, if she's forced to become pregnant and then doesn't miscarry, well, maybe. It is not uncommon for a woman to die giving birth. At a minimum, there is a clear risk to her health: high blood pressure, diabetes, anemia, stroke, cardiac arrest. Perhaps the *SciPhi* editor is unaware of the health risks of pregnancy and childbirth…

But even *with* contraception and abortion, why is she obligated to allow herself to be hurt (yes, men, sexual intercourse against our will, absent our desire, typically hurts) (maybe that's what the *SciPhi* guy didn't get?) so that the man will live? If it's a one-time thing, and the man in question is a good man (yes, that would figure into *my* deliberation), okay, maybe many of us would, and should, say yes. Ten minutes, in and out, go on, live.

But if it's an ongoing thing, like the provision of food (which is what my story suggests), then the scenario would be very much like one sex, male, enslaving another, female; men imprisoning women to ensure continued sexual access and, therefore, their continued existence.

All that aside, the editor said "Art is free, and I won't criticise any apology of anything." Okay, then, an apology for gendercide, should that have been what my story was about, would have been okay. "However," he continued, "all pieces of writing for *SPJ* must have at least a grain of plausibility." When I pointed out that I'd referenced Elliot Rodger and Alex Minassian, he said he hadn't heard of either one. What? *What?* (I keep forgetting that since words like sexism and misogyny aren't used on primetime tv or in mainstream news, most people—in the U.S. and Canada, at least, because their entire worldview is formed by those two media—aren't familiar with the concepts. And it keeps shocking me when I remember that.) (But wait, weren't both Rodger and Minassian reported in mainstream news?) My guess is the editor just didn't read my story very carefully. (Both Rodger and Minassian were referenced in *footnotes*.) And why might that be? Because ... oh, right. It was written by a woman.

He went on to say "As a 100% gay male, I can assure you that your statements about ALL men are quite off the mark ..." Quite apart from the fact that any statements I may have made about ALL men would have been in the context of the story, *a fiction*, I never *made* any statements about ALL men; in fact, I quite deliberately say "Of course not all men" at one point.

"On the other hand," he continued, "the funny notion implied in your story that women don't need sex is also wrong". Oh do tell, please, go ahead and mansplain women's sexuality to me.

"Myself and quite a few of my gay male friends have had experiences of being sexually harassed by women. Therefore, women seem to need sex as well." *Therefore?* Okay, at this point, I'm thinking the editor of a philosophical science fiction journal doesn't have a philosophy degree. Or perhaps a degree of any kind.

In a subsequent email (because yes, I responded to his rejection letter, refuting his points; I'm tired of just letting these things happen without challenge), he said "At any case, there is too much hate shown by the narrator to be humanely appealing." Need I point out all the sf in which male narrators show too much hate of women to be humanely appealing? (Yes, men, any time you write a story or novel in which the males subordinate or sexualize the females, you're expressing hatred of women.)

And, in yet another email, he said "There is no lack of publishing venues that would gladly accept any kind of male-bashing. SPJ is not one of them." To which I replied, "It's just ... disappointing that you didn't see that the story is actually an argument against male entitlement and an exposé of, and a cautionary tale about, toxic masculinity."

On Advertising (again)

Advertising has gained such phenomenal power, it's now allowed pretty much everywhere. And because it's allowed pretty much everywhere, it has gained phenomenal power.

In fact, it has almost single-handedly destroyed the concept of public space because of its invasion of said public space with constant and loudly-proclaimed messages intended for private gain (not for the public good).

This power has increased tremendously with the Internet. No need to go into detail: everyone who uses the Internet is familiar with the intrusive pervasiveness of advertising. More than that, given the addictiveness of online games and social media, advertising in those contexts is especially pernicious.

And who is it who creates all these ads? Who is it who decides which words and which images the rest of us will be forcibly exposed to day and night for most of our lives? Predominantly, male business students. Male business *B* students. (They're the ones who major in Marketing.) That is to say, largely uneducated young men. Who probably didn't take any courses in the sciences or the humanities after high school (and they probably didn't do very well in those courses *in* high school). Who probably took just one psychology course during university, the one focusing on manipulating human behaviour. And who probably haven't read a book, not one, since they graduated (and they probably read as little as possible of the books they were supposed to read *before* they graduated). All of which is to say that they probably have very little comprehension of sexism, racism, environmental responsibility, ... In fact, I remember reading the words of one young man who'd said "I was studying political science at the time, so I had never thought about social processes like misogyny and sexism." (What? *What?!*) And I suspect business students are even less aware, less informed, than poli-sci students.

So they have no clue as to the consequences, for both men and women, of seeing images of subordinated and/or sexualized women every day all day. They are similarly clueless about the consequences of showing pick-up trucks and ATVs driving through pristine forests. They know that attention is grabbed by flashing lights, and they surely know that driving a car requires one's full attention, but apparently they can't put two and two together and so continue to put huge billboards with flashing lights along roads.

And here's the thing: people should understand the consequences of their actions before they're granted unsupervised freedom to act. Certainly before they're granted the power to bombard people with harmful words and images. With power should come responsibility.

So how is it that our government grants them such power? How is it that it allows such harm? On such a large and relentless scale? Legislation is for idiots, for those who cannot govern themselves, and clearly ...

(What's that you say? Freedom of expression? But freedom of expression is not, should not be, *unlimited*. It is justifiably constrained when it violates others' rights ... to privacy (to be free from intrusion), to safety (to be free from harm), to autonomy (to be free of manipulation) ...)

321

To the transwomen who insist they're women

You insist sex isn't binary, but you insist that you're a woman. Why not just be a transwoman, someone between the poles of male and female, somewhere along the spectrum? Wouldn't that make more sense?

The Last Man on Earth
Explains Everything

The Last Man on Earth explains everything. But he's too stupid, too infantile, and too self-centered, to know it. Which is exactly why he explains everything.

1. He enjoys knocking things over, breaking things, destroying things.

He rams his grocery cart into a pyramid of cans. He rolls bowling balls into a row of aquariums.[1] Apparently delighted to hear the smash. His reaction to blowing up one car with another is orgasmic. What does that tell us? *Destroying things gives men pleasure.*

2. He wantonly pollutes the water. That is to say, he does not use resources responsibly. And that is to say, he exhibits extremely short-sighted thinking.

He uses a swimming pool for a toilet.[2] A metaphor if there ever was one. In more ways than one. (In addition to the despoiling of resources, it shows us how full of shit he is.) (And that he is, quite literally, an asshole.)

---

[1] And of course, he won't clean up the broken glass. But, well, he's the last man on Earth, and, hey, if he doesn't bother him … So if, when, he discovers he's *not* the last person on Earth, if, when, he discovers there are other people in the world, other people who might want to walk there without getting cut up, will he go back *then* and clean up the mess he made? Of course he will. And pigs will fly.

[2] It brings to mind the patch of garbage floating around in the Pacific Ocean that's twice the size of the United States. And all the industrial waste—70% of it—that men (most likely) pour directly into our fresh water.

He does this, perhaps, because he figures he can just move into a new house whenever he's finished wrecking the one he's in.[3] Again, such a metaphor. (We've used up our own water and oil, so let's go to someone else's country and use up theirs.) (And when we've used up Earth, we'll go live on the Moon.)

Is it that, like other infants, Phil doesn't understand "All gone!"?[4]

Is it that he lacks the ability to imagine the long-term consequences of his behaviour?

And does he really think he's the only one left? What a special little snowflake he is. Sure, he drove all over the country. Calling out from an RV. Real thorough. Apparently, he didn't consider the possibility that someone might be alive, but be hurt or in other need of help that would require him to actually *get out* of the RV and *walk around* a bit.

But that's Phil. He thinks the world is all about him now. (Actually, he's probably thought that all along.)

3. *He doesn't really do much else.*

Well, he eats a lot of junk food. And he drinks a lot of alcohol.

4. *He thinks about himself.*

He thinks about how lonely he is. Which may seem paradoxical, given how incapable he is of thinking about other people. But he's incapable of thinking about what other people

---

[3] The truly disgusting shape of the house he's living in after a mere five months brings to mind that thing about if the history of the Earth were a year, life wouldn't appear until March, multi-cellular organisms not until November, we'd show up on December 31, by late evening, we'd have well-developed brains—and then it'd take us a mere forty seconds to thoroughly trash the place.

[4] He glories in there being no rules or, more specifically, in there being no rule-enforcer: like a child, he hasn't developed any rules of his own.

might *need* or *want.* He's lonely because of what *he* needs and wants. (Which explains why, when he finds himself so utterly alone, his cry sounds more like the wail of an infant than an existential scream.[5])

No surprise, then, that

5. *He considers half the human species merely as things to be fucked.*

Almost the first words we hear him say are about how much he misses women. Since that comes right after apologies to God for masturbating so much, we know he misses women because he uses them to masturbate. (Not because they might know the cure for the virus.)

And just in case we missed this, we see him choosing porn over food in the grocery store,[6] and we see his lingering gaze at the female-bodied mannequin.

So that's three times in the first six minutes we get this message: women are sexual objects for his use.[7]

When he dreams about a woman eagerly kissing him, the woman is, of course, gorgeous. Why is it that unattractive men always think women will find them attractive? More incredibly, why is it that *un*attractive men think *attractive* women will find them attractive? Seriously. How deluded do you have to be

---

[5] That he continues to believe there's a God also indicates just how child-like Phil is. He may as well be writing Dear Santa letters.

[6] That pornographic magazines, magazines in which women are for the most part humiliated and degraded, are openly for sale, even in grocery stores, without disapproval by the writers or Phil is clear evidence of the rampant misogyny I'm pointing out.

[7] It's pretty much what the writers think about women. In the very first episode, we see there's also a woman alive. But is the series titled, then, *The Last Man and Woman on Earth?* Of course not. Women are not worth mention. (Well, except, as fuckholes.)

about your own attractiveness?[8]

And again, just in case we missed this, when Carol introduces herself as "the last woman on Earth," we see from the look on his face that he's thinking he may have to break the bro pledge, "I wouldn't fuck her if she was the last woman on earth."

Phil thinks he's the last man on Earth because some virus wiped out everyone else. That may have been the proximate cause. (Or just bad writing.) It's likely that climate change, due to melting polar ice, due to increased greenhouse gases, due to relentless fossil fuel use and meat consumption, changed disease vectors which, along with the consequent disruption in the supply of goods and services (food, water, drugs; medical care), created a perfect storm for the virus to become a global epidemic.

He's the last man on Earth because he gets pleasure from destroying things, because he doesn't live responsibly, because he thinks only of himself, his own (primarily physical) needs and wants HERE! and NOW! In short, because he's disgustingly infantile.

I don't find that at all entertaining, let alone insightful, so I stopped watching.[9, 10]

---

[8] But of course, whether or not the woman is attracted to doesn't even cross his mind; can we say 'rapist mentality'?

[9] Who *does* find that entertaining? And *why*?

[10] And does *anyone* find it insightful? I mean, really, is *any* of this *news*?

Why aren't more men insulted by the low standards we set for them?

If he changes a diaper, he's father of the year.

If he cooks something, anything, he's a chef.

If he marries, but otherwise continues to live pretty much as he has to that point, he's suddenly respectable.

If he continues to pay a child's ball game into adulthood, he gets paid a six-figure salary.

If he gets a B.A., he's an expert in his field.

If he writes a book full of incoherence and grammatical mistakes, he gets (edited and then) published.

We don't expect men to pick up after themselves.

We don't expect them to be sensitive to other people's emotions, or even be aware of their own.

We don't expect them to be aware of, let alone appreciative of, natural beauty.

We don't expect them to be interested in children.

We don't expect them to be in control of their sexual impulses or their aggressive impulses.

Do I hate men?

Yes, generally speaking, I do.

I hate the way they take up more physical space than necessary, sprawling over the confines of their chairs, elbowing the people beside them.

I hate the way they take up more conversational space, speaking slowly, repeating themselves, and making irrelevant comments that derail the discussion.

I hate the way they lecture me as if I'm a child.

I hate the way they automatically assume they know more than me. Even when they're students in a class I'm teaching.

I hate the way they feel entitled to tell me what my problems are, to tell me whether I measure up to their standards, to tell me whether I please them or not.

I hate that they work less hard in school, obtain lower grades, and yet receive better job offers.

I hate that they get paid more for work of equal or lesser value.

I hate that they relentlessly sexualize women so we are reduced to nothing but our sex.

I hate that they sexually assault women.

I hate that they kill women who have been sexually assaulted.

I hate that they are entertained by images that humiliate and degrade women, and start watching such images as early as ten years of age.

I hate that they buy and sell girls for their sexual use.

I hate that they enjoy hunting and killing animals.

I hate their reluctance to engage in self analysis, to take responsibility for any of the above, to change any of the above.

I hate that they like the way things are.

So the question that should be asked is not do I hate men, but why do you not?

That said, I also hate women.

I hate the way they defer to men.

I hate the way they expect a man to pay their way through life.

I hate that they accept the privileged status that accompanies being married to a man.

I hate that they sexualize themselves with make-up and clothing as a matter of routine.

I hate that they pretend to enjoy sexual intercourse when they don't.

I hate that they have children even when they don't really want them.

(I like people. People who have not accepted the straitjackets of gender.)

And, possibly related, ...

We're barely in the top quarter when it comes to the gender gap in wages (we're fourth worst).

We're barely in the top quarter when it comes to the gender gap in health (it's safer to be pregnant in Estonia than in Canada).

Speaking of which, we're one of the last six countries *in the developed world* not to have paternity leave.

We're apparently unable to produce even one female Nobel prize winner (every single one of Canada's 21 Nobel Laureates have been men).

We're barely in the top quarter when it comes to the gender gap in political power (even Rwanda, Senegal, South Africa, Mozambique, Costa Rica, Uganda, Angola, Nepal, Serbia, Slovenia, Ethiopia, and Mexico have more women in their parliaments than Canada does).[1]

---

[1] thestar.com/news/canada/2010/02/23/canadian_womens_rights_in_decline_report_says.html

Out with the Literary Canon?

I used to think that 'Out with the literary canon altogether' was going too far, but now ... Name one work conventionally considered part of the traditional literary canon that does *not* subordinate women—their existence, their presence, their importance, what they say, what they do ...

And so by continuing to grant the work such esteemed status, such *legitimacy*, we continue to grant women's subordination legitimacy.

And so works of the traditional literary canon should be studied only in a course dedicated to exposing their misogyny.

On marrying a man
a few years older than yourself

The convention that one marry a man a few years older than oneself allows both partners to pretend that her subordination to him is due her relative age, not her sex.

What I Learned about Men
by Posting a 'For Sale' Ad on Kijiji

The ad said $100. Men offered $70, $80, $90. Every woman who replied to the ad accepted the stated price.

The ad indicated my location, implying pick-up. Men asked whether I'd deliver it (all or part of the way) or simply said my location was too far away. The closest a woman got to that kind of response was 'Are you ever in North Bay?' (And the woman who bought it drove the distance deemed by several men to be 'too far'.)

The ad said nothing about disassembling the item. Men asked whether I would do that (so they could more easily fit it in their vehicle). No woman asked for that.

So. Does this mean that ...

Men are more assertive than women?

Men are more demanding that women?

Men feel more entitled (to whatever it is they want) (and maybe even to things they don't want) (just because) than women?

Men themselves use language loosely (they seldom mean what they say or say what they mean) and so assume others do as well? And so if $100 could mean $70, then $30,000/year could mean $35,000 and 'no benefits' could mean 'Okay, a dental plan'. And 'No' could mean 'Yes.'

Bragging about being beaten

A while ago, I saw a post by a woman bragging about her bruises. (I should've saved the link, but I was just so ... appalled.) In 1976, Women Against Violence Against Women (WAVAW) protested and got the Stones' billboard taken down (it showed a woman bound and bruised, captioned "I'm 'Black and Blue' from the Rolling Stones—and I love it!" In 1978, feminists protested the June issue of *Hustler* that had on the cover a naked woman being shoved head first into a meat grinder and extruded at the other end as raw hamburger: it was called the 'all-meat' issue). We fought against men beating up women and now you're saying you *like* being beaten? What the fuck is wrong with you? Have you no brain?[1]

---

[1] And to all of you wanna-be porn stars, have you not read Linda Marchiano's autobiography?

The Montreal Massacre
(and Donna Decker's
Dancing in Red Shoes Can Kill You)

People who are/were shocked by the Montreal Massacre don't know women's history. Men have been killing us *for centuries*. Simply because we're women. They kill each other too, but in that case, it's mostly because of their target's sexual orientation, tribal affiliation, or skin color. They kill us because of our sex.

Is it more horrible because of that? Perhaps not. Yes, 51% of the world's people are female, whereas only 10% are homosexual, but the target group based on tribal affiliations might be larger than 51% (especially when nations go after each other), and target groups based on skin color are most certainly larger than that (assuming it's 'white' people killing non-'white' people).

Perhaps the horror is that we have been, willingly for the most part, sleeping with the enemy. For centuries.

Donna Decker's *Dancing in Red Shoes Can Kill You* is a must-read. Especially for those too young to have been aware of the Montreal Massacre in 1989. "There were men ... who hated the idea of women's equality so much, they were willing to kill in cold blood. In Canada" (213). Well-put.

Though to be clear, whether we're engineers or prostitutes, whether we're under ten or over sixty, whether we're heterosexual or lesbian, whether we're white or black, whether we're feminist or not—none of that matters. All that matters is that we're female. (Which in itself should make us *all* feminist.) If ever there was a call to arms—

(And yet, before you pick up that gun—yes, even the one that's fallen onto the floor out of the man's hand—know that at least when 'partners' are involved, women who kill men spend an average of fifteen years in prison, whereas men who kill women spend about four years in prison.)

"She had [simply] written down [in her column] everything the guy in the coffee shop had said that morning ... how he was furious with his feminist girlfriend and all feminists. She had embellished nothing. But they had refused to publish it" (321). They had called it anti-male. Note that. Pay attention to that. Simply exposing male hatred of women is anti-male. *How do they figure that?* Speaking the truth about men is anti-male? That means that reality is anti-male. Hm. *What are you going to do with that?*

And men? If this book doesn't make you sick, and then determined to fix your brothers, you should, like Marc Lepine, put a bullet in your own head. (Thank you.)

13 *Reasons Why*:
How to Make a Movie
Without Acknowledging
the Elephant in the Room

So I've just finished watching *13 Reasons Why* and am struck by the completely unacknowledged elephant in the room: *not one character* acknowledges that almost all of the problems leading to Hannah's suicide stem from sexism and its many tumours: misogyny, male entitlement, male privilege, hypersexualization, objectification, the rape culture, etc., etc., etc.

Justin: Being a man is all about getting sex, using women for sex, and bragging about it afterwards to get points, to improve your status (among males). Exaggerating and lying about your 'achievements' is, well, standard operating procedure if you're a guy. 'Bros before hos'—even if it means letting your girlfriend be raped (because hey, what's mine is yours) (and women are just property, after all) (otherwise, it wouldn't even have occurred to him that what he 'owed' Bryce could include Jessica). That said, (weak) applause for his eventual decency, especially given his relative-to-Bryce lack of privilege and the pull of moral obligation for reciprocity (albeit disgustingly overgeneralized, as mentioned).

Jessica: Men are more important than women. One, getting a boyfriend is the most important thing you can do, being someone's girlfriend is the most important thing you can be; your status, your value, depends on your relation to a male—which is why as soon as she and Alex hook up, Hannah is dropped like a second-class piece of shit. Two, what men say

338

is to be believed, they are authorities, about everything; when they open their mouths, truth tumbles out like little golden nuggets—which is why she believes what she's told by Alex et al about Hannah. Three, she's a cheerleader. Her actual 'job' is to cheer and applaud men when they do stuff. (In fact, many of the girls in 13 *Reasons Why* are cheerleaders, and many of the boys are jocks. A whole 90% of the student body is missing. Why? Give you one guess.) (Actually, on second thought, strictly speaking, that's not true. Of the eight boys listed here, only three are jocks. So why did I get that wrong impression? Because the jocks appear as a group, wearing uniforms. They appear as a team, a gang, an army. That's why they seem more … powerful.)

Alex: Women are to be evaluated solely on the basis of their body parts, on whether their body parts please you/men. Again, (weak) applause for his regret and guilt, and his speaking up, but, yeah, men like Alex who confront men like Bryce will get beaten up. Thus, his limited confrontation and his suicide attempt can also be traced to the fucked-up patriarchal culture.

Tyler: Women's bodies are public domain; ergo, photographs of women's bodies are public domain. It's not like there's a person inside or anything.

Courtney: Being lesbian in public means you risk 'corrective rape'; can we blame her for hiding?

Marcus: When a girl agrees to meet you for a milkshake, she's really agreeing to have sex with you. At the very least, she's agreeing to have her genitals fondled by you. In public. In broad daylight. And certainly in the presence of the bros you brought along to witness your conquest. If she objects, well, your outrage is justified. Because you're *entitled* to touch her. In fact, you're entitled to touch any woman. Any time, any place. Simply because you're a man.

Zach: She doesn't particularly like you? She rejected your advances of friendship? Well, yeah, FUCK HER! Because men are entitled to the affection of all women.

Ryan: Sure it's okay to publish someone's work without their permission, without crediting them, perhaps especially if they're a woman and you're a man. Because you, men, know best. What's best for her, women. (Oh, and thanks for carrying on the great tradition of 'Anon' ...)

Sheri: Perhaps the *only* episode that *doesn't* implicate the elephant.

Bryce: Women don't know what they want, but you, *you, a MAN* (well, a boy), *you* know what they want. (And they *all* want you. They all want your penis inside them.) (At least, you *"assume* so.") (And that's good enough.) Thanks to the patriarchy, you can be appallingly deluded about your knowledge and your appeal. You can lie to yourself about it. Again and again.

Mr. Porter: Yes, he goes to regretted sex first, then to alcohol and drugs, but when he gets to rape, Hannah says she didn't tell Bryce to stop, she says she didn't tell him 'No'—so what's he supposed to think? He suggests she may have consented then changed her mind (which she's certainly entitled to do) (and which still leaves the door open to rape), then asks whether they should get her parents or the police involved, but she says 'No'—again, what's he supposed to think or do? And *of course*, he can't promise that Bryce will go to jail. Guess why. He tells her it may be 'best to move on' (but only after he clarifies that Hannah won't give a name, she won't press charges, she's not even sure she *can* press charges), showing that he too is caught in the mire of our fucked-up patriarchy.

Clay: Clay buys into the Prince Charming shit: he blames himself for not saving Hannah. (He doesn't blame himself for

not saving Alex—though perhaps he doesn't know yet ...)
Near the end, he says something like 'We need to start treating each other better, we need to start caring about each other.' Well, as Bryce would surely tell him, caring about others is for sissies—females. And in a patriarchy, male values trump female values (and yes, in a patriarchy there's a difference).

Hannah: She exhibits a lot of passivity, a persistent denial of agency. She wants Clay to kiss her; why doesn't she want to kiss him? (She wants to be kissed; she doesn't want to kiss.) She wants Clay to ask her to dance; why doesn't she just ask him to dance? She wants him to be her Valentine; why doesn't she just tell him that? She tells Clay to go away, but then expects him to stay. Not only is he not a mind reader, but it's that kind of shit that got us to 'no means yes'. (Tony had it right: she asked him to go, he should go, end of story.) Standing outside Mr. Porter's office, she waits to be saved, for him to come running after her.

And of course as soon as Bryce, whom she'd *seen* rape Jessica, gets into the hot tub, she doesn't get out. She probably didn't want to appear rude. You know, hurt his feelings. Once he begins, she doesn't scream STOP; she doesn't scream NO. She just ... accepts it, endures it. (And 'it' looks like it might have been sodomy, not 'just' PIV rape.) That's what women, girls, are supposed to do. That's what we're raised to do. Accept shit. Endure shit.

If girls wore alarm necklaces (instead of short little vagina/anus-easily-accessible skirts), she could've pulled its pin (like a grenade) when she saw Bryce start to rape Jessica ... And again when she was in the hot tub ... And, backing up a bit, why do we keep our teenaged girls so clueless, so desperate (for ... what?) that *they get into a hot tub at a party at a rapist's house in just their bra and panties* (let alone *go to a party at his place in the first place*)? Not to mention, of course, why do we keep our

341

teenaged boys so clueless to the moral wrongness of patriarchy, sexism, misogyny, male entitlement, male privilege ...

So the thirteen reasons why pretty much boil down to one. And it's not even acknowledged.

Feminists have exposed and fought against patriarchy, sexism, misogyny, male entitlement, male privilege, hypersexualization, objectification, rape culture—hell, we *named* most of that shit—for decades. Not acknowledged. Not once. Not even a little bit. It's like Jay Asher was born yesterday and has remained oblivious of such women's voices. Ironic. To say the least.

(I cheered when 'the male gaze' was actually mentioned by the girls, but then they got it wrong, they made it sound like it just describes the attracted look on a guy's face.) (Oh for the love of God!)

And another thing. There are no doubt hundreds of *13 Reasons Why* novels written by women. Have any of them been published? Made into a movie? Received great critical claim? No. But a *man* writes about what it's like to be raped, what it's like to be subjected to misogynistic shit every fucking day, well, world, PAY ATTENTION! Asher is himself a shining example of the male privilege his novel criticizes so unwittingly. Again, the irony.

Furthermore, how many more Sylvia Plaths do we need to see? Why must we keep seeing women kill themselves because of this shit? Why can't we see as many, if not more, saying FUCK THIS SHIT!? Yes, okay, Jessica was drunk, and Hannah isn't a cheerleader, but why couldn't Asher have reversed that? Because, hey, if a girl can do four back handsprings (without mats even), she surely has the strength (shoulders, abs, legs) and the courage (without mats, remember?) to fight back at least *a little*. Why didn't we see a sober cheerleader, or two or three, bustin' Bryce's ass when he tried his shit. Why don't we see more movies like Jodi Foster's *The Brave One?* Give you one guess.

Never mind the elephant. *13 Reasons Why* is a trojan horse.

Ugly, Fat, Hairy Feminists

The reason most feminists are ugly, fat, and hairy is that most feminists are old. That is, over forty.

And there are two good reasons for this. The first is that most living feminists became feminists in the 70s when it was 'in the air' and, therefore, easier to see that women are subordinated in our society. That means they were at least in their late teens in the 70s, which means they're around fifty or sixty now.

The second reason is that too often *it takes until you're forty to figure it out*. Women in their late teens, their twenties, and thirties seem to have it good. They get married. Let's say that means love, a house, and a pension plan. At forty, you get traded in for a younger model. Good-bye to all that.

They have kids. Let's say that means happiness and fulfillment. At forty, they're treated with contempt by their teenagers, dismissed as naïve and incompetent. So much for happiness and fulfillment.

They get interviews; they get jobs. At forty, rather suddenly, it hits you: you're still in the same job, whereas so many of the men around you, even the younger men, have been promoted past you.

So all of this is to say that in your late teens, your twenties, and your thirties, you (seem to) get taken seriously. Sexism? The patriarchy? What are you talking about? But at forty, you stop being taken seriously. You become invisible. No matter what you do. No one hears you. No matter what you say.

And, worse, you suddenly realize that *the only reason* you were *ever* taken seriously was that you were fuckable. Any attention paid to you was pretense. In service to the possibility.

344

You realize that you've been sexualized. Your whole life. Whatever you were had *female* affixed to it. *Prefixed* to it. You suddenly see the sexism you've been swimming in your whole life. And, so, you realize you've been subordinated your whole life. Because *female* means *lesser*. And so you become a feminist.

Of course, there's nothing about being over forty that makes you suddenly ugly, hairy, and fat. (*So-called* ugly, hairy, and fat.) It's being a feminist that makes you so. It's being a feminist that makes you realize that it's against your best interests to accept societal standards about physical appearance—to cover your face with chemical-laden make-up, to inject Botox and silicone (and unless you do that, you're 'ugly'; to volumize and style and colour *this* hair, while shaving and waxing and plucking *that* hair (unless you do that, you're 'hairy'); to eat less than you need (and unless you do *that*, you're 'fat'). Because those standards are set *to attract the male gaze*. Those standards keep us sexualized. (In fact, those standards *are* sexualized: beautiful *means* fuckable—which is in large part means young.) And, so, subordinated.

Plus, quite simply, we have better things to do with our time.

Why more men than women will die of the COVID virus

Why more men than women will die of the COVID virus:

1. Cleanliness is a girl thing. Real men don't wash their hands. (Certainly not several times a day.)

2. The home is the women's cave. So unless it comes with an attached garage, real men aren't going to stay there all day. (Certainly not all week, let alone all month ...)

3. Many of the public health officials we're hearing from are women. Real men don't listen to women. They certainly don't accept their advice.

4. Most men think they're tough, so they figure they're not going to get it. (As if toughness, rather than, oh I don't know, a diet high in fruits and vegetables, and low in beer and cigarettes, has anything to do with immunity to viral infections.)

5. Most men are pack animals; they naturally herd together. So they're finding this whole do-not-congregate thing really hard.

Why more women than men will die of the COVID virus:

1. The men they're living with will get angry and frustrated (at whatever) and as a result kill them. (Because, you know, it's their fault.)

Did men invent this?

So I've been talking with my friend about the effect on the internet (and computers in general) of the overwhelming male influence (the high percentage of male ITers, coders, what have you) and simultaneously formatting the blog-comments sections of my forthcoming novel *Gender Fraud: a fiction* and I realize the 'reply' design (the widgets?) for comments are incredibly not up to the task: a back-and-forth conversation would result in a long horizontal stream which, after just a few exchanges, would mean the replies are squished into a one-inch column. Better to have incorporated some sort of all-comments-on-a-subthread-are-aligned principle. (Assuming the impossibility of incorporating the 'ability' to detect the forementioned 'back-and-forth' between two people.)

Which suggests two questions: Are men in general unaccustomed to extended conversational exchange? Is the ideal conversation for them, the imagined conversation, one in which a reply is a single blow that establishes victory, the end?

Reducing sexism:
non-binary sex and sex-neutral language

That sex is binary makes sexism so easy. What if sex existed on a spectrum?

But, you may reply, it doesn't. Contrary to so many transactivists, sex is a matter of biology, and you are either male or female; barring the exceptional, one has either XY chromosomes or XX chromosomes.

True, but saying that sex is physiological rather than emotional, an objective reality rather than a subjective feeling, *need not* imply that it's binary.[1] Imagine a spectrum: people with XX chromosomes and functioning female reproductive anatomy at one end (implying a certain level of estrogen); people with XY chromosomes and functioning male reproductive anatomy at the other end (implying a certain level of testosterone); in between, pre-puberty people (neither completely female nor completely male yet, post-menopausal people (no longer completely female), people with hormone variations from the norm (due to natural levels or injections), people with surgical variations (for medical reasons or cosmetic reasons—we may want to distinguish between the two), and so on. There could be multiple (physical) determinants of sex, and people would be more or less male or female depending on their particular constellation of chromosomes, hormones, and anatomical bits.

---

[1] Nor need it imply essentialism in the sense that physiological sex is essential to one's identity (for example, although I am female, but I have never referred to myself as a woman because as far as *I'm* concerned, my sex doesn't *define* me except in medical contexts; it *does* imply essentialism in the sense that physiology is essential to one's sex.

In many ways, such a world would surely be more complicated. For instance, competitive sports would have to be completely reorganized not according to sex, but according to height, weight, muscle mass, etc. But surely, it would be, eventually, manageable.

Another way to reduce sexism would be to adopt sex-neutral language, because if you didn't know whether the person was male or female, you couldn't discriminate on that basis.[2] This would involve the adoption of sex-neutral names and sex-neutral pronouns[3] and the elimination of 'man' and 'woman' (as in 'police officer' instead of 'policeman'). We would retain 'male' and 'female', of course, but mentioning sex would be relevant only in biological/medical contexts (and personal contexts regarding sexual interaction); to use 'male' and 'female' in everyday discourse would seem, as it does now, rude.

---

[2] In many cases, given the spectrum mentioned above and the hoped-for elimination of gender, it might not even be possible to know whether the person was male or female if you actually saw them.

[3] Though, please, not 'they' because of the consequent singular/plural confusion; there's no reason we can't use 'ze' for subject, object, and possessive forms.

The Frightening Cluelessness
of PoliSci Students

"I was studying political science at the time, so I had never thought about social processes like misogyny and sexism."[1] What? *What?* (And you're in *PoliSci?* On your way to some sort of career in politics, government ... ?)

---

[1] narratively.com/i-was-an-angry-mens-rights-activist-now-im-a-fierce-feminist/

Another reason to hate men

Premise 1: "By 2050 at the latest, and ideally before 2040, we must have stopped emitting more greenhouse gases [typically caused by the burning of fossil fuels] into the atmosphere than Earth can naturally absorb through its ecosystems (a balance known as net-zero emissions or carbon neutrality). In order to get to this scientifically established goal, our global greenhouse gas emissions must be clearly on the decline by the early 2020s and reduced by at least 50 percent by 2030." *The Future We Choose: Surviving the Climate Crisis*, Christiana Figueres and tom Rivett-Carnac, pxxii

Premise 2: Snowmobiles and ATVs "emit 25 percent as many hydrocarbons as all the nation's cars and trucks put together, according to an EPA study." products.kitsapsun.com/archive/1999/02-19/0062_environment__snowmobiles__atvs_du.html

Premise 3: For every hour of operation, over one gallon of uncombusted fuel is produced by jetskis, and what doesn't evaporate into the air settles onto the water. nonoise.org/resource/jetskis/jsmemo.htm#WaterPollution

Premise 4: An overwhelming majority of those who drive snowmobiles, ATVs, and jetskis are men. castlesales.com/facts-and-statistics-about-snowmobiling, stopthrillcraft.org/statistics.htm, stopthrillcraft.org/kind_jetskis.htm

Conclusion (That is to say): Men are producing fossil fuel emissions—lots of fossil fuel emissions—*just for fun.*

And here's something else
that would never happen to a man

I posted these on tumblr (jass-richards.tumblr.com), hoping it would become viral like 'Everyday Sexism' and 'Why I'm a Feminist' with a great many additions, but, sadly, it did not. Pity: if something happens to a woman that would never happen to a man (or vice versa), that's sexism. And if the distinction-on-the-basis-of-sex is unjustified (yes, sometimes sexism is justified—for example, providing ob/gyn services to females but not to males), well, that's sexist shit (or gender shit, since gender is aligned with sex). And it should piss us off. All of us.

So this guy in our neighborhood has early Alzheimer's and dizzy spells. He's looking for a babysitter (his word) and someone to cook for him and do his cleaning so he doesn't have to go into a home. And he asked me.

I have no experience babysitting. And absolutely no aptitude for it. Yes, I do my own cooking and cleaning, but I have no interest in it, at all, and do as little as possible. So why did he ask me? Because I'm a middle-aged woman. Apparently that's what middle-aged women do, that's what we are, that's what we're for.

Yes, I've been friendly with him, stopping to chat or at least wave when I walk by (as a result of which he once asked me if I like sex and whether I'm any good at it—apparently that's another thing women do, are, are for), but I doubt that friendliness on the part of a man would have indicated that he's available for babysitting, cooking, or cleaning (or sex).

I've got three degrees, I used to be a philosophy instructor, I've published several books, and I'm currently making a living as a consultant. Would a man with such credentials be asked to be someone's babysitter and do their cooking and cleaning?

Ah, but this guy doesn't know I'm all that. And that's also telling. If I were man who has lived in this neighborhood (small, rural) for twenty-five years, everyone would likely know all of that about me. But I don't go around announcing these things, and no one's ever asked. Because they just assume I'm—well, none of that. After all, I'm just a middle-aged woman.

*

Many years ago, I attended a talk by the President of the CCLA, and at the end, I approached him about something he'd said or something the CCLA was doing, and I was summarily dismissed. He barely looked at me; his assistant simply waved me away, saying that he had no time for questions now. I suspect that if I'd been a young man, the man might have considered me a potential member, perhaps, recognizing my initiative, intelligence, and passion, even an up-and-coming protégé, someone to whom he'd extend an invitation to go for a beer, carry on the conversation ...

*

I joined the Green Party, and when, at a meeting, I objected to something the leader said, he practically had a heart attack: he started shouting at me, all blustery and red-faced, and jabbing his finger in the air at me ... (Geez louise, get a grip!)

*

I was interested in renting or buying a cottage on a river and found something on Kijiji, so I sent a message with a few questions:

353

Hello, I'm interested in renting, maybe purchasing ...

1. Is the power by generator, propane, or electricity?
2. Kayaking up the river—how far before I hit rapids or have to walk my kayak through a 'rock garden'?
3. Would I see other docks/houses every 100M or so?
4. Is there a sunset view anywhere on the property during July or August?
5. How busy is it during July and August with ATVs and motorboats?

Thanks.

And the guy replied with this:

Too many questions for me to bother with.

Seriously? Five questions. All of which required no more than a one- or two-word answer. And note the dismissive language: "... to bother with." The guy was asking $600/week for rent, $129,000 for sale. And he can't answer five frickin' questions?

My guess is if I were a man, his response would've been quite different. My guess is if I were a man, he would've taken my query SERIOUSLY. Because does he really think someone's going to buy or even rent WITHOUT knowing, for example, the power source?

*

Being expected to be a size zero.

*

Being asked to train the guy who becomes your supervisor.

*

When I arranged to have an electrician come and do some work at my house, he called the next week, on the day we'd arranged for the work to be done, saying he couldn't help me out, he was busy that day. Yeah, you're busy doing work at my house, I wanted to say. Then it hit me. 'Help you out'. Like he was doing me a favour. WTF. I'd hired him! I would be paying him! (Why is it so many men just can't seem to work for a woman?)

*

Telling someone your name is 'Peg' and they immediately call you 'Peggy'. (Or 'Patty' or 'Janey' ...)

Acknowledgements

"Figure Skating: A Very Gendered Thing" (an earlier version) and "Bambi's Cousin's Gonna Tear You Apart" (titled "Hunting") appeared in the *North Bay Nugget*.

"I'm too drunk ... " appeared at Transhumanity.net.

"Let's Talk about Sex" appeared in *Herizons*.

"Permitting Abortion and Prohibiting Prenatal Harm: Reconciling the Contradiction" was presented at the Bioethics and Medical Ethics Section at the Twentieth World Congress of Philosophy (August 1998) and also appeared at the Institute for Ethics and Emerging Technologies website (ieet.org).

"Why isn't being a soldier more like being a mother?," "Transgendered Courage," and "Mr. and Ms." also appeared at the Institute for Ethics and Emerging Technologies website (ieet.org).

"Mr. and Ms." also appeared at Pagan Spirits (erinoriordan. blogspot.com).

"Transgendered Courage" and "What's so funny about a man getting pregnant?" appeared at *The Canadian* (agoracosmopolitan.com).

"School Crossing Signs" appeared at fbomb (fbomb.org).

"Whose Violence" appeared in *Philosophy Now*.

"Against the Rape Shield," "An End to War," "Arrogance, I think," "Bambi's Cousin is Going to Tear You Apart" (titled "Hunting"), "Bang Bang," "Boy Books," "Casual Day at the Office" (titled "Grub Day at the Office"), "Gay Bashing," "Impoverished Scientists," "King of the Castle," "Marriage: a sexist affair" (titled "Marriage"), "Mr. and Ms." (titled "An Apartheid of Sex"), "Population Growth (i.e., rape)," "Power or Responsibility?," "Sex and Salespeople," "Suicide, Insurance, and Dead Sugar Daddies," "The Part-time Ghetto," "The Political is Personal," "The Sexism Compensation Index," "To the Morons who wear Make-Up," "War Rape," "What's so Funny about a Man getting Pregnant?," "Why Do Men Spit? (and women don't)" (titled "On Spitting"), and "Women's Fiction" appeared in *The Philosophy Magazine's* online Philosophy Café, often as earlier versions.

"Boy Books" also appeared in *Teaching and Learning Literature* and *Indirections*.

"Marriage: a sexist affair" (titled "Sexism in Marriage") and "The Political is Personal" also appeared in *Humanist in Canada*.

"Sex and Salespeople" also appeared in *Victoria Times Colonist*.

"The Part-time Ghetto" also appeared in *Links* and *Academic Exchange Quarterly*.

"The Sexism Compensation Index" also previously appeared in *Canadian HR Reporter*.

"Responding to Wolf Whistles," "Stop Being Complicit," and an earlier version of "And here's something else" appeared on BlogHer.